THE ENERGY VIEW OF ECONOMICS

Yajun Adam Chen

经济学能量观

陈亚君 著

中国商业出版社

图书在版编目（CIP）数据

经济学能量观 / 陈亚君著. -- 北京 : 中国商业出版社, 2021.5

ISBN 978-7-5208-1491-1

Ⅰ.①经… Ⅱ.①陈… Ⅲ.①经济学—研究 Ⅳ.①F0

中国版本图书馆CIP数据核字(2020)第250229号

责任编辑：于子豹　袁　娜

中国商业出版社出版发行

010-63180647　　www.c-cbook.com

（100053　北京广安门内报国寺 1 号）

新华书店经销

福建省天一屏山印务有限公司

★

787毫米 × 1092毫米　16开　13.5 印张　200 千字

2021 年 5 月第 1 版　　2021 年 5 月第 1 次印刷

定价：98.00 元

谨以此书献给

我的同学、同事兼挚友丁文先生

This book is dedicated to

my schoolmate, colleague and intimate friend Mr. Ding Wen.

The Energy View of Economics

— A novel Economic View, through which a Seamless Organic Connection among the Theories of William Petty, Francois Quesnay, Adam Smith, Thomas Malthus, Karl Marx, and Alfred Marshall etc., can be obtained.

经济学能量观

——一种能将自威廉·配第、弗朗斯瓦·魁奈、亚当·斯密、托马斯·马尔萨斯、卡尔·马克思、阿尔弗雷德·马歇尔等的理论进行有机连接的经济学新观点。

PREFACE

Observing this world by standing on the earth, seeing the sun, the moon, and stars rising from east and falling in west, our forefathers concluded naturally that the sun, the moon and stars rotate around the earth, which is known as the geocentric theory. With observing more and more meticulously and precisely, more and more deviations between the results of observation and results of calculation according to the theory were identified.

Before the heliocentric theory is recognized, in addition to one epicycle, astronomers had to use up to 80 deferents trying to make the geocentric theory fitting the observation of the reality well. However, a concise heliocentric model explains all of the phenomena in solar system (We all know now that the sun is not the center of the universe in deed). The similar situation is happening nowadays in economics study just like what happened in astronomy prior to the heliocentric theory. There are so many doctrines available, Freiburg School, Supply-side Economics, Monetarism, Keynesian School, Rational Expectation School, London School, Sweden School, Institution Economics, so on and so forth, but each of which explains economic phenomena well only partially but not wholly. It cannot make up an integral system like classic dynamics supported by only three laws of Newton. There must be some bias existing on the

前言

当我们的祖先站在这个地球上观察这个世界，看到日月星辰从东方升起，从西边落下，他们自然而然地得出如下的结论：日月星辰是围绕着大地转的。这就是所谓的地心说。可随着观察精准与细致程度的提高，人们发现观察结果与根据理论计算的结果并不完全吻合。

在日心说没有被认可之前，那时的天文学家们只能用一个本轮加上多达80道的均轮才能让地心说更吻合现实的观察。而一个简洁明了的日心模型，就能说明太阳系里的所有的天文现象了（现在大家都明白，太阳其实也不是宇宙的中心）。现在的经济学界的状态就像是日心说面世前天文学界的状态，众说纷纭，弗莱堡学派、供给学派、货币学派、凯恩斯学派、理性预期学派、伦敦学派、瑞典学派、制度经济学派，莫衷一是。虽然每种学说都能解释一部分而非全部的经济现象，却又似乎不能成为一个像牛顿三大定律构成的完整的古典力学体系。究其原因，应该是在立足点上就存在着某种未被认知的偏差。

stand points of observation unrecognized.

Incidentally, I realized a truth that the fundamental concept of economics — VALUE, is essentially the synonym of the fundamental concept of physics — ENERGY. A set of new economical explanations hereby are deduced. And many definitions of economic terms therefore need to be upgraded or adjusted. And amazingly, the true face of the anchor of currency in circulation, which has been exploring by many economists for quite a long while, is unveiled eventually.

机缘巧合，我发现了这样一个事实：经济学的一个基本概念——价值，与物理学的一个基本概念——能量实质上是同一回事。由此可以推演出一系列新的经济学解释，许多经济学术语的定义也因此要被升级或修正。令人惊诧的是，被许多经济学家苦苦探索多年的流通货币之锚也最终被揭开了神秘的面纱。

Value is nothing else but the energy in both real (contained) and imaginary (dissipated) forms. As a science, economic doctrine has to follow not only the law of conservation of matter but also the law of conservation of energy, based on which, it is concluded naturally that the currency in circulation is anchored by the gross dissipation of energy in both real and imaginary forms during productions and transportations of the goods in circulation.

价值实质上是能量的实项（内含的）和虚项（消耗的）表达，作为一门科学，经济学说不仅必须遵循物质守恒定律而且还必须遵循能量守恒定律，据此我们可以自然得出如下结论：流通货币是由生产运输流通中的商品消耗能量的实项和虚项的总和来锚定的。

In eyes of the author of this article, except the time, there is only one basic independent variable in economics, which is very “ENERGY”.

在本书作者的眼里，除时间外，经济学里只有一个基本自变量，那恰恰是“能量”。

Last but not the least, one thing has to be kept in mind that, in the context of energy, there is no multiplication/magnification but only addition and subtraction. Although the “Rate of Surplus Value” is used in this book, it just means the degree of obtaining (adding) extra energy from the Nature by spending (subtracting) the energy human owned. This is the key to understand clearly the rule of economy.

最后，重要的一点必须牢记：在能量的语境里没有乘法 / 放大，而只有加法和减法。尽管本书里用到了“剩余价值率”这样的术语，但它真正含义是指，花费（减法）人类拥有的能量来从大自然获得（加法）额外能量的程度。这是正确理解经济规律的关键所在。

目 录

目 录

PART ONE: ON WEALTH

第一篇 财 富

Ⅰ. O Sole Mio — the Source of Wealth

Ⅰ. 太阳 —— 财富之源

Different people have their different definitions of wealth. The following is the definition of mine. Wealth is a set of "beings", of either biological, mechanical or pure logical structure, in either tangible or intangible form, which were produced and saved for current and/or future use per the organization of human. We may say it in short, wealth is reserve.

不同的人对财富有不同的定义，我的定义是：财富是在人类组织下生产和储存的，以备当下和未来之用的，以生物学结构、机械学结构甚至纯逻辑结构存在的，有形及无形的"存在"。简言之：财富即储备。

Simply looking around us, we will find out the following facts which are indeed the natural basis for humankind to be able to collect and accumulate the wealth:

看看我们的周边，我们可以立即发现如下人类能够借以获得并积累财富的自然基础：

●Far away beyond the top of our heads, there is the sun, which is sending us the energy through sunshine constantly;

● 远在我们的头顶之上，通过阳光，太阳在源源不断地向我们输送能量；

●Under our feet, there is the earth which contains all chemical elements listed in the Periodic Table of Elements by Mendeleev, of fixed amounts in total respectively beside a few aerolites falling from the outer space occasionally in a handful amount;

● 在我们的足下，大地向我们提供了门捷列夫的元素周期表所列的总量一定的所有元素，另外还有从天外偶尔陨落下来的数量极少的陨石；

●On the earth, there are varieties of species which can reproduce themselves in geometrical ratios when unchecked, among which humankind

● 在地球上，存在着包括人类也位列其中的，各种各样的物种，在没有制约的情况下，按几何比率

sits on the top. All together, they form the ecosystem of the earth;

●The photosynthesis of plants and algae transforms the solar energy into chemical energy saved in their bodies, which may become the energy source for other organisms with helps of enzymes, and ultimately for human being; or for mechanical engines made by human through burning;

●The last but not the least for sure is the intelligence of human, which is the promoter and the binder in the forming of the wealth.

Human body itself is one kind of the energy converters invented by Mother Nature just like all machines invented by human brain, but auto reproduction. Man eats foods, which are the carriers of the energy sourced from the sun; and thereby gains sufficient materials for growth and metabolism of his body and the energy for conducting series of actions organized by his brain to fulfill certain tasks, which is called labor of human. Following the notion of Marshall, we say that, man gains the energy from the sun indirectly and sacrifices his labor directly onto the wealth-to-be by either "readjusting matter so as to make it more useful", or "putting it in the way of being made more useful by nature".

Hundreds of thousands of years ago, men, women and even their children wandered around day after day, migrated from one place to another for collecting fruits on or under trees, vegetables on or underneath the ground, and cereals on the land, occasionally, if lucky enough, they captured small, slow moving, or wounded animals as food

进行自身繁殖，它们形成了地球上的生态系统；

● 植物和藻类等的光合作用能将太阳能转换成化学能并存储在它们的体内，通过酶的作用，它们能成为其他有机体，最终成为人类的能量来源，或者通过直接燃烧为人造的机器提供能量；

● 最后，但也是最主要的，人类智慧是财富形成的推动剂和黏合剂。

就像其他由人类自己发明的机器一样，人类的身体不过就是自然之母创造的，能自我繁殖的能量转换器而已。人，吃下源自太阳的能量载体——食物，由此得到身体成长和新陈代谢需要的物质和足以从事一系列由其大脑组织的活动的能量，我们称这些活动为人类的劳动。仿照马歇尔的说法，我们说：人类间接地从太阳获得能量，并直接对财富标的施以劳动，“调整物质形态使得它更有用”，或者“使它在自然的作用下变得更有用”。

数十万年前，男人、女人甚至他们的孩子，整天在外转悠，从一个地方转移到另一个地方，为的就是从树上树下收集果子，地上采集蔬菜，田间地头收获谷物。如果幸运的话，偶尔他们也能够逮到些小型的、慢速的或者是受伤的动物作

as well, just for getting themselves stuffed therefore energized for subsistence. They always bothered by an issue as such though: sometimes they encountered plentiful of food, portion of which had rotten before their stomachs had room again, and some other times found very few so that they had to be in hunger for a while. Is there any way to keep the food for a longer while? Learning by surveying, eventually, they mastered the methods of preserving food through drying, salting, boiling, baking, fermenting, refrigerating, so on and so forth. They got their wealth reserved for future use the first time.

为食物来充饥，获取能量，从而能够生存下去。可他们总是受到一个问题的困扰：有时他们会碰到充足的食物，部分食物甚至在他们没来得及享用前就腐败掉了；而有时他们只能得到非常少的食物而不得不忍饥挨饿一段时间。有没有什么办法使得食物的保存时间长一些呢？通过观察学习，他们掌握了通过干燥、腌制、蒸煮、烘烤、发酵、冷冻等方法来保存食物。他们第一次有了财富的储备。

Still learning by surveying, they eventually realized that crop and livestock farming could make the food supply more constantly and evenly, so long as they could keep the crop growing on a sufficiently ventilated, fertilized, and sun shined land; and protect the livestock from illness and beast of prey. People possessed their wealth in other fashion.

仍然是通过观察学习，人们最终认识到，只要能保证庄稼耕作期间有足够的通风、肥力、光照；保证家畜远离病害和野兽的攻击，耕种庄稼和饲养家畜可以使得食物供应更持久、更均衡。人类以另一种形式拥有了财富。

Cave was too crowded along with the growth of the family/tribe. The air inside the cave was stinky. Part of the family/tribe had to move out. Probably being inspired by the crowns of trees, people started to build up their sheds with wood and mud, stone and straw. With proper maintenance, they could keep their wealth for a quite long time.

随着家族和部落的增长，以前居住的洞穴太挤了，空气也太污浊，部分成员必须搬出去，也许受到树冠的启迪，人们开始用木材和泥土，石料和草料来搭建棚屋。通过恰当的维护，他们便拥有了耐久的财富。

Nowadays, we do more or less the same things as our ancestors did hundreds of thousands of years ago but only making the food lasting longer and testing more flavored; and the shelter more durable and more comfortable. On top of that, instead of the

如今我们实际上多多少少从事着与先辈们所做的相似的活计，只是让食物味道更好，住房更舒适而已。当然，现在我们已经使用上结构复杂的机器来替代由石头和木头

tools made of stones and woods, we are now able to make amazingly complicated machines, which are used by ourselves.

做成的工具。

All these progresses happen only because of the development of the intelligence of the human being. So, we may regard the knowledge of experience accumulated by human ever since as the subjective catalyst for the wealth production and accumulation. I would like to revise the discourse on the wealth by William Petty a little bit as: The Sun is its father and the Earth its mother; the knowledge of human being makes it possible the bond of the father and the mother to yield wealth in a miraculous productivity.

所有的这些进展都是随着人类智力的发展而发生的。我们可以说，人类一直以来的知识积累是财富生产和积累的主观催化剂。让我们修改一下威廉·配第的一句名言来表述：太阳是父，大地为母，人类的知识促使了两者的结合，并以奇迹般的效率促使财富产生。

From natural science, we know that the saving of food is essentially the saving of solar energy. Generally speaking, the solar energy from the sun is not able be saved directly (on the base of thermal balance in the atmosphere formed already above the earth). However, it can be saved in the roots, trunks, stalks, leaves, and grains or fruits of the plants on the earth through photosynthesis indirectly. Coal, crude oil and natural gas are nothing but savings of solar energy in other deposit forms.

自然科学告诉我们，食物的储存实际上就是太阳能的储存。一般来说，太阳能是无法直接被储存的（假设地球大气层的温度是平衡的）。但它可以通过光合作用，以另一种形式间接储存在植物的根部、枝茎、叶片和果实当中。煤、原油、天然气也只不过是另一种形式的太阳能储存。

All products out of the processing industries are only available with dissipation of certain amount of energy through variety of means per the organization of human. First of all, man power and intelligence need to be nourished every day with suitable food in quality and in quantity. We need heat to smelt ores to make copper, iron, tin, and all other metals. We need heat to make dinner ware and brick out of clay; cement and glass out of stone or

所有的由人类组织的加工过程也离不开各种形式的能量。首先，人的智力和体力每天需要一定数量和质量的合适的食物来供养。我们需要热量来熔化矿石生产铜、铁、锡等金属。我们需要热量来烧制泥坯成砖块，焙烧沙石成水泥或玻璃。没有能量，任何过程都无法进行。Goudsbiom 先生认为火是人类文明

sand. We find nothing functioning without energy's presence in initiation, in between, and even in the very end of the stage of all of the procedures. Mr. Goudsbiom regards the fire as the cause of the human civilization, and fire is just a sensible form of energy.

的动力，是重要的能量来源。

Terrestrial heat and radioactive substances are other sources of energy on the earth, but usage of which is much less than of solar energy. Ignoring the contribution of terrestrial heat and the nuclear energy which takes only little portion, we may say, all the wealth on the earth is just reserve of the solar energy.

在地球上，地热和放射物质是另一类的能源，只是与太阳能相比，它们的用量实在微不足道，甚至可以忽略不计，因此我们可以说：财富就是太阳能在地球上的储备。

Zhang Jingyue, a Chinese doctor in Ming Dynasty, said in his medical book *The Pandect of Jingyue* that "The big treasure in the sky is only the Sun; and the big treasure in the body of human is only the positive energy."

中国明朝的一位名医张景岳在他的《景岳全书》中写道: 天之大宝，只此一丸红日；人之大宝，唯此一息真阳。

Ⅱ. Fuels & Tools — the Essence of Material Wealth

Ⅱ. 燃料和工具 —— 物质财富的实质

For easy subsistence, man invents tools and methods of using them. For better subsistence, man invents more and more sophisticated tools and methods.

Besides food necessary for keeping man's body energized for thinking and acting, man needs means for keeping his body warm in winter and cool in summer. So, varieties of wears are invented to serve such needs. Man needs means for keeping himself and his family away from attacks by beasts. So, varieties of shelters are built to serve such needs. Man needs means for making food inviting and

为了方便生存，人类发明了工具及其使用方法。为了更好地生存，人类发明了越来越精致复杂的工具和方法。

除了为人类思想和行动提供能量所必需的食物外，人类需要工具来保证其身体冬天温暖，夏天凉快，各色各样的服装因此被发明；人类需要工具来保护他们自己和家庭不受猛兽的侵犯，形形色色的棚屋因此被建成；人类需要工具烹制易于消化的食物，各种各样的炉子和锅

easy for digesting. So, varieties of stove and pans are invented to serve such needs... So, we have diversiform living tools.

因此被创造……我们统称这些为生活工具。

Making garment needs needle. Man needs tools like hammer and grinder to make needles. To make hammer and grinder, man needs other tools. Building house needs wood and brick. Man needs tools like saw and knife or ax to cut trees; and kiln to bake the adobe. Making pan needs iron. Man needs furnace to smelt the ore; mold to cast the pan; and grinder to polish the surface... So, we have other kinds of tools, which are used for producing other tools. We may call them producing tools.

制造服装需要缝衣针；人们需要锤子、磨针石来制造缝衣针；为制造锤子和磨针石，人们又需要其他的工具。建造房屋需要木料和砖头，人们需要像锯子和刀斧那样的工具来砍伐树木；同理，需要砖窑来焙烧砖坯。锅子是由铁制成的，人们需要熔炉来熔化矿石，需要砂石抛光表面……因此，我们有了各种形式的用于生产的工具。我们称之为生产工具。

Some tools can be used for both living and producing purpose. Hammer can be used for cracking nuts for living and forging the needle for producing. Knife can be used for cutting meat for living and chopping wood for building. Telephone can be used either in a plant or in a house.

有些工具可以被同时用于生产和生活。比如锤子，可以用来砸开核桃取仁为食，也可以用来锻打铁条使其成针。刀子可以用来切肉，也可以用来砍木造屋。电话机可以用于工厂，也可用于家庭。

Marx said in his book *Das Kapital*: “An instrument of labour is a thing, or a complex of things, which the labourer interposes between himself and the subject of his labour, and which serves as the conductor of his activity. He makes use of the mechanical, physical, and chemical properties of some substances in order to make other substances subservient to his aims.” (Vol. 1, Chapter 7, Sec. 1) We now call all the instruments tools here in this article in general.

马克思在他的《资本论》中说：“劳动器具是一种置于劳动者与劳动对象之间的，助以实施其行动的物件，或者是它们的组合。他利用一些物料之机械的、物理的及化学的特性做成另一些达成其目的的物件。”(第一卷第七章第一节)我们在本书中将器具统一称作工具。

From the view of labor process, Marx regarded the tool as one of the three elementary factors as he said. “The elementary factors of the labour-process are

从劳动过程来看，马克思将工具看成劳动三要素之一。“劳动过程的要素是：1.人的行动，如工作

1, the personal activity of man, i.e., work itself, 2, the subject of that work, and 3, its instruments." (Vol. 1, Chapter 7, Sec. 1).

本身；2.劳动对象；3.劳动器具。"（第一卷第七章第一节）

Actually, besides the work of food making for subsistence of human, all other subjects of man's labor are materials which are to be integrated into tools in the end. Now we may give the wealth in a narrow sense an annotation as the following,

实际上，除了为人类生存必需的食物生产外，其他的劳动对象都是最终归于工具的材料。现在我们可以给财富另外做一个狭义的注释:

In addition to energy carriers which are used as the power source of labor, the so called wealth of the society is just whole set of tools, and materials which are on their way to be tools in the end through the process organized and implemented by human.

除为劳动提供动力的能量载体之外，所谓社会财富就是一堆工具，以及即将在人的主导和实施下最终成为工具的物料所组成。

We can simply say: besides semis, the wealth consists of just fuels, which are the first tier of the material wealth; and tools, which are the second tier of the material wealth.

或者说：除了中间产品，物质财富是由称之为第一层次物质财富的燃料，和称之为第二层次物质财富的工具所组成的。

Ⅲ. Organization — the Cause of Utility

Ⅲ. 组织 —— 效用之因

On www.wikipedia.org the definition of the organization is, "An organization (or organisation) is a social entity, such as an institution or an association that has a collective goal and is linked to an external environment." In this article however, organization means not only the entity of human but also entity of substance, which are organized with its elements in a certain structure and/or in a certain sequence so that a constant performance can be expected.

维基百科（www.wikipedia.org）对组织的定义是："组织(organization或 organisation)是一种社会实体如机构、联盟，它具有一个关联外部环境的共同的目标。" 但在本文中，组织不仅仅是指由人组成的实体，也包括由物质组成的实体， 它们由各种元素以一定的结构或顺序形成，它们的功效是可以被预测的。

Organization is a word opposite to chaos.

与组织一词相对的是混沌，处

Chemical elements in chaotic status do not possess utility at all. We need hardness of a material to make tools. The hardness of a metal is formed because of its crystallite, which is a kind of organization of the molecules of metal. The hardness of pure copper is of 35 HB, we may change the crystallite by adding 10% of tin and 5% of lead, and get the copper alloy with hardness of 70 HB immediately. By adding carbon into iron, we can get even higher hardness. Tools are organizations of certain substances in certain connections for getting certain task fulfilled. A head of a solid body with a long handle forms a hammer for beating. A head of a sharp blade with a long handle forms an ax for chopping. We say that a hammer possesses its utility of beating, and an ax possesses its utility of chopping therefore.

于混沌状态的化学元素是不具有任何效用的。制造工具我们需要硬度，金属的硬度是由其晶粒的排列结构，即金属分子结构决定的。纯铜的硬度只有 35HB，加入 10% 的锡和 5% 的铅后，我们马上可以得到 70HB 的硬度。在铁中增加碳元素，我们可以得到更高的硬度。工具是以完成某种任务为目的的由一定的物质构成的组织。一个实心的头部和一根长柄的结合就构成了一个用于敲击的榔头。一个有锋利刀锋的头部和一根长柄的结合就构成了用于砍剁的斧子。我们说：榔头具有敲打的效用，斧子具有砍剁的效用。

A dress is made of fabrics, which are made of yarns, which are made of fiber from cotton, flax, wool, or even synthetic materials; through spinning, weaving, dying, tailoring, sewing, so on and so forth, in a production organization consisting of managers, designers, spinners, weavers, dyers, tailors and needlewomen respectively. Dress is a form of organization of thread and fabric mainly, which is the organization of yarns, which is the organization of certain fibers... In total, dress possesses therefore its main utility of keeping human body warm.

一件衣服由布料组成，布料又由纱线构成，纱线可以由棉花、亚麻、羊毛，乃至合成纤维制成。在由经理人、设计师、纺线工、织布工、印染工、裁剪工和缝纫工等组成的工厂里，经过纺线、织布、印染、裁剪、缝制等工序，衣服才能被制成。衣服主要是由缝线和布料构成的组织，布料是由纱线构成的组织，纱线又是由纤维构成的组织…… 总而言之，衣服从而具备了为人体保温的主要效用。

Utility is the external performance of an organization as a whole.

效用就是组织作为一个整体的外部功效。

Organizations of the same structure but of different materials create the same utilities but in different qualities. We may have a hammer with

由不同的材料按相同的结构组成的组织可以产生不同质量的效用。榔头的头部可以由铁、木头或

a steel head; we may also have a hammer with a wooden head or rubber head. With the same stroke, we will have different beating qualities.

橡胶做成，在相同的一挥之下，它们的敲击质量是不同的。

Different organizations of same raw material may generate different utilities. When a log is split in half vertically and hollowed in middle, a canoe is formed for ferry. When logs are joggle jointed each other, a frame of a house is formed; with the attachment of the wooden pieces as the walls, a house is formed for residence. From the logs, we may make furniture of all kinds such as, case, desk, chair, bed, cabinet, etc.

由相同的材料按不同的结构组成的组织产生不同的效用。如果把一根木头对半劈开，并将当中掏空，一条渡河的独木舟就做成了；如果将一些圆木榫接在一起，就能构成房屋的框架，装上由木板做的墙，一座供居住的房子就造好了；用圆木，我们还可以制造各色各样的家具，如箱子、桌子、椅子、床、橱，等等。

From natural science, we know that all different kinds of inorganic substances are certain organizations of molecules, which are smallest units of keeping the property of such inorganic substance; all different kinds of organic substances are certain organizations of cells, which are the smallest units of keeping the property of such organic substance. We then have a bunch of materials available on the earth to be reorganized as our tools for producing and eventually living.

自然科学告诉我们：不同的无机物是由其不同的分子构成的组织，分子是保持其性质的最小单元；不同的有机物是由其不同的细胞构成的组织，细胞是保持其性质的最小单元。我们因此在地球上可以找到众多的可用材料，重新组织它们来制造工具用于生产以及生活。

Now, we may say that, a tool is just a certain kind of organization, which creates certain utility for living and/or producing.

现在我们可以说：工具就是一类能为生产和生活提供效用的组织。

Not only all artificial organizations have their utilities, but also some natural organizations have their utilities, like diamond has its utility for cutting due to its already well formed crystallite; grain has its utility for energizing human body due to its well-formed organization of nutrition; Log has its utility for carrying people across a river due to the low

不仅人造的组织具有效用，自然的组织也具有其效用，比如，钻石能切割，是因为它业已形成的晶格；谷物能为人体提供能量，是因为其自然形成的营养组织；木头可以直接用于渡河，是因为它细胞构成的较低的比重；秸秆可以用于燃

density of the organization of cells. Straw has its utility of heating due to its organization of the fiber containing carbohydrates.

烧供热，也是因为其碳水化合物的纤维组织。

Intangible organizations like working instruction on a workshop, a procedure during a massage, even the note flow in a music piece are pure mental organizations, but they have their utilities just as any tangible organizations. Strictly speaking, the proper combination of tangible organizations and intangible organizations, which means a higher level organization, is the only way of the realization of the utility.

无形组织，如车间里的作业指导书、按摩程序乃至音乐中的音符流，都是一种纯智力的组织，它们与有形组织一样具备效用。严格地讲：有形组织和无形组织的恰当结合而形成的更高层次的组织才是实现效用的唯一途径。

Ⅳ. Reorganization — the Cause of the Value of Labor

Ⅳ. 再组织 —— 劳动价值之因

Prior to the prehistoric period of time, the Mother Nature was the only organizer on the earth. Plants and animals grew and died as per the scheme designed by the Mother Nature. All other natural resources had been sleeping on or underneath the earth since the form of the earth until the wake-up of the human being's intelligence.

在史前时代以前，自然之母是地球上唯一的组织者。植物和动物们按照自然之母的安排而生长和毁灭。而其他的自然资源从地球形成开始一直在地球中沉睡，直到人类智慧的苏醒。

Besides using the fruits of trees, grains of crops and fleshes of animals as the material of food, man started to use body of living animal as the power source of labor, skin of animal as material for garments; use branches of trees as fuel and trunks as rafts; use diamond as tool of cutting hard surface, use stone as a tool of grinding and beating… From the human survival and better living perspective, the utilities of natural resources are either limited or even merely potential in the most cases.

在利用树木的果、植物的谷、动物的肉作为食物之外，人类开始利用家畜的身体作为劳动的动力，动物的皮毛作为衣服的原料，树枝作为燃料，树干作为筏子；使用钻石刻划坚硬的表面，使用石头来制造敲击和研磨的工具……从人类生存和发展的角度看，自然资源的效用是有限的，大多数情况下甚至只是潜在的，人类或多或少需要对自

The reorganizations by human are more or less necessary. The effort taken for reorganization of the natural resources and their derivatives as per the design of human being is called labor. Both thinking and acting on purpose are all labors of human.

然资源进行再组织。根据人类的设计，对自然资源及其衍生物进行再组织的努力就是劳动，有目的性的思考和行动都是人类的劳动。

The trunk of pine tree is a good material for being beams and columns of a house; Man has to change the status of the trunk of pine tree from a living plant to a piece of long log; Man has to change the location of the log from the place of its growth to the place where the house is built; Man has to make joints among the beams and columns. For building a house, man has to change the form of mud to adobe as the material of the wall. For furnishing the house, man has to change the shape of the log to become the table, chair, and bed...

松树的树干是做房梁和房柱的好材料，人必须将它生长在树林里的状态改变成木头状态，人必须将它的位置从原生地改变到造房地，人必须改变木料之间的关系，对木料进行榫接以构成房梁和房柱。为了造房子，人们必须将泥土变成土坯，作为墙的材料。为了添置家具，人们将木头改制成桌子、椅子和床……

"Change" means reorganization and surely extra effort is needed to get the work done. From the stand point of human being, the more effort man applies on it, the more value, man believes, it possesses. Easy come, easy go.

"改变"意味着重新组织，也就理所当然需要额外的努力来完成。从人的观点看，付出的努力越多，他（她）就会觉得越有价值。来得容易，去也易。

With only human effort, we are not able to obtain metal out of ore. We need heat to purify and thereafter to reorganize the crystallite of the metal. Heat in such cases plays a role just as important as human direct effort.

仅仅依靠人的努力，我们并不能从矿石中提取出金属。我们需要热量来纯化然后重新组织金属的晶粒，热量在此起着和人的努力一样重要的作用。

To distinguish from the natural resources, which exist by themselves without any intervention of human, we call a thing resulted from any intervention of human a product.

为了与那些没有人类的干预就存在于自然界的自然资源做区分，我们称人为干预的结果为产品。

A tree in the forest is a kind of natural resource, but a log of a tree is a product since human had cut the tree off and moved it out of the forest. A fish in

一棵长在森林里的树是自然资源，而一根原木却成了一种产品，因为人已经将树砍倒并将它运出了

the sea is a kind of natural resource, but a fish in the market is a product because man had caught it with some means of fishing.

森林。一条在海里的鱼是一种自然资源，而市场上出售的鱼是一种产品，因为人用某种捕鱼工具逮到了它。

Ⅴ. Dust thou art, to dust returnest — the Life Cycle of Wealth

Ⅴ. 来自尘土归于尘土 —— 财富的寿命周期

Besides a few substances like gold and diamond which has almost unlimited natural life, all other things have their own limited natural life and functioning cycle in general. The value of a product is therefore a function of time. It takes time to form the value of certain utility thereby to satisfy some of the human wants. Time wears and tears the value out, even if a product is just rested on the shelf, as the rust to iron, mold to wheat, decay to wood, weathering to stone, and degradation to plastics. At certain point of time, the value of the utility of an organization collapses into none.

Different product has different shape of life cycle. However, they mostly follow one pattern as following figure illustrated.

除了极少数物品，像钻石和黄金有无限的自然寿命外，几乎所有的物品一般都有一个自然寿命和效用周期。因此，一个产品的价值是时间的函数，满足人类需要的产品效用价值需要时间来形成，时间又不断噬蚀着价值，即便该产品只是被放置在货架上，就如锈蚀之于铁器，霉变之于小麦，腐朽之于木头，风化之于顽石，降解之于塑料。在某个时间点，组织的效用价值会坍塌而归于无。

不同的产品有不同形状的寿命周期图，但它们基本与下面的图形相似：

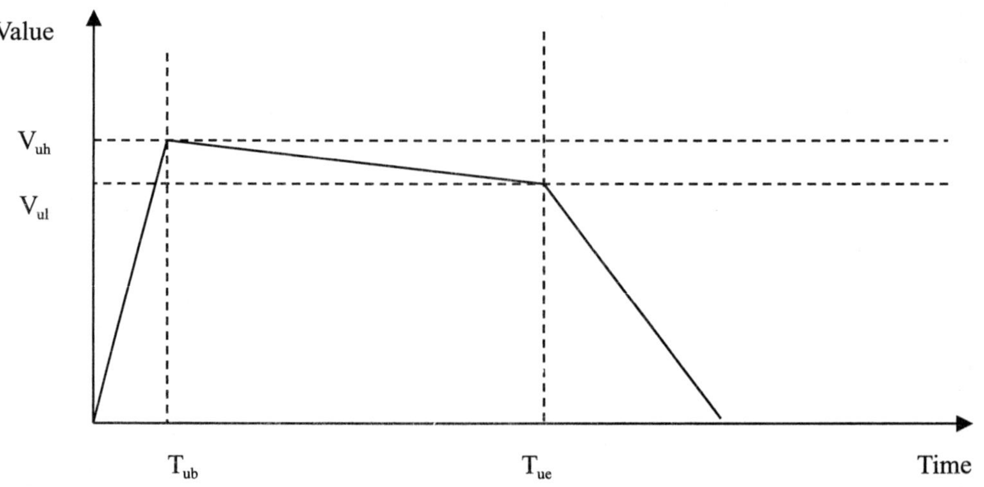

Figure 1. Natural life cycle pattern of a product

图 1. 某产品的自然生命周期

T_{ub} represents the time point when the utility begins; and T_{ue} represents the time point when utility ends.

The value may collapse earlier than its natural T_{ue} anytime if the product is engaged in application or destroyed by accident.

To a house, we can be consuming its value for even more than 100 years if we get it maintained properly.

Before going further, we have to make a clear understanding of what the Consumption is. We consider that the Consumption is a process which starts as soon as the product reaches the users' hands to perform its utility; not only the families of individuals are the consumers but also the firms and social organizations are consumers in a broad sense as well. As Marx said: "Labour uses up its material factors, its subject and its instruments, consumes them, and is therefore a process of consumption. Such productive consumption is distinguished from individual consumption by this, that the latter uses up products, as means of subsistence for the living individual; the former, as means whereby alone, labour, the labour-power of the living individual, is enabled to act. The product, therefore, of individual consumption, is the consumer himself; the result of productive consumption, is a product distinct from the consumer." (Vol. 1, Chapter 7, Sec. 1)

According to the different periods of the development of value, we divide the life cycle of a product into four phases, namely, wealth in process (hereinafter: WIP), wealth in stock (WIS), wealth in consumption (WIC), and wealth consumed (WC).

T_{ub} 表示效用的开始时间点，T_{ue} 表示效用的终止时间点。

当一个产品被使用或被损坏，其价值的坍塌点可能会比 T_{ue} 提前。

如果我们对一座房屋进行适当的维护，它能被我们使用上百年。

至此，有一个概念必须先予以澄清，那就是关于消费的理解。我们认为：一旦产品到达使用者之手开始发挥它的效用时，消费过程即开始了；不仅家庭的个体是消费者，公司及社会机构从广义上说也是消费者。正如马克思所说："劳动者用尽其物质元素、劳动对象及工具，消费它们，形成一个消费过程。这样的生产消费有别于个人消费，后者用尽产品作为个体生存的手段；而前者则通过劳动，形成个体行动的劳动力。因此，个人消费的产品是消费着他自己；而生产消费结果是消费有别于消费者的产品。"（第一卷第七章第一节）

根据价值形成的不同阶段，我们将产品寿命分成四个阶段，分别是：形成期（WIP）、储存期（WIS）、消费期（WIC）、和耗尽期（WC）。如果我们不考虑维护的存在，使用

If we don't take the maintenance into consideration the actual life curve of a product in use shrinks as the following Figure 2 illustrated.

中的财富寿命将比上图有所收缩，如图二所示：

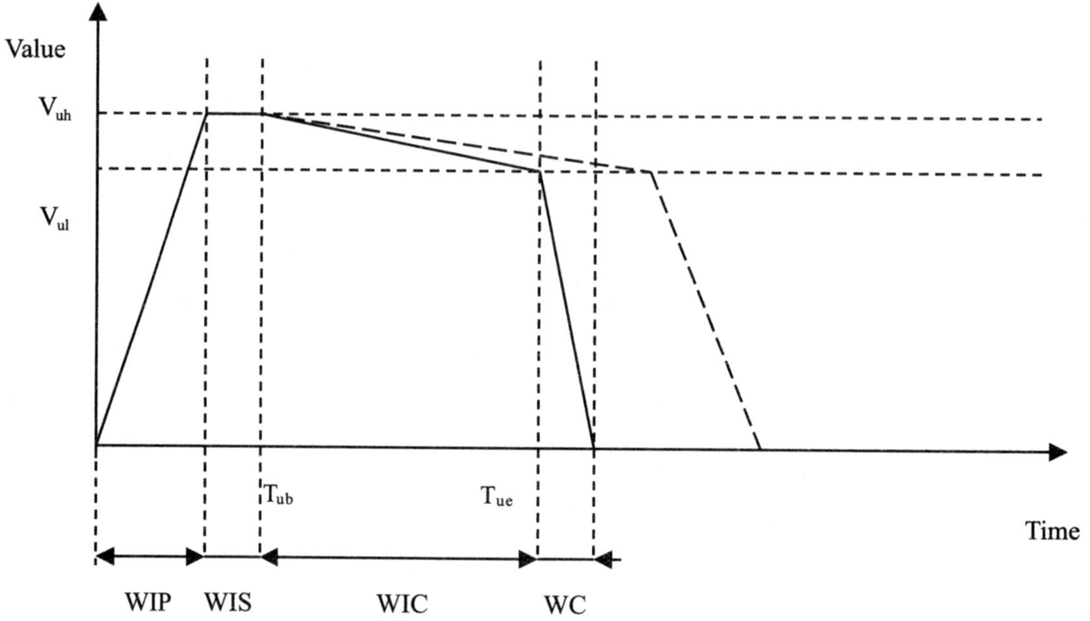

Figure 2. Actual life cycle pattern of a product

图 2. 某产品的实际生命周期

From a grain being seeded into the land to a bunch of new grains being harvested, the wheat plant on land is called WIP. When wheat stored in farmer's house or dealer's stockroom, it is still WIP. The wheat is grinded into flour and the flour is used by the baker for making bread, all of which are called as WIP. Bread on the shelf of bakery for sale is recognized as WIS. Bread in family's refrigerator is in period of WIS. Bread is on the dinning table is beginning of WIC. When bitten and chewed by man, it is recognized as in WIC; and eaten up by man or mould off in the refrigerator, we say bread is now a wealth consumed (WC). (see further discussion in Chapter ⅩⅩⅫ)

从一粒种子播入泥土到一捧新长成的麦粒被收获，小麦在地里是处于 WIP 阶段，小麦在农户和商贩的仓库里仍然是处于 WIP 阶段，被研磨成粉制成面包还是处于 WIP 阶段。面包放在面包房的货架上是处于 WIS 阶段。面包在某家的冰箱中处于 WIS 阶段，餐桌上的面包是 WIC 的开始，在口中咀嚼，吃进肚里后或者在冰箱中霉掉了，我们说面包被消费掉了，即处于 WC 阶段。（第三十二章有更进一步的讨论）

Generally speaking, in farming industry, the WIP takes months from seeding to on shelf; the WIC takes about seconds. The duration of WIP is usually much longer than that of the WIC.

通常，农业产品需经数月的形成期，而消费期可能是分分秒秒的工夫。WIP 的阶段远远长于 WIC 阶段。

From the ore mining all the way to the fulfillment of needle making, we call all the semis the WIP. Needle in grocery store is WIS. Needle on house wife's hand is WIC. In case the needle is broken accidentally, we call it WC.

从采矿到缝衣针的制成，我们称所有的中间产品为 WIP，杂货店货架上的缝衣针为 WIS，主妇手中的缝衣针是 WIC，如果某天缝衣针不小心被弄断了，则是 WC。

On the contrary to the products from farming industry, the period of WIP of a product in processing industries is usually much shorter than that of WIC in the processing industry in general. The WIP usually takes time measured in week while the WIC takes time measured in year.

与农产品相反，工业产品的 WIP 通常会比 WIC 短，WIP 一般以周计，WIC 一般以年计。

Proper maintenance to a product, may improve its life cycle. Some can be even lasting forever. However, extra efforts are needed for keeping the value of a product away from collapsing. The life cycle is therefore extended.

对一个产品进行恰当的维护可以延长其寿命，有些甚至可以无限地延长。但这需要额外的努力来保证产品的价值不至于坍塌，即寿命的延长。

The wheat flour can be kept good for food in house in an open atmosphere for probably three months. It can be extended to probably three years if kept in a dry, sealed and cool environment.

在一般开放的家庭环境中，面粉差不多能保存 3 个月不变质，但在一个干燥密封低温的环境下，它也许能保存 3 年。

The wheat grain can be kept good for reproduction for more than one year under a common environment. It could be extended to five years if kept in a dry and cool environment.

在一般环境下小麦能在 1 年后保持发芽的能力，在干冷的条件下 5 年之后照样能发芽。

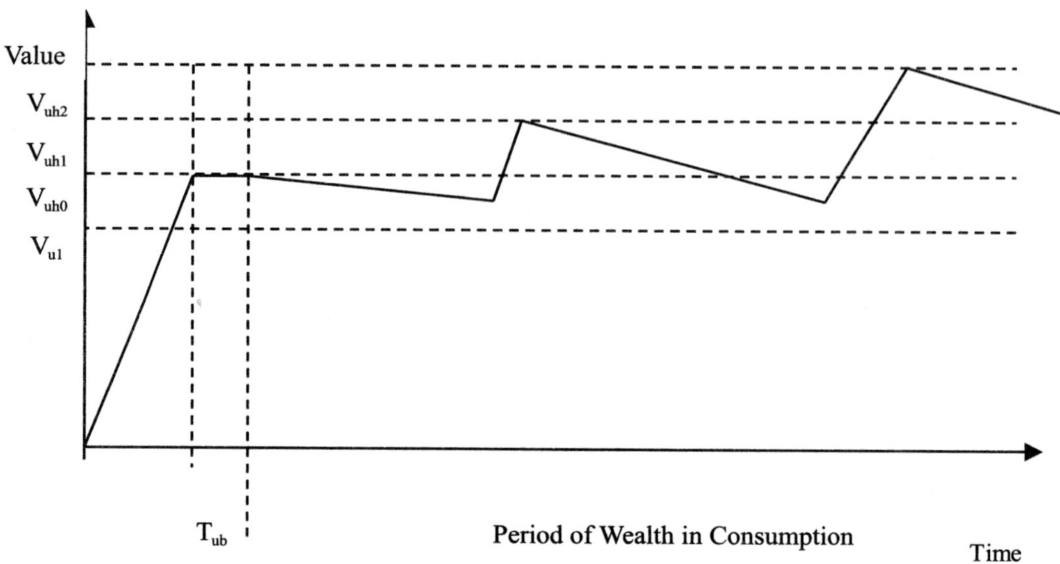

Figure 3. Life Curve with proper maintenance

图 3. 经恰当维护后的生命曲线

The designed life of Eiffel Tower is only 20 years. Under the proper maintenances by French, this beautiful tower built in 1889 passed its anniversary of 130 years already.

埃菲尔铁塔的设计寿命只有 20 年，但在法国人的恰当的维护下，这座建造于 1889 年的铁塔，过完了它 130 岁的生日。

Some services of pure labor like massage, entertainment, education, etc., the WIP and WIC are overlapped together, that means when the WIP starts the WIC starts simultaneously and WIC ends when WIP ends at the same time.

一些纯服务性的劳动产品如按摩、娱乐、教育等，它们的 WIP 和 WIC 是重叠的，也就是说：当 WIP 开始了，WIC 也随即开始；WIP 结束时，WIC 也同时结束。

PART TWO: ON VALUE

第二篇 价 值

Ⅵ. Review of the Theory of Value

Adam·Smith said: "The word value, it is to be observed, has two different meanings, and sometimes expresses the utility of some particular object, and sometimes the power of purchasing other goods which the possession of that object conveys. The one may be called 'value in use'; the other, 'value in exchange'."

"But experience has shown that it is not well to use word in the former sense." Marshall commented and continued, "Thus the term value is relative, and expresses the relation between two things at a particular place and time."

Marx stated in his book *Das Kapital* that "The utility of a thing makes it a use-value. But this utility is not a thing of air. Being limited by the physical properties of the commodity, it has no existence apart from that commodity. A commodity, such as iron, corn, or a diamond, is therefore, so far as it is a material thing, a use-value, something useful. This property of a commodity is independent of the amount of labor required to appropriate its useful qualities. When treating of use-value, we always assume to be dealing with definite quantities, such as dozens of watches, yards of linen, or tons of iron. The use-values of commodities furnish the

Ⅵ.价值理论回顾

亚当・斯密说："细观价值一词，含义有二：其一为表达某物的效用；而另一则表达用其购买他物的能力。前者可表为使用价值；后者可表为交换价值。"

"经验表明，运用前者含义稍欠妥当。"马歇尔评论说，"因此，价值是相对而言的，它表达在特定时间和地点的两物之间的关系。"

马克思在他的《资本论》里说："某物的效用使得它有使用价值，但其效用不是空穴来风，它受某物品的物理性质所限制，并不能脱离该物而存在。一个物品，如铁、玉米或钻石，只要是一种物质，就是有使用价值、有用的事物。物品的这种特性与所需要的形成其有用的品质的劳动量无关，当讨论使用价值时，我们总是假设以一定的数量为前提，如数块手表，数尺亚麻布，或者数吨铁。物品的使用价值为一些特殊的研究即物品

material for a special study, that of the commercial knowledge of commodities. Use-values become a reality only by use or consumption: they also constitute the substance of all wealth, whatever may be the social form of that wealth. In the form of society we are about to consider, they are, in addition, the material depositories of exchange-value.

的商用知识的研究提供素材。只有被使用或消费，使用价值才成为现实，它们构成所有财富的物质，不管该财富的社会形态是什么。此外，以社会的形式，我们认为它们是交换价值的物质载体。

"Exchange-value, at first sight, presents itself as a quantitative relation, as the proportion in which values in use of one sort are exchanged for those of another sort, a relation constantly changing with time and place. Hence exchange-value appears to be something accidental and purely relative, and consequently an intrinsic value, i.e., an exchange-value that is inseparably connected with, inherent in commodities, seems a contradiction in terms." (Vol. 1, Chapter 1, Sec. 1)

“交换价值在第一层面上表示的是一种数量关系，是一类使用价值与另一类使用价值交换的比例，是一种随时间地点不断变化的关系。因此，交换价值看起来具有偶然性和相对性，从而是固有的，也就是说：交换价值是不可分离地与宿主物品联系在一起的。这似乎是一个有些矛盾的定义。”（第一卷第一章第一节）

My interpretations on utility and purchasing power are however that, the utility is the external performance both subjectively and objectively of an organization as a whole caused by both the Mother Nature and human being. The power of purchasing is expressed according to the aggregated efforts of reorganizations in the reality initiated by human being only.

而我对效用和采购力的注释如下：效用是一个由自然之母和人类共同构造的组织的整体的主观的和客观的外部功效；采购力是仅由人类发动的再组织的努力的总和的表达。

A natural diamond possesses its utility of cutting hard surface already before it is unearthed, since Mother Nature had organized a diamond with carbon under high pressure and high temperature for quite a while so that the crystallites of carbon were well organized, the hardness of a diamond was therefore formed even without any exertion of

一颗天然的钻石在它出土之前已经具有了刻划坚硬表面的效用了，因为自然之母已经让碳元素经历了足够长时间的高温高压，形成其特有的晶粒结构，钻石硬度的形成并不需要人类的任何干预。所有天然晶体包括黄金都是一样。

human effort. The same thing happened to all kinds of the natural crystals including gold.

Take a plant as another example. A small piece of seed can grow into a big tree of tens meters height without any human's intervention at all. The utility of the trunk of the tree is there available potentially. The labor of cutting the trunk of a tree into a log is definitely not all about the value-in-use of a log. First of all, a log has its intrinsic property of heating things up via burning. Secondly, the cells of the tree were so organized by the Mother Nature that a log is a good material for making different kinds of furniture.

再来看看植物的例子，一粒小小的种子在没有人类的干预下也能长成数十米的参天大树。树干的效用已经潜在地生成了，将树干砍下成为原木的劳动绝对不是其使用价值的全部。首先，原木具有其天然的可以燃烧发热的特性。其次，原木的细胞被自然之母如此组织，从而成为制作家具的绝好材料。

However, most of the substances on the earth are in a quasi-chaotic status initially. The intervention of human plays a very important role in all the cases. The utilities of all of the tools are more or less associated with the reorganizations by human, since all the tools are designed, made, and used by human. Utility makes sense only to human being therefore. Utility deals with the relationship between human being and the nature. The term of Value-In-Use (hereinafter: VIU) is used for expressing the total efforts contributed by both nature and human in an abstract scenario, where the organization occurs at a single spot and all the elements necessary are immediately available at that spot.

当然，地球上绝大多数物质开始时都处于准混沌状态。人类的干预在所有情况下都起着相当重要的作用。所有工具的效用都或多或少地与人类的再组织相关联，因为所有的工具都是由人设计、制造和使用的。因此，效用是仅对人而言的。效用涉及的是人和自然的关系，使用价值（VIU）这个术语被用来表述在一个抽象的环境中（所有必备的条件在该处都是完备的），自然和人努力的综合贡献。

Goods exchange is basically the ownership exchange, which deals with the relation among the human beings. It makes natural sense for people to exchange goods based on the exertion of human efforts. The term of Value-In-Exchange

商品的交换也就是物权的交换，它涉及的是人类之间的相互关系。以人们投入的精力的总和来作为商品交换的依据成了一件很自然的事。这时我们需要用交换价值

(VIE) applies. This implies the hypothesis that Mr. Average Person A can get the same amount of products done as his next door neighbor Mr. Average Person B with the same effort under the same circumstance.

In the past, our economists were so concentrated on the process of construction of an organization that the process of deconstruction of an organization was literally ignored. Or, in other words, the effects of construction and deconstruction were treated the same in the past, which unfortunately led us into an economic labyrinth with no easy way out. From the natural science we know that, generally speaking, the process of the construction of an organization absorbs heat/energy while the process of the deconstruction of an organization generates heat/energy. Actually, the study on the deconstruction of an organization is as important as the study on the construction of an organization because the energy needed for construction of an organization comes from the deconstructions of other organizations. We have to use another term in addition, Value-In-Heat (VIH), to express the other aspect of an organization.

Food contains heat. When we eat food, the enzymes in our stomachs help us to deconstruct the organization of the food and to generate energy for our body. Therefore, we have power to do thinking and acting, and to bestow the value of labor into its subject thereby. This is a process of transferring the VIH of food into the VIE of the labor and the VIU of the subject through increasing the degree of the

（VIE）这个术语来表述。这里隐含下列假设：用相同的精力，凡人A先生在相同的条件下能与他的邻居凡人B先生生产一样的产品。

过去，我们的经济学家们只关注组织的建构过程却并不关注组织的解构过程，或者换句话说：组织的建构和解构被用相同的观点来认知。而由此导致我们进入一个不容易找到出口的经济学迷宫。自然科学告诉我们：一般而言，建构组织吸收热量/能量；解构组织释放热量/能量。事实上，研究组织的解构与研究组织的建构具有相同的重要性，因为建构组织的热量/能量来自另一组织的解构。我们使用热能价值（VIH）来描述一个组织的这项特性。

食物中含有热量，吃下食物后，我们胃里的酶帮助我们解构食物组织并为我们的身体提供热量。因此，我们有了精力去思考、去行动，从而将我们的劳动价值通过增加劳动对象的组织度而植于该对象中，这就是一个将食物的热能价值转化成劳动的交换价值和劳动对象使用价

organization of the subject of the labor.

When we burn coke together with ore in a furnace, the fire helps us to deconstruct the organization of the coke, which is made from wood, to generate the heat for causing the formation of the crystallite of the metal. The VIU and VIE of the metal are increased by the same amount of VIH the coke contained in addition to the direct human labor.

As a piece of wheat grain is put into the earth, it grows up into a strain of wheat seeding, under a suitable condition including water, fertilizer, air, sunshine, temperature, etc., through a long time photosynthesis, which turns the solar energy into chemical energy and saves it in the grain, straw, leave and root of the newly grown plant. The matured grain is used by human being as food; straw is used as fuel for cooking, as feed for herbivores, as fertilizer for land, or for other uses; and root may be kept in the land somehow as fertilizer with help of germ for next crop.

Let's focus on the grain only then. In the eyes of a natural scientist or a nutritionist, a kilogram of wheat grain consists of carbohydrates of so much, fat of so much, protein of so much, fibrin of so much, and over all containing heat of 13.260 kilo-Joules or 3.17 kilo-Calories. Finding another kind of grain, say rice, of the same Calorie-per-kilogram (It is called heat-value in natural science), and he says the wheat grain and rice grain are of the same value in heat. He doesn't count in how much effort the farmer has already contributed and how much effort the food dealer has contributed for

值的过程。

当我们在熔炉里用焦炭熔炼矿石时，火帮助我们解构由木头制成的焦炭的组织来产生热量，以促成金属晶粒组织的形成。金属的使用价值和交换价值的增加量等于焦炭所产生的热能价值与人类直接劳动的交换价值的总和。

当一粒小麦种子被播进土里，在适当的水、肥、气、阳光及温度的条件下，它能长成一株小麦苗，经过长时间的将太阳能转化成化学能的光合作用，化学能被储存在新长成的植株的谷、秆、叶和根中。成熟的谷子可以作为人的食物；秸秆可以被用作做饭的燃料，或者动物的饲料，或者肥料，或者派作他用；根部可以留在地里在细菌的帮助下成为下一季庄稼的肥料。

让我们将注意力放在谷物上来。在自然科学家或营养学家的眼里，1公斤小麦谷物含有碳水化合物若干，脂肪若干，蛋白质若干，纤维素若干，总共含有13.26千焦耳或3.17大卡热量。如果另一种谷物，如稻谷含有相同的每公斤单位热量（物理学中称为热值），那么，他就会说：小麦和水稻的谷物是（热能价值）等价值的。他并不关心农夫花了多少心血或者商贩花了多少精力将它们带到市场上，他

making them available in the market. He concerns only the amount of the heat, which determines the subsistence duration of human.

只关心维系人类生存时长的热量。

In the eyes of a farmer situated in dry land, because he has to convey plenty of water from distance besides the same plough, fertilization, and field management exerted, he believes 1 kilogram of rice shall be worth of 1.2 kilograms of wheat, no matter if the Calorie-per-kilograms of both wheat and rice are the same, since he spent more efforts for rice farming than wheat. To his neighbor, another farmer situated in wet land, he treats 1 kilogram of rice worth of only 0.9 kilogram of wheat since he has to dig an extra deep drainage network for wheat farming.

对劳作在旱地里的农夫而言，由于除了同样的耕地、施肥、田间管理外，他必须从远处引来很多的水对水稻进行灌溉，即便水稻和小麦的每公斤的卡路里的含量相同，他也会认为 1 公斤水稻的价值抵得上 1.2 公斤小麦的价值，因为他认为他种水稻花的精力比种小麦多。对于劳作在湿地的邻居来说，1 公斤水稻只能抵得上0.9公斤的小麦，因为他必须在地里挖掘额外的排水沟网才能收获小麦。

For the consistency of analysis, we have to isolate all the minor interferences by assuming an abstract situation that all the resources for production of a specific product are available on a single spot. The accumulation of total efforts forms the VIU of this product.

为了分析的一致性，我们必须将一些次要的干扰因素排除在外，以营造一个抽象的环境，在这样的抽象环境中，所有生产某产品所必需的自然资源都在该处唾手可得，所有努力的总和就形成了该产品的使用价值。

Now, as long as the VIHs are the same, the VIU of the wheat produced on dry land is the same as the VIU of wheat produced on wet land; the VIU of the wheat produced trough summer is the same as the VIU of wheat produced through winter; even though the VIEs of them are different.

这样，只要热量价值相同，生长在旱地的小麦价值与生长在湿地的小麦的使用价值是一样的；小麦的夏熟品种与秋熟品种的使用价值也是一样的，哪怕它们的交换价值并不一样。

In the eyes of a dealer, based on the 1 kg of rice produced in Japan, which will be sold in London; there are additional contributions being considered in, which are the contributions from the following aspects.

在粮商的眼里，一公斤在伦敦市场上出售的日本生产的水稻，还有以下因素的贡献需要被包括进来一道考虑：

●The family offering living conditions (same to a farmer);

●The firm of his own (same to a farmer);

●The transportation (same to a farmer);

●The possible lose during the transportation(same to a farmer);

●The government maintaining a good order of the society (farmer, too);

●The bank offering initial capital (farmer, too);

●The land lord for land and facility (farmer, too);

●There is a wear and tear during the transportation (farmer, too);

●There is a risk of damage caused by human's fault (farmer, too);

The above mentioned factors are all the contributions to the value-in-exchange.

Now we have gone through the illustrations of the concepts of VIH, VIU, and VIE in farming. Let's have a look at iron bar manufacturing as the second example which belongs to the processing industry.

Man started the iron making 3400 years ago. Main process is roughly as following described.

●Ore mining;

●Ore grinding;

●Ore sintering;

●Smelting under high temperature by burning coal/coke with oxygen;

●Decontaminating;

●Casting.

Assuming all the processes from mining to

● 家庭提供的生活环境（对农夫同）；

● 他自己的商号（对农夫同）；

● 运输（对农夫同）；

●运输过程中可能的损失（对农夫同）；

● 维护社会秩序的政府（对农夫同）；

● 提供初始资本的银行（对农夫同）；

● 设备与土地的拥有者（对农夫同）；

● 运输过程中的损耗（对农夫同）；

● 人为损失（对农夫同）；

以上这些都是形成交换价值的因素。

至此，我们已经诠释了农产品的热能价值、使用价值和交换价值。让我们再看一个铁坯生产的加工行业的例子。

人类在 3400 年前就开始炼铁了，基本的流程如下：

● 采矿；

● 研磨；

● 烧结；

● 熔炼；

● 去渣；

● 浇注。

假设从采矿到浇注的所有工序都

casting are done on the same spot, the VIH of the coal/coke and the accumulation of the labor, in a broad sense, are contributed into the VIU of the iron bar. In the reality, however, the ore from different mine carries different VIE because the difficulties of the mining in different mines are different and the distances from different mines are also different ,therefore the labor of transportations are different, too. The same principle applies onto the fuel supplying and even the supply of laborer as well.

是在相同地点完成，所消耗的煤/焦炭的热能价值与劳动的总和，在广义上，增加了铁坯的使用价值。而在现实世界中，从不同的矿区开采出来的矿石有不同的交换价值，这是因为，每个矿区开采难度并不一样，矿区到炼铁厂的距离也不一样，因此所需开采和运输的劳动成本也就不一样。同样的事情也会发生在燃料供应，甚至劳动力供应上。

Dress making is the last example which covers farming and processing. Through cotton farming, carbon dioxide and water are organized into the fiber via the photosynthesis therefore the initial VIH of the cotton fiber is formed. Taking the farmer’s efforts, which include ploughing, seeding, fertilizing, harvesting, and sorting, into consideration; the VIU/VIE of the fiber is thereof formed finally. Through spinning, weaving, dying, tailoring, sewing, packing, and distribution; the VIE of the dress is available for trade and VIU of it for use, while VIH stays in this dress until it is worn out and/or simply discarded into trash can. The waste of the dress is still valuable for generating heat by consuming the VIH of the cloth through burning. Until now, the VIE and the VIU are reset to zero, or to be precisely, approaching zero, while the VIH of the dress is transferred either onto the subject heated or none, meaning vanished into the air.

最后，让我们来看看一个横跨农业和加工业的制衣过程。在种植棉花的过程中，二氧化碳和水在光合作用下形成了纤维，棉花纤维的VIH由此形成。计入农夫的耕种、施肥、收获及梳理等努力，棉花纤维的VIU和VIE也最终形成了。经过纺线、织布、印染、剪裁、缝纫、包装及分销，衣服的VIE就可以被交易，且衣服的VIU可以被使用，而衣服的VIH则被保留在衣服里直到它被穿破或直接被扔进垃圾桶，被扔进垃圾桶的衣服仍然可以通过燃烧其VIH而产生热量。到此为止，衣服的VIE和VIU被清零，或者更准确地说逼近于零，而其VIH通过燃烧，将其价值转移到被加热的对象上，或者直接耗散在空气中。

In the VIH world, we see only the energy contained in an organization, which offers

在VIH的世界里，我们只看见组织所包含的能量，这些能量经

driving power to change the substantial world by deconstructing itself. VIH of a specific material is assigned by the Mother Nature. It is fixed in all circumstances.

In the VIU world, we see not only the contribution of labor, which is directly involved in production by ignoring the effects of location and season; but also the contribution of the Mother Nature. VIU is determined by the procedure of organizing a product starting from chaotic status. It is stable in certain period of time unless a technology break-through invented

In the VIE world, we see the contributions of all different kinds of people in the reality, who play different roles in the society, as the officers in the government; as the soldiers in the military; as the instructors for education and training; as the engineers for research and design; as doctors in hospitals; as clerks in bank or shop; as actors in show and performance; as porters in transportation; as lawyers; as house servants etc.; to keep the organization of society in order so that the production may be conducted safely, efficiently, and constantly; which is our vivid social ecosystem, as matter of fact. VIE is influenced by variety of social and geographic factors in addition. The products, which are of the same internal organization, sourced from same location, and exchanged at same place through same channel, are of the same VIE in a certain period of time even though that the price, as the external expression of VIE, changes quite often due to the current and/or the predicted future situation of supply vs. demand in general; even lies

由其自身的解构而释放出来作为改变物质世界的驱动力。某个物质的VIH是由自然之母赐予的，它在任何情况下都是确定的。

在VIU的世界里，我们看到的，不光是去除了地域和季节因素影响的直接劳动的贡献，还有自然之母的贡献。VIU是由从混沌状态开始到产品形成的整个组织过程来决定的。除非发生新的技术突破，它的值是稳定的。

在VIE的世界里，我们看到是在这个现实世界里所有各种不同的，在社会中发挥不同作用的人的贡献，比如政府的官员、部队的士兵、教育和培训机构的讲师、设计研究院的工程师、医院的医生、商店和银行的职员、表演的演员、搬运的工人、律师、家政服务员等，他们的存在使得整个社会组织运行得更安全、更有效、更确定。事实上，这就是我们生长于斯的活生生的社会生态。VIE受各种社会和地理因素的影响，但在相同的组织形式，相同的地点，通过相同的交换渠道进行交换的产品的VIE在一定的时期内是相同的，尽管作为VIE的外部表述的价格经常由于供求关系变化而变化，有时甚至一个谎言也会导致价格的波动。

may cause price fluctuations sometimes.

To human body, the VIH/VIU of the rice of 100 kg in town and those of the rice of 100 kg in distance of 100 km are the same in deed. However for some reason, say due to flooding, people need to transport rice from distance to the town by some means, say porters. It might take four days for a porter to carry in 100 kg of rice. During these four days, porter needs eat out about 5 kg of rice plus cooking charge and family support, only 90 kg of the rice are left for his boss in town. The boss needs the same amount of rice to make his family and himself survival. There are only 80 kg of rice available for sale in town. Therefore the VIE of the 80 kg of rice from distance is equivalent to the VIE of 100 kg of local rice in town even though the original unit VIU/VIH in distance was the same as that in town. It leads us to the conclusion that the same products with the same VIU/VIH from different location may have different value-in-exchanges at a specific spot. The VIE of 1 kg of rice from Thailand is surely different to the VIE of the 1 kg of rice from Japan in the market of London.

对于人体来说，本地产的100公斤稻谷的VIH/VIU与来自远方的100公斤稻谷没什么区别。可由于某种原因，比如发大水，镇子里的人们必须从远处以某种方式，假设是采用人工运输运进稻谷。一个运输工可能需要花4天将100公斤稻谷运进镇子，可是在这4天里运输工需要吃掉5公斤粮食，再加上他的家庭的需要，可能只剩下90公斤稻谷给他的雇主了。而老板自己和家庭在这4天里也需要粮食生存，因此，只留下80公斤的稻谷在市场销售。尽管原先的单位VIU/VIE是相同的，而这从远方运来的80公斤稻谷的VIE却与本地产的100公斤稻谷的VIE是相等的。我们因此可以说：尽管原始的VIH/VIU是相同的，但从不同地点来的产品，在确定地点的交换价值是不同的。在伦敦出售的泰国大米与日本大米的VIE是不同的。

Ⅶ. Measure of the Value

There is a more precise way to formulate the value of a commodity. On top of the man labor-power-time, all other forms of energy, including animal labor-power-time and machine labor-power-time, dissipated in the product forming process shall be integrated together to express the value exerted onto the product. The unit of measure of the value is

Ⅶ. 价值的计量

我们给商品的价值构建一个精确的公式如下：在人的劳动力—时间之上，所有其他形式的能量贡献，包括用于生产过程的畜力—时间和机械劳动力—时间，都应该累加起来计算该产品的价值。价值的计量单位是焦耳。财富是物化了的价值，

Joule. Wealth is the materialized value, so the unit of measure of the wealth is also Joule.

所以财富的计量单位也是焦耳。

Let's take a survey on the following case for proof. For a farmer, there are three ways to plough his land; the first of which is to hire three persons to do the job, two of whom to drive the plough through pulling ropes in the front and one other to control the plough at the back; the second of which is to hire one ox to drive the plough in the front and one human to control at the back; or the third of which is to hire a person to drive a motor tractor with a plough.

让我们以下例为证。一个农夫有三种方法来耕地，其一为：雇佣三人，两人在前拉犁，一人在后扶犁；其二为：一牛在前拉犁，一人在后扶犁；其三为：一人开着带犁的拖拉机耕地。

I believe the value adding to the crop of the farmer in all three ways shall be about the same by comparing the total net energy dissipated in three different methods since all of them did the same work, that is to overcome the friction caused by the earth through the same distance they drive through (we will discuss the values of these three scenarios in later Chapter further). Only difference is though that; pure human configuration may take three days, while the total mass of which is the lightest; the human plus ox one may take one day, while the total mass of which is in the middle; and the tractor plus human one may take only a few hours, while the total mass of which is the heaviest; to finish the plough, just because the power of an ox is higher than that of two men; and the motor tractor is even of much higher power, which means much higher efficiency in scale of time than the former two configurations.

我认为，这三种方法给农夫庄稼增加的价值应该是差不多相同的，因为这三种耕地方法就克服泥土的阻力而做的功而言是相同的（后面将会做进一步的探讨）。不同的恐怕只是因为拖拉机的功率最大；牛的功率居中；两人的总功率最小。人拉犁可能需要三天完成；牛拉犁可能需要一天完成；而拖拉机耕地仅需要个把小时完成。而三人组合的总质量最小；人牛组合的总质量居中；人开拖拉机组合的总质量最大。

To avoid the paradox of "the more idle and unskilful the labourer, the more valuable would

为了避免"闲散的欠技能的劳动者越多，增加的价值越多"的悖

his commodity be, because more time would be required in its production", we can easily treat the idle time of person in the value adding process as the invalid work time. An unskilled person spends a longer time for getting the job done is just because his efficiency is lower than a skilled person. Or in Ricardo's words, he has poor comparative advantage. Generally speaking, it needs same amount of energy in net to get a certain work done, no matter what the working style and arrangement is.

论，我们能够容易地将劳动的空闲时间作为无功时间；一个欠技能的劳动者只是他的劳动效率比其他正常人低从而需要较长的工作时间而已，或者用李嘉图的话来说：他不具备比较优势。一般说来，无论工作的方式是什么，完成一个特定工作的所需的净能量是一定的。

From now on, we refer to the labor, in this article, not only as the labor of human but also labor of animal and labor of mechanical engine in the reorganization process; Instead of labor-time, we are going to use labor in Joule to express the work fulfilled by men, animals, and/or mechanical engines.

从现在起，本文中所述的劳动，指的不仅是人类的，还包括牲畜和机械引擎的在再组织过程中的贡献。我们用焦耳为单位取代劳动—时间，来表述人、牲畜及机器所做的工作。

Ⅶ. Expression of the Value

Ⅶ. 价值的表达

With the introduction of the energy into the value definition, we found that the value of a product has two faces in deed, especially of products, which are carriers of energy, from farming and other energy industries. For example, a piece of log contains certain amount of VIH, which can be used for smelting ore to make iron by burning, through which the VIH of a log is transferred into the VIU and VIE of the iron; or it can be used for making a quite good desk with certain amount of the VIE of labor added to the initial VIU/VIE of the log by extra labor while the portion of the VIH

随着能量的概念引入价值的定义，我们发现：一个产品，特别是由农业或其他能源行业生产的能量载体，具有了两张面孔。比如一段原木，通过燃烧可以将其 VIH 转移给被其加热的由矿石冶炼成的铁的 VIU/VIE；或者被用于制作一张漂亮的书桌，劳动的价值加上原木的原始 VIU/VIE，构成了书桌的 VIU/VIE，而部分原木的 VIH（假设 70% 的原木 VIH 保留，30% 的 VIH 随着刨花木屑而变成废料）保留在

of the log (say 70% of the original VIH remained since 30% of the wood was scrapped during the process of desk making) is still retained in that desk until someone breaks the desk and uses the broken desk to make heat by burning. The VIH of the desk is therefore transferred into the VIU/VIE of the hot water or food cooked no matter how much VIU/VIE of the desk was before.

书桌里直到某日书桌被损坏，而损坏的书桌被拿去当燃料烹制食品。这时，留在书桌里的 VIH 会因此转移到被烹制的食品的 VIU/VIE 中，而不管这书桌的 VIU/VIE 曾经有多高。

For better expressing the double faces of the value, we have to use complex number to describe it instead of real number in the past. We may use form of (H+iL) to express value of any substances. The real part of the value expresses the energy a certain amount of substance containing, which supplies heat for bodies of human and animals, or heat for varieties of mechanical engines; while the imaginary part expresses how much allocation of labor, in a broad sense, is bestowed into such amount of substance. We may say, one kilogram of local wheat contains (13260+i5000) Joule of value, which means one kilogram of wheat offers 13.26 kJ of energy to the human body as food, meanwhile it embodies 5 kJ of labor in total (no matter in forms of labor of human, labor of animal, and/or labor of engine) used for producing and marketing such wheat locally. Or, one kilogram of wheat from Ohio, US to Shanghai, China contains (13260+i6000) Joule of value, which means one kilogram of wheat offers 13.26 kJ of energy to the human body as food, meanwhile it embodies 6 kJ of labor in total covering production, transportation, public service, etc. We may express the value of one gram of diesel as (40320+i20000) Joule; the value of one gram of

为了更恰当地表达价值的两面性，我们必须放弃以往使用实数形式来表达价值的方法，转而使用复数形式。我们使用 (H+iL) 来表述某物的价值，实部表述该物所含可以作为人体或牲畜的食物，或者提供机械引擎的能量的大小；虚部表述该物广义劳动的投入。我们可以说一公斤小麦含有 (13260+i5000) 焦耳的价值，这就是说，作为食物它能向人体提供 13.26 千焦耳的热量，同时说明本地生产销售此食物共花费了 5 千焦耳的劳动（不管是人的劳动，牲畜的劳动还是引擎的劳动）。或者一千克由美国俄亥俄州生产，在中国上海消费的小麦含有 (13260+i6000) 焦耳的价值，说明其含有 13.26 千焦耳可供使用的热量，同时含有包括生产、运输、公共服务等贡献的 6 千焦耳的劳动。我们可以将 1 克柴油的价值表述为 (40320+i20000) 焦耳；1 克汽油的价值表述为 (46000+i22000) 焦耳；1 克地产松树的价值为 (12000+i9000) 焦耳；1 克地产标准煤的价值为

gasoline as (46000+i22000) Joule; the value of one gram of local pine wood as (12000+i9000) Joule; one gram of local standard coal as (29000+i6000) Joule.

(29000+i6000) 焦耳。

Ⅸ. Consumption Way of Value

Let's look at a pride of lions first. When they are hungry, they organize themselves to prey, which is the only form of their labor. The prey caught is their product of labor. Eating up the body of the prey is the consumption of their product. Being stuffed, they find a place to rest (by females), to play (by cubs) and to patrol (by male) until they feel hungry again and therefore prey again, so on and so forth.

Upon eating up the body of a prey, the energy is therefore taken and saved in the belly of a lion, portion of which will be spent/consumed on preying/laboring next time for the sustaining of life while rest of which will be spent/consumed on just leisure. We categorize the first case, which the energy is consumed for getting the new energy for next cycle, the samsaraous (reincarnational) consumption, and the second one, which the energy is consumed just for "being" basically, the terminal consumption.

A pride of lions could keep preying whole daytime long. Minus the amount the whole pride eats to obtain the energy for preying the next time, the rest of what they got would be the surplus of their preying. But they don't do so because it makes no sense for them to just pile up the prey they

Ⅸ. 价值的消费途径

让我们从观察一个狮群开始，饥饿了，它们就自动组织起来去猎食，猎食是它们唯一的劳动。捕来的猎物是它们的劳动产品，吃掉猎物就是对产品的消费。吃饱后，它们就找个地方休息（母狮）、玩耍（小狮）、巡逻（公狮），直到下次饥饿袭来而再次捕猎，如此等等，循环往复。

吃完猎物后，能量被吸收并存储在狮子的肚子里，部分能量将被用于维持生命的下次捕猎活动的耗费 / 消费中，另一部分则被用于休闲的耗费 / 消费中。前一种情况，是为获得新能量的能量消费，我们称之为轮回消费；而后一种情况，能量的消费基本上只是为了“存在”而发生，我们称之为终极消费。

狮群是有能力在整个白天捕猎的，扣除狮群为获得下次捕猎的能量而吃下的猎物，剩下的就是这个狮群捕猎的剩余。但它们却不会这样去做，因为只是堆积捕得的猎物看着它们腐烂，对狮群来说毫无其

caught and watch them in decay with no benefit at all to the pride. The accumulation of surplus makes no sense to the lion pride.

他益处。因此，剩余的积累对狮群来说毫无意义。

Having a look at the whole world of all the animals other than humankind, we will soon realize that, averagely speaking, all the animals produce/collect only energy just for satisfying the needs by their bodies. We may call this phenomenon the Elementary Equilibrium of Being.

考察一下所有的除人类之外的整个动物世界，我们会发现：平均来说，所有的动物只会生产 / 采集仅仅它们的身体所需的能量， 我们称这种现象为生存的初级均衡。

Our ancestors did almost the same thing in million years ago. Naked men, women and even their children wandered around in daytime, moved from one place to another for collecting fruits on or under the trees, vegetables on or underneath the ground, and cereals on the land, occasionally, if lucky enough, they captured small, slow moving, or wounded animals as their product as well. Sometimes, products might be over produced a little bit and saved for the season when food is in shortage. Averagely, they produced (or more precisely, found) just enough food for the family's living. After mastering fire, the whole family/tribe might sit together around the fire on the wood collected by the family member; cooking, eating, chatting, entertaining, or just resting while some of them were guarding, when food and wood were their main products for their consumption sooner or later. In addition to food and wood; through surveying and thinking; people started to make tools for the efficiency of production or the convenience of living, garments for the comfort of body, and ornaments just for good looking; by utilizing the leisure time. Both the producing tools

数百万年之前，我们的祖先也是一样，裸体的男人、女人甚至他们的孩子成天在外游荡，一处一处地收集树上树下的果子，地上地下的蔬菜，田间地头的谷物；运气好的话，逮到一些跑得慢的、受伤的小动物作为他们的收获。有时产品可能会超量，然后被存储起来以备食物短缺之时。平均来说，他们只生产（准确地讲是找到）正好满足家庭生活的足够的食物。掌握了火的使用方法后，整个家庭 / 家族可以一起围坐在由家庭成员收集来的木材燃着的火堆旁，烹饪、取食、聊天、娱乐或仅仅是休息，同时有一部分人为保护家族的安全而警戒。那时，食物和木材是他们用于消费的主要产品。在食物和木材之外，经过观察和思考，人们开始利用空闲时间制造用于提高生产效率的生产工具；方便生活的生活工具；舒服身体的服装；或者仅仅是为了好看的饰品。不管是生产工具

and living tools, garments, ornaments, etc. are all the products of the human labor other than direct food/energy production. All producing tools are used for producing new energy or improving the energy efficiency eventually, so the energy/value used for making producing tools belong to the samsaraous consumption while the energy used for directly making living tools, including garments and ornaments, belong to the terminal consumption, which maintains man not only being but also feeling good.

还是生活工具，还有服装、饰物等都是人类的有别于食物 / 能量直接生产的劳动的产品。所有生产工具最终都是被用于生产新能量或者提高能量的使用效率的，所以用于制造生产工具的能量消耗属于轮回消费；而用于直接制造生活工具、服装、饰品的消费则属于终极消费，这些不仅维系人的存在而且使他们感觉良好。

Crop farming and animal farming made it possible that not all the members of the society were necessary out whole day long for making food and wood. There were laborer surplus available for doing something else. There came professional wizard, priest, monk, imam, poet, actor, scholar, doctor, and artisan, so on and so forth in the society, to whom the farmers pay partial of their food and wood for forecast, pray, consolation, knowledge, cure, and tools. Besides food and wood, people started to consume other products just mentioned.

作物种植和家畜养殖使得整个社会不再需要所有的家庭成员成天在外采集食物和木柴，剩余劳动力便可以用来制作其他产品。因而社会上有了巫师、牧师、僧侣、阿訇、诗人、演员、学者、医生和工匠，诸如此类，农民通过支付他们部分食物和木材来换得预告、祈祷、慰藉、知识、医药和工具。人们开始消费食物和木柴之外的其他产品了。

X. Transfer of Value

X. 价值的转移

A. Simple Transfer

Now, we all know that almost all the values are sourced from the sun, considering that the contributions of the terrestrial heat and the nuclear energy are so far so little that it is almost ignorable. Through the sunshine, the sun passes the energy onto the plants, algae and atmosphere on the earth.

A. 简单转移

至此，我们已知道几乎所有的价值都源自太阳，因为地热和核能的贡献可忽略不计。通过阳光，太阳将能量输送给地球上的植物、藻类和大气层。通过光合作用，植物和藻类将地球上的自然资源（主要

By means of photosynthesis, the plants and algae convert the natural resources on the earth, mainly water and carbon dioxide, into the fibrin, starch, protein, oil and sugar; within which the energy from the sun is converted and saved. The VIH of a plant/alga is therefore created.

是二氧化碳和水等）转化成纤维素、淀粉、蛋白质、油和糖，从而光能转换成了化学能并得以储存。植物和藻类的 VIH 由此形成。

Let us take an apple tree as the example. From a seed to a mature tree, it takes certain amount of energy to grow the roots, trunk, branches, leaves, and fruits. The energy dissipated for growing the roots, trunk, branches, leaves, and flowers create the VIUs of roots, trunk, branches, leaves, and fruits respectively; and the energy reserved in roots, trunk, branches, leaves, and fruits, which can be recalled again by burning or digesting, generate the VIHs of roots, trunk, branches, leaves, and fruits respectively.

以苹果树为例，从一粒种子到长成一棵成熟的苹果树，用于其根、干、枝、叶及果等的生长的总的能量消耗，构成了根、干、枝、叶及果的 VIU；而储存在根、干、枝、叶及果中的可以通过消化或者燃烧的能量分别构成了根、干、枝、叶及果的 VIH。

Now, here comes Adam and Eve. They eat apples dropping from the trees, of which the VIH is 2.17 kJ per kilogram, and they eat so many apples that they are energized to be able to do something other than just lying and eating. Say Adam eats 3 kilograms of apples, Eve eats 2 kilograms. By eating apple fruits, Adam and Eve possess ability of laboring worth of the VIH of the apple fruit they eat if they keep working whole day long except reasonable rest and eating time. To measure the value created by their labor we use VIE. The total VIE they created in that day equals to the total VIH of the apple they ate in the same day in general, with assumption that the energy consumption for reasonable rest and eating time is null, that is to say the transfer ratio of energy is supposed as 100%.

这时，来了亚当和夏娃，他们吃从树上掉下来的苹果，苹果每公斤的 VIH 为 2.17 kJ，食用足够的苹果，他们获得了比让他们躺在地上继续吃苹果还要多的能量。假设亚当每天吃 3 公斤苹果，夏娃每天吃 2 公斤苹果。一天内，除了吃饭和适当的休息时间，亚当和夏娃获得了与他们所食用的苹果的总的热量价值 VIH 相同的劳动的能力，我们用 VIE 计量他们劳动的价值，即总的来说，假设吃饭和适当休息的能量消耗为零（假设能量转移率为 100%），一天中，他们总的劳动价值 VIE 等于当天所食用的苹果的总的热量价值 VIH。

Adam spends a half day to get some flints back home and to make three stone axes (without handle) from them; and another half day to cut a log of a tree into a canoe with using out those three axes at all.

亚当花了半天时间寻找到三片燧石并制成了（无柄）斧子，在另一个半天里，磨好了那三把斧子来砍树和掏空树心，制成一艘独木舟。

Eve has to take care of two children of them the whole day, meanwhile she usually can do some other work simultaneously, which can be treated as, a quarter day in total to collect the fruits from apples trees, which weigh 10 kilogram in total; and the second quarter day in total to collect the branches and leaves from the trees; and a half day in total for housekeeping, food preparation and children fostering for the family. So, Eve does only half day direction production and half day house work necessary for the family subsistence.

夏娃必须整天照看孩子，但同时她也可以做些其他事情，累计计算：四分之一天用来摘树上的苹果，共有 10 公斤重；四分之一时间用于收集树叶树枝；另外半天是整理家务、准备食物和照料孩子。夏娃从事了半天的直接生产和半天的维系家庭长久生存的家务劳动。

Adam eats 3 kilograms of apple fruit a day, which is worth of 6.51 kJ of VIH. Half of this 6.51 kJ of VIH is transferred into those three stone axes. So, one ax carries (0+i1.085) kJ of value. Since all of these three axes are worn out in making canoe, we therefore say that the values of these three axes are transferred into the canoe. Plus half day's effort Adam exerts, the value of the canoe is therefore (70000+i6.51) kJ, which is equal to (100000+i0) (the supposed initial VIH of the log) + 3×(0+i1.085) (the values of three axes) + (0+i3.255) (the value of the labor of Adam's half day's labor) – (30000+i0) (supposing that VIH of scraped wood of the log takes 30%). For simplifying the calculation, we ignore the value contribution by Eve of her house work at this moment.

亚当一天吃3公斤苹果，折合6.51kJ的VIH，6.51kJ VIH的一半被转移到那三把石斧上，一把斧子携带了(0+i1.085) kJ的交换价值。因为在制作过程中全都磨损掉了，所以三把斧子的价值又被转移到那艘独木舟中了，加上另一个半天的投入，那艘独木舟的价值为(70000+i6.51) kJ，其明细为：(100000+i0) (假设原木的热量价值) + 3 × (0+i1.085) (三把斧子的价值) + (0+i3.255) (亚当半天劳动的价值) – (30000+i0) (假设有30%的木料被挖掉成木屑了)。简单起见，我们这里暂时忽略夏娃做家务的贡献。

Eve eats 2 kilograms of apple fruit a day, which

夏娃一天吃 2 公斤苹果，能产

creates labor value in (0+i4.34) kJ a day in total. 1/4 of her daily labor value goes to those 10 kilograms of apple fruits making (21.7+i1.085) kJ in total; another 1/4 of the daily labor value goes to that pile of branches and leaves making (1000+i1.085) kJ in total (the real part is just an estimation); a half of her labor value goes to her house work, including housekeeping, food preparation, child care, etc., which is consumed by the family members in the same day.

生总共 (0+i4.34) kJ 价值的劳动，1/4 转移到那 10 公斤的苹果中，折合 (21.7+i1.085)kJ，另四分之一转移到那一堆树枝树叶中，折合 (1000+i1.085)kJ（实数部分为估计数）；还有半天的家务劳动的价值被家庭成员们当天消费掉了。

Cain and Abel were interested in fishing. As grew up, they decided to find a way for capturing fish effectively. Working together, they tried many different designs and materials collected by themselves. Eventually, they invented a cone like basket made of bamboo twigs with a wide open on bottom and a small open on top. It took 100 days of two brothers in total through many times of trial. How much VIE of the invention is worth of then? It is 868 kJ, which is the product of 2.17 ×4×100. When the old fishing basket is broken, they need probably only half day of one person to duplicate another fishing basket afterwards, which is worth of 2.17 kJ in value. Since the knowledge of making fishing tool invented by the brothers can be used almost forever, the value amortization of the invention onto every new fishing tool is therefore very little and usually ignored.

该隐和亚伯对捕鱼很感兴趣，长大后，他们决定找到一种有效的捕鱼方法。他们在一起试验了很多种想法和材料，最后终于找到了一种方法：用竹条制成的上下开口的上小下大的罩来捕鱼。他们一共花了 100 天完成这项发明，那么这项发明的交换价值是多少呢？它应该是以下三个数的乘积 2.17× 4×100 等于 868 kJ。如果一个旧的这种捕鱼罩用坏了，他们可能只需要半天的工作时间复制一个新的捕鱼罩，因为由兄弟俩合作发明的制作捕鱼罩的方法可以被一直使用下去，该发明的交换价值分摊到每个捕鱼罩上的部分非常之小，通常可以忽略不计，因此一个捕鱼罩的交换价值就是 2.17 kJ。

Here is the rule: During the process of deconstruction of the energy carrier, only the VIH portion are transferred to the labor value which is the VIE of the labor, no matter how much the VIE of such food/fuel itself contains; and, during the

规则：当能量载体解构时，无论其本身所载的交换价值为何，仅其所含的热量价值 VIH 部分被转移到新的劳动中成为劳动的交换价值 VIE；而在产品的建构过程中，所

process of construction of a product or products, all the VIEs of the means of production, ultimately VIEs of labors, are transferred into the product(s) and the VIH of the materials for the production are distributed in proportion among the new products and the scraps if any.

有生产工具的VIE，追根溯源地说，就是所有劳动的交换价值都被转移到新产品中，且原材料中的VIH将会按比例地分配到新产品（有效部分）和废料中。

Supposing a man consumes, equivalently in total, 1 kg wheat a day averagely, it means that he can do the labor worth of 13.26 kJ in a day with ignoring the energy saved in his belly. We say that he is only able to offer value to the society worth of 13.26 kJ maximal in a day no matter he is a laborer or a banker.

假设一个人平均一天消耗1公斤当量的小麦，在不考虑在他肚子里的能量储存的话，他就只能干价值13.26 kJ的活儿，即无论是一个普通的工人还是一个银行家，他一天最多只可能向社会提供价值为13.26kJ的劳动。

B. Equation of Value

B. 价值等式

With the understanding of the value in heat (VIH) and the value in exchange (VIE) transferring into the new product, based on the law of conservation of energy, we then naturally have the following equation in terms of the gross wealth created by an independent society, produced in certain period of time, as,

在理解了热量价值和交换价值向一个新产品转移的原理后，我们就自然会得出如下基于能量守恒定律的有关一个独立社会的，在某个时间段内创造的毛财富总价值等式：

$$(1) \quad \sum_{i=1}^{P} \mathrm{VIE}i = \sum_{j=1}^{M} VIE_j + \sum_{k=1}^{N} VOT_k$$

Where: P represents the total number of different kind products in both tangible and intangible forms being/having been newly produced, that is to say, all the finished products, semi-products, and work-in-processes are included, in certain period of time, say one day, one week, one month, one quarter, or one year, etc.;

其中，P表示在一定时期内，如一天、一周、一月、一季或一年内，所有以最终产品、半成品、在制品等形式存在的有形和无形的新产品的品种数；

M represents the total number of different kind of energy carriers being deconstructed in the same

M表示这段时间内被解构的各种形式的能量载体的品种数；

period of time;

N represents the total number of different kind of producing tools in use in the same period of time;

VIE_i represents the value in exchange of the product #i in total;

VIH_j represents the value in heat of the energy carrier #j in total for production;

VOT_k represents the value transfer of the producing tool #k in total for production;

In the real world, there are many different societies, which possess different energy efficiencies in terms of production style people master or prefer. Comparatively, it might need different amounts of the total VIH and VOT to produce the same total amount of VIE. The above equation shall be adjusted as the following by adding the factors of comparative advantage into consideration, meaning that, to produce the same set of products, different society dissipates different total amounts of energy in both real form and imaginary form.

N 表示这段时间内被使用的生产工具的品种数；

VIE_i 表示第 i 种产品的总的交换价值；

VIH_j 表示第 j 种能量载体的总的热量价值；

VOT_k 表示第 k 种生产工具在生产过程中价值的转移。

在现实世界里，存在许多具有不同的能量效率的社会，在这些社会里，人们能掌握的或是愿意使用的生产方式各有不同，相比较而言，同样一个产品组合的价值可能是由不同总量的 VIH 和不同总量的 VOT 构成。将比较优势因子考虑进来后，上述等式应调整为如下的表达形式，也就是说：不同的社会生产相同配置数量的产品所消耗的实项和虚项的能量总和是不同的：

(2)

$$\sum_{i=1}^{P} VIE_i = \left(\sum_{j=1}^{M} (\upsilon j' * VIH_j') + \sum_{k=1}^{N} (\upsilon k' * VOT_k')\right) = \left(\sum_{j=1}^{Q} (\upsilon j'' * VIH_j'' + \sum_{k=1}^{R} (\upsilon k'' * VOT_k'')\right)$$

Where: υ' and υ" represent the different factors of comparative advantage of two specific societies of different living and producing styles.

One society always set all of its own factors of comparative advantage to 1, and calculates out the factors of comparative advantage of the other society by comparisons.

其中：υ'和υ"分别代表两个特定社会环境的针对其不同生活/生产方式的比较优势因子。

一个社会总是将自己的比较优势因子设置成 1，再通过比较计算出另一个社会的比较优势因子。

PART THREE: ON SURPLUS-VALUE

第三篇 剩余价值

Ⅺ. Three Sectors of the Social Economy

Ⅺ. 社会经济的三大产业

Nowadays, most of countries follow more or less the classification of industries suggested by Mr. Fisher and Mr. Clark to do the statistics, namely primary industry, secondary industry, and tertiary industry. The primary industry covers basically all kinds of farming; the secondary industry covers basically all manufacture, construction, mining, and energy; the tertiary industry covers basically trade, communication, and variety of services. But I would like to make a slight modification according to the manner of energy application in the production as the following.

在当代世界，大部分国家都按照费雪和克拉克的提议进行产业分类统计，分别是第一产业、第二产业和第三产业。第一产业基本上涵盖各种农业；第二产业基本上涵盖了所有加工业、建筑业、采矿业和能源产业；第三产业基本上涵盖贸易、通讯及各种服务业。但我将根据能量在生产过程中的存在形式对其进行一个稍稍的如下调整：

1. Fuel Industry (FI), the Primary Sector of the social economy, the products of which are used for supplying either bodies of humans and animals or engines of machines with the energy, which are either embedded in produces like cereal, poultry, livestock, fish, vegetable, fruit; including all their derivative products, which are used as food or drink such as, bread, cookie, liquor, wine, juice, vinegar, pickle, etc.; or embedded in cotton, wood, crude oil, coal, radioactive materials; and their derivative products, which are treated as the source of energy

1. 燃料产业（FI），是社会经济的第一产业，该产业的产品，被用于向人体和牲畜或者是机械引擎提供能量，这些能量不是包含在诸如谷物、禽类、牲畜、鱼类、蔬菜和水果以及它们的衍生产品，如面包、饼干、烈酒、红酒、果汁、酸醋、腌菜等食品或饮料中，就是包含在诸如棉花、木料、石油、煤炭、放射性材料以及它们的衍生产品，如汽油、柴油、电力，或者转换为直

such as, gasoline, diesel, electricity; or directly in forms of terrestrial heat, sunshine, water flow, wind.

Sometimes, the products of FI can be used not only as the energy carriers but also as the raw materials for making tools when the physical structure of which are utilized. For example, the cotton can be of cause used as a fuel to create heat. But it's mainly used for making clothes for human while the heat value of the cotton is embedded in clothes. A log can be used as fuel of heating, too. But people use it mostly as the material of making furniture. When the furniture is broken into garbage, it can be used again as fuel to generate heat eventually. All the plastics are made from the crude oil. Plastics are usually treated as tools. When broken, they can be simply sent to a garbage burning station to generate electricity.

2. Tool Industry (TI), the Secondary Sector of the social economy, the products of which are solely tools of all kinds, which are used for living such as pan, stove, vase, car, house, etc.; and for production such as spade, warehouse, factory, engine, crane, truck, etc.; or for both such as phone, computer, etc.; and none-energy-carrier materials, too, for example metal ores, which will be intergraded into tools eventually.

3. Service Industry (SI), the Tertiary Sector of the social economy, the products of which are mental and/or physical services of all kinds such as, security service, health service, educational service, design service, amusement service, communication service, trading service, etc.

The FI is the fundamental section of the

接的能量形式，如地热、阳光、水流以及风等。

产自第一产业（FI）的产品有时不仅可以作为能量载体而且因为其物理结构也可以作为制造工具的材料。比如棉花自然可以用作燃料产生热量，但它通常却是被用来制造人类的衣服，而棉花的热量价值被保留在衣服里。原木也可以被用作燃料产生热量，但人们通常将它们用作制造家具的材料，如果家具受损成了废物，这些物料仍然可以最后通过燃烧来产生热量。塑料来自原油，塑料通常用来制造工具，当工具损坏了，我们可以直接将它们送到垃圾发电厂发电。

2. 工具产业（TI），社会经济的第二产业，其产品全都是形形色色的工具，它们被用于生活，如锅、炉、罐、车、屋等；用于生产，如铲子、仓库、工厂、引擎、吊车、卡车等；或兼用于两个方面，如电话、电脑等。制造工具的非能量载体的材料（如金属矿物）的生产也属于此产业。

3.服务产业（SI），社会经济的第三产业，该行业的产品全属于各类脑力或体力服务，如安全服务、健康服务、教育服务、设计服务、娱乐服务、通信服务和贸易服务等。

燃料产业是社会经济的基础产

economy. Only the VIH of the product out of FI exceeds the consumption of the labor required for producing it, could the TI and SI exist. FI is the basis of the whole economy of the society. We call all the products of the Fuel Industry the energy carriers, which is the first tier of the material wealth.

业，只有当该产业产品的VIH总量超过消耗在生产这些产品上的劳动总价值时，工具产业和服务产业才有可能存在，FI是整个社会经济的基石。我们将燃料产业的产品称作能量载体，它们是第一层次的物质财富。

All the products from TI are tools or the raw materials which will become tools eventually, which form the total material wealth of the society together with the energy carriers from FI. The productivity of the TI determines the level of the accumulation of the material wealth. We call all the products of the Tool Industry the Utility Carriers, which is the second tier of the material wealth.

工具产业的产品是工具或者是制造工具的材料，它们与燃料产业的产品一起组成社会的总物质财富，TI的生产效率决定着物质财富积累的水平。我们将工具产业的产品称作效用载体，它们是第二层次的物质财富。

SI is a support sector of the social economy. First of all, it maintains and offers the knowledge of human society. It keeps the economic system in a stable status so that the economy develops in a sustainable way. SI adds the value by either attaching it to the products produced by FI or TI, or transferring the value to the laborer of FI or TI.

服务产业属于一种支持产业，首先，它提供并维护人类社会的知识，它保证经济系统处于稳定状态，社会经济因此得以持续发展。服务业通过给FI和TI产品增加价值，或者向FI和TI的劳动者转移价值来实现价值的增加。

Ⅻ. Surplus-Value is an Objective Phenomenon

Ⅻ. 剩余价值是一种客观存在的现象

Many economists are suspicious of the existence of Surplus-Value stated by Marx if looking only through the circulation of the value of a specific product, just as Marx described, “Our capitalist stares in astonishment. The value of the product is exactly equal to the value of the capital advanced. The value so advanced

许多经济学家对马克思阐述的剩余价值存有疑虑，如果他们仅仅着眼于某个产品的价值流通的话，正像马克思描述的那样：“我们的资本家惊恐地瞪着眼睛（发现），产品的价值正好等于垫付资本的价值，垫付的资本没有被扩大，剩余

has not expanded, no surplus-value has been created, and consequently money has not been converted into capital. The price of the yarn is fifteen shillings, and fifteen shillings were spent in the open market upon the constituent elements of the product, or, what amounts to the same thing, upon the factors of the labour-process; ten shillings were paid for the cotton, two shillings for the substance of the spindle worn away, and three shillings for the labour-power. The swollen value of the yarn is of no avail, for it is merely the sum of the values formerly existing in the cotton, the spindle, and the labour-power: out of such a simple addition of existing values, no surplus-value can possibly arise. These separate values are now all concentrated in one thing; but so they were also in the sum of fifteen shillings, before it was split up into three parts, by the purchase of the commodities".

价值没有被创造，由此金钱也没有被转化成资本。棉纱的价格是 15 先令，而在市场上这 15 先令全都花在了组成这个产品的元素上了，或者说是从劳动过程的因素看，加起来相等；10 先令用来买棉花，2 先令支付纺锤的磨损，3 先令支付劳动力。吹大棉纱的价值亦属徒劳，因为它只与业已形成的棉花、纺锤和劳力的价值之和有关。从如此简单的算式中，剩余价值没有产生的可能。这被分割的价值现在又被聚集到在被分成三份采购不同的商品之前的 15 先令上了。"

As of the reason, why the surplus-value exists, Marx said only in one sentence in his book as, "The fact that half a day's labour is necessary to keep the labourer alive during 24 hours, does not in any way prevent him from working a whole day". (*Das Kapital* Volume 1, Chapter 7, Section 2).

至于剩余价值存在的原因，马克思进而用了一句话来说明："事实是，半天的劳动就可以维持劳动者24小时的生存，但这并不能阻止让他工作一整天。"（《资本论》，第一卷第七章第二节）。

Let's do some further analysis here to explore where the surplus-value comes from.

让我们在这里做进一步的分析，来探索剩余价值到底是从哪里来的。

Tens thousands years ago, people were struggling around for finding enough food for survival until a wise man, who was Emperor Shennong (神农氏, in Chinese, 神means God; 农 means agriculture; 神农氏means The God of

数万年以前，直到辨五谷创农具的神农氏的出现，人们一直挣扎在为寻找足够的粮食以维持生计的努力中。从那以后，人们才可能有足够的粮食来满足需要。随着农

Agriculture) according to the Chinese legend, invented many farming tools, identified five different crops and their farming schemes for his people. Since then, it was possible for the society to have enough food to feed all of the people. With the development of the farming skill and farming tools, only portion of the population of the society is necessary for farming, while the other portion could be doing something else or be just idled. The value of the food supplied to those people of doing something other than farming or simply being idle was the surplus-value of the farming, therefore the surplus-value of the society.

业工具的改进和农业技术的提高，社会仅需要部分劳动力就能生产出全社会所需的粮食，而另一部分人口就可以从事其他活动或者赋闲在家。提供给那些从事其他活动或者赋闲在家的人员的食物的价值，就是农业生产的剩余价值，也就是全社会的剩余价值。

How does it happen? One may ask. We have to realize one fact that the real value of food is not created by labor of human only but by the Mother Nature also through converting the solar energy into the chemical energy saved in the grain, straw, and even the root of the crop. The contribution of labor of human in farming is just to improve the growth condition of the crop therefore to assure the harvest as great as possible. The farmers need food to energize their bodies to get the work done for sure. When the total amount of energy of the food produced by the farmers exceeds the total amount of energy needed by the bodies of the farmers, however, an energy surplus, the surplus-value therefore is generated. The surplus-value was enjoyed by the kids and disables of the families, the lords of the lands, the officers of the nation, artisans and servicemen in town, and even other idle people around. Let's call all these people the idled out of farming, all the values of the products created by

有人会问：这是怎么发生的？我们必须认识到一个事实：食物的价值不仅是由人的劳动创造的，而且也是由自然之母通过光合作用将太阳能转化成化学能并储存在庄稼的果实、秸秆乃至草根里的。人在农业生产中的贡献仅仅是改善庄稼成长的环境，以便有个尽可能好的收成。农夫当然需要粮食给他提供劳作所需要的能量，可一旦农夫收获的粮食所能提供的能量总和超过了他耕作这些粮食所耗费的能量，能量剩余也就是剩余价值便产生了。这个剩余价值被提供给家里的老人、小孩，土地的所有者，国家的官员，镇上的工匠和服务人员以及其他闲散人员享用。我们称所有这些人为非农人员。而所有这些非农人员所能创造的任何产品的价值，就是被转换了的农业产业的剩

whom, if any, are transformed surplus-value from the farm industry, which is treated as the surplus-value of the society, too.

余价值，也被认作全社会的剩余价值。

The same principle applies onto the coal mining, crude oil mining, and all other energy generation industries like wind power, hydroelectric power, and photo-volt power in the Fuel Industry of the social economy. If the total energy needed by human labor and other forms of labor for getting the products of energy carrier available for the society is less than the total energy the products can offer. The surplus-value of the FI is therefore generated.

同样的原理也适用于采煤、采油以及其他能源工业，比如风电、水电、光电等社会经济的燃料产业。如果生产能量载体所需的人力劳动和其他形式的劳动的总和小于能量载体能提供的能量总和，则燃料产业的剩余价值就产生了。

Actually, the phenomenon of the surplus-value exists not only in the society of human but also other societies such as, of bee, and of ant. There are many worker ants, many soldier ants, several male ants and a couple of queen ants forming a society of ant. Only a portion of the worker ants are in charge of food “farming”. The rest ants, which are in charge of house building, home guiding, and egg laying and hatching are just sharing the surplus-value of the food produced by those worker ants. The only difference between human society and other societies is though, on top of housing, guiding, and propagation, human also produces a lot of other tools for themselves to get the work done more quickly, more easily and more efficiently therefore the life of them getting more and more comfortably.

事实上，剩余价值现象不仅存在于人类社会，也存在于诸如蚂蚁和蜜蜂的社会。一个蚂蚁的社会由很多工蚁、很多兵蚁、少数雄蚁和几只蚁后组成，只有部分工蚁负责食物的采集，其他负责蚁穴建造、看家护院、后代繁殖的蚂蚁，只是享用那部分工蚁创造的剩余价值。人类社会与之有别的是，除了造房、警卫、繁殖外，人类还为自己工作生活更加方便、更加舒适和更加高效而制造很多其他工具。

Since the Industrial Revolution, many new technological inventions made it possible for the tool industry to employ more and more the idled out of farming to produce products other than food. The entrepreneurs borrow the surplus-value from

工业革命以来，许多技术发明使得工具产业雇佣越来越多的非农人员来生产非食物的产品成为可能。企业家们从农夫/领主那里借得剩余价值，用来雇佣非农人员以

the farmers/landlords; hire employees, who are the idled out of the farming, to produce variety of tools; and sell them in the market to make profit.

生产和销售各种工具并取得利润。

XIII. Profit — the Allocation of Surplus-Value

XIII. 利润——剩余价值的分配

For easily understanding, we have to conceive an abstracted society of 1000 people as the start point, which consists of only farming and tool-making industries; and all the people in this society are fully employed. We suppose that people exchange products based on their effort of producing such goods, in the other words, in labor-in-Joule spent onto the goods. To make calculation easier, we also have to ignore the contribution of the existing tools and other form of fuel at beginning, or, we suppose that all the productions are made by hand purely. We will discuss the situation of involving the contribution of tools of production in the other Chapters.

为了方便理解，我们首先假设一个抽象的有1000人的简单社会作为起点，那里仅有农业和工具制造业，社会中所有人员都有活干。我们还要假设人们以他们生产付出的努力，即劳动焦耳数交换产品。为了计算方便简洁，在开始时，我们忽略已有工具以及其他燃料的贡献（或者将劳动仅限定在纯手工劳动），我们将会在其他的章节中讨论工具的贡献。

Let's assume that, there is 70% of population is employed in farming and 30% in tool-making by pure human labor. The food, worth of 10 TJ (trillion Joule), produced by the farming industry is just enough for all the people in the society in one year. The total value of food of the society in the year can be expressed as (10+i7) TJ. And the total value of tools of the society in the year can be expressed as (0+i3) TJ. That is to say, the total VIE of the food of the society is 7 TJ, and the total VIE of the tool of the society is 3TJ. The total Value-In-Exchange of the products produced by the society in this year is

我们假设：70%的人口从事农业生产，30%的人口从事仅需人工劳动的工具制造。一年中，农业生产出的总热值为100亿焦耳的食物正好够全社会所有的人食用。即，那年的全社会粮食价值总额为：（100+i70）亿焦耳；那年的全社会工具价值总额为：（0+i30）亿焦耳。也就是说，全社会生产的粮食的总交换价值为70亿焦耳；全社会工具的总交换价值为30亿焦耳。全年全社会生产产品的总交换价值为

10TJ.

Now, we say that, 70% of the total food of the society is consumed by the population in farming industry and 30% of the total food of the society, which is the food surplus from the farming industry, is consumed by the population in tool-making industry. 70% of food, consumed by farmers, takes 70% of the total heat-in-Joule out of the farming industry (that is 70% of the 10TJ = 7TJ), and 30% of food, consumed by tool-makers, takes 30% of the total heat-in-Joule out of the farming industry (that is 30% of the 10TJ = 3TJ). The total labor-in-Joule spent in farming is 7 TJ. So, the farmers transfer 30% of their product to the tool-makers in the value-in-exchange of 2.1 TJ (30% × 7). In the other words, the tool-makers get 30% of food of the society (with 3TJ value-in-heat) in the cost of 2.1 TJ in VIE. This 30% of food of the society eaten out by tool makers in the year, means that the value-in-exchange of the whole tools produced by these tool makers in the year is 3TJ.

We now can end up with the following conclusion, the tool-making industry makes 3 – 2.1 = 0.9TJ profit for the society, the profit rate of which is 30% (= 0.9 / 3×100%); while the farmer takes 2.1TJ as their own profit, the profit rate is 30% (= 2.1 / 7×100%) as well in this case.

In case of that 30% of the population is in farming and 70% in tool making, we may conclude easily as following, farming industry consumes 3TJ VIH (= 30% × 10TJ) and rest 7TJ VIH is transferred to tool-making industry in VIE of 2.1TJ (=70%

100 亿焦耳。

现在我们说：社会 70% 的粮食被农业人口所消耗，30% 的粮食作为农业生产的剩余粮食，被工具制造业人口所消耗。占人口 70% 的农夫消耗的粮食占 70% 的农产品的总热值焦耳数（也就是 100 亿焦耳的 70%=70 亿焦耳）；占人口 30% 的工匠消耗的粮食占 30% 的农产品的总热值焦耳数（也就是 100 亿焦耳的 30%=30 亿焦耳）。而农业产品的总交换价值是 70 亿焦耳，因此，农业以 30% × 70 亿焦耳 = 21 亿焦耳的交换价值将社会 30% 的粮食出让给了制造业，换句话说：制造业以 21 亿焦耳的交换价值得到了占社会总量 30% 的粮食（总热值为 30 亿焦耳），这 30 亿焦耳的热量被工具制造者在年内吃掉了，也就意味着制造业年内生产出的工具的总交换价值为 30 亿焦耳。

结论是：工具制造业新创造出了 30 – 21= 9 亿焦耳的社会利润，利润率为 30% (= 9 / 30 × 100%)；而农夫们将那交换价值为 21 亿焦耳出让的粮食作为自己的利润，利润率在这个例子中也是 30% (= 21 / 70 × 100%)。

如果农业人口为30%而制造业人口却是70%，则我们可以同理得出以下结论：农业消耗了30亿焦耳（= 30% × 100亿焦耳）的总热值，剩下的70亿焦耳的热值被以21

×3TJ), which is treated as the profit of farming industry. The profit rate of farming is 70% (= 2.1 / 3×100%); And tool-making industry takes 4.9TJ (= 7 – 2.1) as the profit of the industry. The profit rate of tool-making is 70% (= 4.9 / 7×100%) as well in this case.

Let's go further by taking the none-full-employment into consideration. The total food of the society is consumed by farmers, which takes 30% of the population; by tool-makers, which takes 50% of the population; and the idlers, which takes 20% of the population. Instead of 70%, the farming industry can reach only 30% profit rate if the idlers are solely supported by farming industry as the following deduced, farmers, taking 30% of total population of the society, produce 10TJ of value-in-heat worthy of 3TJ in value-in-exchange. As the profit of the farming, 1.5TJ (50%×3TJ) in VIE is transferred to tool-making. The profit rate of farming industry is therefore 30% [=1.5 / (3+2)]. And the profit rate of the tool-making is however 70% [=(5-1.5)/5×100%]

Or, farming industry reaches 70%[=(70%×3)/3] of profit rate and tool-making industries gets profit rate of 41.43% [= (5-70%×3) / (5 + 2)] only if the population of the idlers is fully supported by tool-making industry.

In case of that the population of the idlers is split according to the proportion between farming and tool-making, the situation will be as following, the farming takes 75 (3/8 of the idlers) more people to support and tool-making takes 125 (5/8 of the

亿焦耳（= 70% × 30亿焦耳）的交换价值卖给了工具制造业，利润率为70%（= 21 / 30 × 100%）； 而制造业创造49（= 70 – 21）亿焦耳的总利润，利润率也是70%（= 49 / 70 × 100%）。

让我们将非充分就业的因素考虑进来，社会总粮食由占人口30% 的农业人口、50% 的工业人口和 20% 的闲散人员所消耗。如果社会闲散人员全部由农业负担，则农业的利润就会从应有的 70% 的利润率降为 30%。推导如下：30% 的农业人口生产出 100 亿焦耳的粮食值 30 亿焦耳的交换价值；50% × 30=15 亿焦耳的交换价值被出让给制造业，也就是农业的利润，农业的利润率为 30%［=15 /（30+20）× 100%］，而工具制造者的利润率却涨到了 70%［=（50–15）/50 × 100%］。

或者，如果闲散人员全部由工业负担，则农业的利润率保持在70%［=（70% × 30）/30 × 100%］而工业的利润率降为41.43% ［= (50–70% × 30) / (50 + 20) × 100%］。

如果两个产业按比例分摊闲散人员的负担，则相当于农业要负担额外的 75 人 (闲散人口的 3/8)，工业要负担额外的 125 人 (闲散人口的 5/8)，由于仍然只有总人口的

idlers) more people to support. 10 TJ of the food produce by farming is worthy of 3 TJ in VIE still, 62.5% of which, that is 18.75TJ, will be transferred to tool-making as the profit of farming meanwhile. The real tool makers, who take 50% of the total population of the society, produce 5TJ of value-in-exchange in forms of tools. The profit of the tool-making is 50-18.75=3.125(TJ). And the profit rate of the tool-making is 3.125/(50+12.5)=50% therefore; meanwhile the profit rate of the farming is 18.75/(30+7.5)×100%=50%.

As we said in the previous Chapter, the energy in other labor form functions just as the energy in human body. It's still true when we include the energy of all forms on one hand, and engines of all kinds on the other hand into our consideration. That is to say, if the 20% of the total energy is used for production of the of energy carriers themselves and 80% for tool making, the profit rates of the FI and the TI are all 80%, on condition that the contribution of the SI is dissolved into the FI and the TI in the same proportion in advanced.

30%从事农业生产，所以，生产出的100亿焦耳的粮食的交换价值依然是30亿焦耳，其中62.5%的交换价值，即18.75亿焦耳，被作为农业的利润出让给了制造业；制造业有占50%总人口的人在真正从事工具制造，其产品的总交换价值为50亿焦耳，制造业的利润为50–18.75=31.25亿焦耳。因而，制造业的利润率为31.25/（50+12.5）×100%=50%；农业的利润率为18.75/（30+7.5）×100%=50%。

如前所述，能量的其他劳动形式与人体的能量劳动形式作用是一样的。如果我们一方面将所有形式的能量消耗考虑进来，另一方面将各种引擎的劳动也考虑在内，以上的演算依然成立。也就是说，如果20%的能量用于能量载体的生产，80%的能量用于工具制造（服务产业已由燃料产业和工具产业按比例分解在先）的情况下，燃料产业和工具产业的利润率皆为80%。

XⅣ. Accumulation of the Wealth of the Society

XⅣ. 社会财富的积累

The wealth of the society can be categorized into two parts, one of which is the mental wealth, or knowledge in other words (we will discuss it in detail in later Chapter), which is intangible; and the other is the material wealth, which is tangible.

社会财富分为两大类，其一为智力财富，或者说是知识财富（后面讨论），属于无形财富；其二为物质财富，属于有形财富。

Food, bio-fuel, fossil fuel, electricity generated from all kind of resources are primary material wealth of the society. All of the energy carriers are of the same property that it can be utilized only once. So long as the energy carrier is deconstructed for heat/power generation, the life of the energy carrier is ended. However, the lives of the tools and the materials for making tools produced thereby can be lasting for much longer time generally as we discussed in the previous Chapter. Tools of all kinds are the secondary material wealth of the society. The accumulation of all the tangible and intangible products in phases of WIP, WIS and WIC forms the total wealth of the society.

粮食、生物燃料、化石燃料以及利用各种资源产生的电力属于社会的第一层次的物质财富，所有的能量载体都具有一个共同的特性：只能被利用一次。一旦能量载体被解构用来产生热量，它作为组织的寿命就终结了。而如前所述，工具以及制作工具的材料的组织寿命一般却可以延伸许久。所有的工具组成社会的第二层次的物质财富。所有处于 WIP、WIS、WIC 状态的有形和无形产品的累加组成了社会的总财富。

There are two factors affecting the material wealth accumulation of the society, which are technology of the farming and the technology of tool making. The farming productivity determines the ceiling of human resource available for all other industries. And tool technology level determines what kind of tools can be made, in what rate of comparative advantage, and how much energy in forms other than food can be transferred into the tool-to-be and the materials which are used for making tools.

社会物质财富的积累受两个大因素的影响，其一为农业生产的技术水平，其二为工具制造的技术水平。农业的生产效率决定着其他行业可用人力资源的上限；而工具制造的技术水平则决定了可以按什么样的比较优势率来制造什么样的工具，以及将多少食品以外的能量形式转移到多少新工具及其原材料的价值中去。

The annual consumption of energy in all kinds determines the ceiling of the annual wealth increase. Suppose that all the energy carriers produced in a year are consumed at all in the year. The net national wealth increase can be expressed in the following formula,

一年的总能耗决定着当年国民财富增加的上限，假设当年生产的能量载体就在当年被消耗掉了，那么当年新增国民财富可以由下列等式表述：

$$\triangle NW = (\sum EC + \sum VOT) - (\sum VOT + \sum WC)$$
$$\triangle NW = \sum EC - \sum WC \quad (3)$$

Where: △ NW represents the net national wealth increase in the year;

∑EC represents the total energy consumed in the year;

∑VOT represents the total value of transfer of the producing tools, which are therefore total samsaraous consumption, in the year;

∑WC represents the total wealth terminal-consumed by the society in the year;

We have to be noted that the value depreciations of producing tools do not fall into the category of wealth terminal-consumed, but only value transferred. The total amount of value transferred onto the new products from the tools equals to the total amount of value depreciated from the existed tools in certain period of time.

So long as a producing tool is put into the phase of WIC, the compensation of the depreciation will usually be used for either buying the same tool or upgrading with a new generation of the tool in the future. That is to say in general, the value of this tool will stay in the national wealth for ever, even if a specific tool itself is replaced, and then its replacement is replaced again, so on and so forth. It sounds like a process of propagation of tools, which is very similar to the process of propagation of human being. This is the cause why the national wealth has been getting bigger and bigger for ever in general, with the exception of natural and man-made catastrophe.

My notion on value/wealth follows not only the Law of Conservation of Matter but also the Law of Conservation of Energy.

其中：△ NW 表示年度国民财富的净增加；

∑ EC 表示当年总的能量消耗；

∑ VOT 表示当年总的工具价值转移量，即轮回消费；

∑ WC 表示当年社会财富的总的终极消费；

我们必须认识到：工具的折损不属于终极消费的范畴，而只是价值的转移。在一定时期内，转移到新产品中的工具的价值等于工具的折损。

只要工具在被使用，其折损补偿一般会被用来采购新的同样的工具或者该工具的升级产品，也就是说，尽管作为某工具本身会被一再地替代，但该工具的价值一般会永远被保留在社会财富里，听起来就像工具也能像人类进行繁衍一样。而这正是人类财富，在没有自然或人为灾难的通常的情况下，会越积越多的原因。

我的财富 / 价值观不仅遵循物质守恒定律也遵循能量守恒定律。

ⅩⅤ. All Because of the Existence of Surplus Value

A. Duty Factor of Obtaining Energy

Millions years ago, a man started his daily life after getting up in the morning. When he was hungry, he went to a forest, walked around in the forest for searching mature fruits in trees, then climbed the tree and picked up fruits and ate them. He might switch from one tree to another until he was full. The energy spent for his actions of walking, searching, climbing, picking, switching, and even chewing and digesting was for obtaining energy for prolonging his life. We call the dissipation of energy for obtaining energy again the samsaraous dissipation.

Between current time full and next time hunger, he could nap for rest; jump on trees for exercise; chase rabbit for fun; or play with his companions around for entertainment, etc. Or, he might need to swing a leaf on hand to ventilate for himself in hot day, to prepare some heavy clothes made of leaves for winter, to train his kids with skills. When thirsty, he had to go to a pond to drink water. He had to safe guard himself through frequent watching around. All these actions need the dissipation of energy, too, which is a surplus of above mentioned energy obtaining action. We call this portion of energy the surplus-value, and dissipation of which is called terminal dissipation, if we don't take tool making into the consideration.

The necessary time for a man to collect enough

ⅩⅤ. 一切皆因剩余价值的存在

A. 获能占空比

百万年前，一个人醒来后就开始了他一天的日常生活，感到饿了，他走进树林，来回寻找成熟的果子，然后爬上树，摘下果子并吃掉它们。他可能会从一棵树转到另一棵树，直到他吃饱了。他用于行走、寻找、攀爬、采摘、转移甚至咀嚼和消化的能量是为了获得能量来延长自己的生命。我们称为了获得能量而消耗的能量为轮回消耗。

在饱食之后到下一次饥饿之前的时间段里，他可以打个盹儿，也可以在树上荡来荡去锻炼身体，还可以追逐兔子以获得快乐，如此这般。或者，他也可以在大热天摇动手中的树叶使得空气流动；用树叶制作为冬天准备的厚实的衣服；教会孩子生存技巧。渴了，他必须走到池塘去喝水。他必须经常观察四周保证安全。所有这些动作也需要消耗能量，而这些能量就是上面提到的摄取能量行动的剩余部分，我们称之为剩余价值。而在不考虑制造工具的情况下，这部分能量的消耗为终极消耗。

一个人获得足够食物所需要的

food for himself depends on the surrounding environment, season, and his skill. We may borrow a term from the natural science, which is Duty Factor of Obtaining Energy (DFOE), to measure man's capability of creating surplus-value. DFOE equals to the necessary time for a man to collect enough food/energy for his own samsaraous dissipation divided by the time span of a day, which is 24 hours. The less the DFOE is, the more capable for a man to create surplus-value.

时间随周边环境、季节和他自己的技能的不同而不同。我们借用一个科学术语“获能占空比”（DFOE）来度量一个人的创造剩余价值的能力。DFOE 等于一个人为自己的轮回消耗获得足够食物 / 能量所必需的时间除以一天的时间长度——24 小时。一个人的 DFOE 越小，他创造剩余价值的能力就越大。

B. DFOE determines the possible living standard of human life

B. 获能占空比决定了人类可能的生活标准

Surplus-value is the energy gained less the energy spent for getting it. Surplus-value phenomenon is universal in all the animated nature including human world surely. We may say, that no surplus-value, no propagation of all the animals, therefore no animals in the nature.

剩余价值是生产出的总能量与生产中所消耗能量之间的差额。剩余价值现象是包括人类在内的动物界普遍现象。我们可以这样说：没有剩余价值就没有动物的繁衍，因而也没有动物世界。

A silk worm keeps eating all the day and night. The energy spent for eating is just a portion of the energy eaten in. The saved energy, which is surplus-value, in its body is used for cocoon knitting, eclosion and egg-laying later on. The next generation of silk worm is therefore produced.

蚕宝宝没日没夜地一直吃，用于吃这个动作而消耗的能量并不是吃进去的能量的全部。它肚里保存的能量，也就是剩余价值，会被用于今后编织蚕茧、羽化成蛾以及产卵，下一代蚕宝宝就由此而生了。

The surplus-value created by honey bees is sufficient not only for the species propagation but also for enjoyment of bears or human beings unwillingly.

由蜜蜂创造的蜂蜜剩余价值不仅足以用于物种自身的繁衍，而且并非情愿地为熊或人所享用。

Squirrel helps to plant pine trees by applying the surplus-value it gained.

松鼠利用剩余价值帮助种植松树。

Human ranks on the top intelligence wise. By applying surplus-value, man is able to build more

人类具有顶级的智能，通过利用剩余价值，人可以建造出越来越

and more complicated, more and more durable organizations for his better living in addition to just survival.

复杂、越来越耐久的组织，用于简单生存之外的更好的生活。

Let's look at a scenario first: It took 100 man-hours to build a shed in 10 square meters in some ancient time, when the DFOE was 50%. Minus 8 hour sleeping time, there was only 4 (= 24 hr. × 50% – 8 hr.) hours per day left for a man to build the shed. It would take 25 days for him to finish the shed in 10 square meters. If the DFOE was reduced down to 25% thanks to some technology progress, this man would have 10 hours per day to build the shed, meaning it needed only 10 days to finish the same shed. In other words, he was able to build two and half sheds in 10 square meters or a shed of 25 square meters during 25 days for his family. Living standard of his family is therefore improved.

让我们先来看一个场景：在某古时，需要100个工时搭建一个10平方米的棚屋，而当时的DFOE是50%，刨去8小时的睡觉时间，他一天只有4小时可以用来搭建棚屋。他需要花费25天来搭建10平方米的棚屋。如果DFOE由于某种技术进步降低到了25%，则此人一天将会有10个小时来搭建，即10天便可以完成一个相同的棚屋。或者说，他可以在25天内为他的家庭搭建两个半10平方米或者一个25平方米的棚屋，他的家庭的生活水平就因此得到了提高。

Of course, we all acknowledge that technologic innovation is the key of reduction of DFOE.

当然，众所周知，技术创新是降低获能占空比的关键。

At the beginning of the Industrial Revolution in 18th century, people had to work 12 hours a day and 7 days a week, but the living standard of an average family was quite poor. Nowadays, we work 8 hours a day and 5 days a week. We have cars for transportation, air conditioning for living, even long break to tour the world. We have more and more time and money for entertainments and sports. All of these are due to the existence of the surplus-value and the increase of the capacity of creating more and more surplus value caused by technology progress.

18世纪的工业革命之初，人们必须一天工作12小时，一周工作7天，而当时普通家庭的生活水平相当差。如今，我们每天工作8小时一周工作5天，可我们拥有汽车作为交通工具，空调机用于生活，甚至可以休个长假，去周游世界。我们有越来越多的时间和财力用于娱乐和体育活动。而这一切都归功于剩余价值的存在以及技术进步导致的创造越来越多剩余价值的能力。

C. Surplus Value determines not only the Wealth Accumulation but also Morality of Society

At very beginning, ancient human had to be searching almost all the day long, except dark night for rest, to find enough food for survival, due to the poor Duty Factor of Obtaining Energy. There was rarely wealth left. The security of survival was therefore very low. When any adult's DFOE was greater than 50%, he will be probably casted away by his family and his society since he couldn't supply enough food for himself therefore needed support from the family or the society, if the general DFOE of the family or the society was just about on the 50% level. People were struggling for survival by all means including stealing, plundering and even massacring. Person, who had the capability of reducing DFOE, no matter how it was, took the lead of the family and the society. There was no such a word of charity.

Farming technology helped reduction of the DFOE of the society. One couple was able to support a family of 10 more or less in general, that means the DFOE then was down to the level of 10%. Being luxury, charity was available though.

What happens when the DFOE is down to about 1% now? Man cares not only human being but also pets and wild animals; not only animals but also plants.

C. 剩余价值不仅决定了社会财富的积累而且决定社会道德

最初，基于可怜的获能占空比，古代的人们除了用于休息的黑夜，不得不成天在外寻找足够的食物来维持生命，几乎没有什么财富积累下来。因此，生存的安全系数非常低。当一个成年人的获能占空比大于50%时，他恐怕会被他的家庭和社会所抛弃，因为他不能为自己提供足够的食物从而需要家庭或社会的救济，而当时家庭和社会的获能占空比也差不多在50%。人们会为了生存不择手段地去偷盗、抢劫甚至屠杀。不管用什么方式降低获能占空比的人，会成为家庭和社会的领袖。那时是不存在慈善这个词的。

农业技术帮助社会降低了获能占空比，一对夫妇通常能养活一个十口之家，也就是说，这时的获能占空比已经降到10%的水平了，尽管是一种奢侈，但慈善已经存在。

当获能占空比降到了1%，会发生什么事呢？人类现在不但关注自身而且也关注宠物乃至野生动物；不仅关注动物还关注植物。

PART FOUR: ON ORGANIZATION

XVI. Essence of Knowledge

The brain of a new baby born in seconds ago is just like the brain of a baby born in a hundred thousands of years ago, which is almost in void with only instinct embedded, which is organized according to the organization of gene. Through his intrinsic sensing organs, he smells, he hears, he touches then sees, tastes the outside world in a multi-dimensional way. With the capability of his brain, he organizes the neurons in his amazing brain to reflect the images and connections of the outside world by the stimulations from his smelling, hearing, touching, seeing, tasting, or in general, surveying in a multi-dimensional manner. Along with his growth second by second, hour by hour, day by day, and year by year, he surveys, memorizes, and then compares the images in memory and makes some adjustment and abstraction for his future reference. He does even induction and deduction trying to conclude a reason behind and to predict trend ahead of the development of a thing. A logic sequence is therefore organized and memorized in his mind as well. It is obvious to us that the knowledge is the performance of a set of the ORGANIZATIONS in human brain, which are

第四篇　组　织

XVI. 知识的实质

几秒钟之前出生的婴儿与几十万年前出生的婴儿，除了由基因组织形成的本能外，大脑几乎同样都是一片空白。透过本身的感觉器官，他嗅、听、触然后视、尝外部的世界，即对世界进行多维度的观察，借助大脑的能力，将神经元组织起来用以反映外部世界的景象和关联。随着分分秒秒、日日夜夜、年年月月的成长，他观察、记忆，然后比较记忆中的景象并做出调整和抽象，以备今后之用。他甚至能够采用归纳和演绎的方法来琢磨一件事情的前因和后果。一个逻辑顺序因此而形成并被记忆。很明显，知识即是人类大脑里的反映真实世界的一组组织的表述。

reflections of the organizations in the real world.

However, all the images, reflections, connections, and sequences in man's mind are pure subjective. They may be true, false, or true and false in a probable manner. According to what he learnt and/or believed, man makes practices accordingly, surveys the result of his action by comparing with his expectation in his mind so that his knowledge is refined and expanded via the update and accumulation of the organization of his brain. He confirms what he believes correct and discards what doesn't fit. That is so called, learning by mistaking.

可是所有的景象、反射、关联和顺序都属于人的纯主观的东西，它可能是对的，可能是错的，也可能是有时对有时错的。依据他的所学所信，人做出相应的行动，观察他行为的后果并与他期待的愿景进行比较，以对脑中的组织进行纯化和扩展。他接受他认为是正确的，摒弃他认为是不适的，所谓通过试错法学习。

The organization in human brain is dynamic. It is a constant life time process of iteration. The living environment including family status, tribe culture, and level of the civilization of the society, influences the forming of man's knowledge. First of all, seeing is believing. Man trusts the knowledge coming from his own experience. The knowledge of human can be inherited more or less to their successors through education by using library, which carries, maybe not precisely, the records of the knowledge in the brains of the predecessors for the successors; and functions as the external brains of human race. The library of human knowledge has therefore been iterating ever since and for ever. Oracle augury was one part of knowledge in 3000 years ago in China. Nobody uses it at all nowadays. Instead, we had a lot of new knowledge like genetics and economics collected into the library of human recently.

人脑中的组织是动态的，是一个终身迭代的过程。家庭状况、部落文化、社会文明等生活环境都会影响其知识的形成。首先，眼见是实，人坚信亲身的经历。人的知识，通过书传口授，人类的知识宝库，或多或少地、或精或概地从上一代传给下一代，承载知识的书籍就相当于人类的外部记忆。因此，人类的知识库得以从古到今直至永远地迭代。甲骨占卜在3000年前的中国是一种知识，现在已经没人在用了。基因学、经济学等被新近收集进了人类知识的宝库。

The organizations of all kinds, sensible in the real world, can be found in human brains of their mirror images. Knowledge in both human brains

现实世界中所有的可感知的组织都能在人的大脑里找到它们的镜像。储存在人脑中和书库中的知识

and libraries is the mental wealth of the society. The knowledge in brain is just a mental scheme but nothing else. But it needs also energy dissipation to keep brain running healthily, and to keep the knowledge inheriting constantly. Therefore, certain piece of knowledge possesses its value-in-exchange just like any piece of material wealth.

都是社会的精神财富。人脑中的知识就是智力构造而非其他，但它仍需要能量消耗来维持大脑健康地运行，保持知识的永续传承，因而，知识就像任何一件物质财富一样具有其交换价值。

There is no such a single brain in the world that whole set of the knowledge about the real world are held in. Human knowledge is a collective system, which includes all the knowledge embedded in every people's brain. The throughputs of two nail making factories of the same organization of production and management may be different due to the different people involved therefore the knowledge sets of those two factories are different in deed.

在这个世界上还没有一个大脑能装得下有关这个世界的所有知识，人类的知识是一个集合体，是包含每个人大脑里的知识的总和。两座以同样结构组成的制钉工厂的产出可能并不一定是一样的，因为事实上不同工厂的工人可能具有不同的知识集。

Man is such a creature that he can not only learn the world by organizing his brain to reflect it passively, but also change the world by organizing his activities with his peers and tools, per his preference in mind, actively. Most amazing part is tool making, which leads us to the accumulation of wealth. Tool itself is sort of organization, which is the realization in the real world of the knowledge in human brain.

人是这样一种生物，他不光具有被动地认识世界的能力，而且具有主动地将他自己和同伴及工具组织起来改变世界的能力。最惊人的是制造工具的能力，它导致我们能有财富的积累。工具本身也是一种组织，它是人类大脑中的知识在现实世界中的实现。

XVII. Tools in Economy

XVII. 经济中的工具

The tools take the most portion of the material wealth of the contemporary society. The reasons for human to invent and use tools is listed as following,

当今社会，工具占据了物质财富的绝大部分。人类发明和使用工具的原因如下：

- To protect the human being themselves and

- 保持人类自己及其财产处于

their wealth in a good condition.

- To make hard thing easier;
- To get things done faster;
- To make impossible thing, as it seems, possible.

Houses in all kinds are built for mainly protecting human being and their wealth in good conditions. It's hard to break a walnut with bare hand or teeth; it's easy to use a stone/hammer. One man is only able to carry 50 kg for long distance transportation in speed of about 5 km/hr.; with a wheeled cart, he is able to transport cargo weighing 500 kg in speed of about 5 km/hr.; with a powered motor truck, he is able to transport cargo weighing 100,000 kg in speed of 100 km/hr.; by driving a train, he is able to transport even 1,000,000 kg in speed of 200 km/hr. It was impossible for man to travel to the moon a hundred years ago; it's possible now by using very sophisticated tools in a very sophisticated way organized by human.

In a narrow sense, we have two kinds of tool, which are sheltering tool and implementing tool. Chair, bed, cabinet, workshop, railway station, and family house are all sheltering tools.

We classify the implementing tools further by three criteria, namely, source of power, engagement in application, the existence of logic respectively.

According to the source of power, we have manual tools and powered tools. Man has to apply his own muscle power to drive and to control the manual tool. Ax, knife, plough, vice, shovel, and needle belong to manual tool. The mechanisms

良好状态；

- 变难事为易事；
- 变慢事为快事；
- 使看起来不可能的事成为可能的事。

各种各样的房屋主要用来保护人类自己和他们的财富处于良好状态。用手很难打开一个核桃，但有了锤子就很容易。一个人只能挑 50 公斤重的货物以每小时 5 千米的速度进行长途运输；利用带轮子的小车，他能以每小时 5 千米的速度运输 500 公斤的货物，利用机动卡车，他就能以每小时 100 千米的速度运输 100 000 公斤重的货物，如果驾驶一列火车，他还能以每小时 200 千米的速度运输 1000000 公斤重的货物。100 年前，去月球旅行是不可能的事，人类尽管需要采取非常复杂的方法和工具来完成，但现在它却成为可能。

从狭义上讲，我们有两类工具：庇护工具和执行工具。椅子、床、柜子、车间、火车站、家居房屋都是庇护工具。

我们又可将执行类工具按三个判据——动力来源、应用状况和逻辑存无来进行进一步分类。

根据动力的来源，我们有手动工具和助动工具。人必须用自身的体力来驱动和控制手动工具。斧头、砍刀、犁具、台钳、铁锨和缝衣针属于手动工具，手动工具的机理相

of the manual tools are relatively simple by, 1) to extend and/or expand the limbs and trunk of human such as chopsticks, spoon, fork, ladder, etc.; 2) to apply Lever Principle in all kinds to get a job done, which is out of the natural capability of human or too exhausting for a man to keep operating all day long. Lever, pulley, gearbox are of this kind. Manual tool is the externalization of some of the actuating organs of human.

对比较简单，主要是由：（1）人体四肢和躯干的延伸，如筷子、汤勺、叉子、梯子等；（2）运用杠杆原理及其变形来完成人体自身难以完成的，或者是相当吃力的工作，如杠杆、滑轮、齿轮等。手动工具是人的执行器官的外延。

For powered tools, man need only to control the tools. Ox, horse, pneumatic hammer, steamer, motor truck, and wind mill are all powered tools. The mechanism of a powered tool is quite complicated either in biological view or in mechanical view. Specialists are needed for making them realized.

对于助动工具，我们只需要对其进行控制。牛、马、气动锤、蒸汽机、机动卡车和风车都属于助动工具。助动工具的机理从生物学和机械学的角度来看，相对比较复杂，需要专家来实现。

Just like the human body, in which there are sensing organs and actuating organs. We have actuating tools and sensing tools according to the engagement of tools in application. Actuators are used directly in the changing process while the sensors are used just for checking if the object is existing/functioning well as per the request so that the human's want may be well satisfied.

正如人体有感觉器官和执行器官一样，根据应用的状况，工具也有实施工具和测量工具。实施工具直接参与改变的过程，而测量工具是用来测量结果是否符合人们的要求。

According to presence of logic in the output of a tool, we have simple tools and complex tools. If there is any logic with regard to either time or space, or other measures embedded in a tool, we call it complex tool. Otherwise, it belongs to simple tool. The most sophisticated complex tool so far is computer. Weaving loom is a typical complex tool, by using which, man is able to make patterns of the fabric through pulling the warp up and down. In this

根据工具使用的结果是否有逻辑关系的存在，我们有简单工具和复杂工具。如果工具里植入有空间和时间的关系，就是复杂工具，其他的则为简单工具。至今为止，最繁复的复杂工具是电脑；织布机就是一个典型的复杂工具，利用它，人们通过改变经线的上下就可以织出不同的花样；而一口井、一个风

sense, well, pneumatic hammer, motor truck, and steamer are all simple tools. But punching die is a complex tool since there is position logic defined in the die. Actually, the complex tool is somewhat the extension of the organization in the human brain. We may call it the externalization of the organization in brain.

锤、一辆机动卡车乃至一台蒸汽机都是简单工具；而一个冲压模具却是一个复杂工具，因为模具定义了空间关系。实际上，复杂工具是人脑的某个子组织的延伸，我们可称其为：人脑的外延。

In one word, tools are externalizations of sole or combined physical and mental organs of human. The organizations like governments, militaries, shops, bands, hospitals, schools, families, factories, in a broad sense or in a higher level, are social tools, which are externalizations of the logic in mental organs of human, too.

总而言之，工具就是人类身体和大脑器官的单一或组合的外延。诸如政府、军队、商店、乐队、医院、学校、工厂是广义上讲或者是更高层次上讲的社会工具，它们也是人脑组织中逻辑的一种外延。

Besides food, drink and all other forms of energy source, and semi-products which are on their ways to be tools, we treated all man-made things and some natural resources the tools. Horse, ox and donkey are human raised tools for power; roads are the tools for transportation; rivers are tools for transporting water and boats; caves and houses are tools for sheltering; even the land itself is an instrument of labour, in some sense, just as Marx said.

除了食物、饮品以及其他的能源加上即将成为工具的半成品，我们将其他所有人造的甚至一些天然的物件称作工具。马、牛、驴是人饲养的助动工具，道路是运输工具，河流是运送水和船的工具，洞穴和房屋是居住的工具，甚至土地本身从某种意义上正如马克思所说的，也是一种生产工具。

By using tools, man changes the world meanwhile changes himself both physically and mentally as well. Under the organization of human, tools create more tools by consuming additional energy. It means that, the result of using tools is that human has been getting more and more wealth accumulated for the society. Or, on other words, tools are the accelerators of the wealth creation of the society; the degree of the complexity of the

通过使用工具，人类改变了世界，同时从身体和精神两个方面改变了自己。在人的组织下，随着能源的消耗，工具创造出了更多的工具。也就是说，人类使用工具的结果是使得人类社会的财富得以积累得越来越多。换句话说，工具是创造社会财富的加速器，工具的复杂程度决定了创造

tools determines the capacity of the wealth creation for the society in the scale of time.

社会财富的能力。

XVII. Engine — the Amplifier of Value-In-Exchange

Engine is a special kind of tool. It plays a crucial role in the development of the economy. It always causes a revolution in the social economy once a new type of engine is employed.

At the very beginning, human body is the only engine available in economy, the productivity then was very very poor. Man was only able to manage keeping himself and his family survival. When furnace is employed, human is able to make ceramics and to purify ores to get different kinds of metal. When horse and camel are domesticated, human is able to move heavier goods faster and further. Windmill and watermill saves a lot of human power for grinding. Sail is an ancient engine for driving boat. The first industrial revolution is realized upon the invention of steamer. The popularization of car is only available after internal combustion engine was invented. Electrical motors in sizes from small to big make the automation realistic.

When only the engine of human body was employed, the global population was just several millions. When the other engines like ox, horse, and smelting furnace were employed, the global population reached something like 550 million. When the steamer was employed, the global population went up to 2 billion. It is over 7 billion

XVII. 引擎——交换价值放大器

引擎是一类特殊的工具，它在经济发展中起着关键作用，一种新型引擎的应用总是会引发社会经济的革命。

起初，人体是经济中唯一的引擎，那时的生产力非常非常的低下，人只能勉强维持自己和家庭的生存。使用了火炉后，人类就能够制造陶器和熔炼金属；当马匹和骆驼被驯化后，人类能够以更快的速度运输更重的物品到更远的地方；风车和水车为人类提供了很多研磨动力；风帆是一种驱动船只的古老的引擎；蒸汽机的发明促成了第一次工业革命；内燃机的发明使得汽车的普及成为可能；大大小小的电动马达使得自动化变成现实。

在人体是唯一引擎的时代，全球人口只有几百万。在牛、马及火炉等其他引擎投入使用后，全球的人口达到了近 5.5 亿。蒸汽机的应用使得全球人口达到20亿。而如今，各色各样的引擎的使用，使得全球人口超过了 70 亿。

as all varieties of engines are employed now.

There are many different kinds of engines available in the world. We have bio-engine like horse, ox, camel, donkey, etc., which offer power by converting feeds through digesting. We have mills in different kind, which offer the rotating power by converting the flow power of air or water. We have heat engines like furnaces, steamers, diesel engines, gasoline engines, etc., which offer power by burning fuels. We have electrical motors, which offer drives by converting electrical power to the mechanical drive.

世界上存在很多形式的引擎，我们有生物引擎，如马、牛、驼和驴等，它们通过消化食物来提供动力；我们有风车水车，通过转化气流和水流成旋转动力；我们有炉子、蒸汽机、柴油机、汽油机，通过燃烧燃料提供动力；我们还有电动马达，将电力转换为机械驱动力。

From perspective of value, engine in all kinds can be treated just as an amplifier in terms of Value-In-Exchange.

从价值的角度看，所有的引擎都可以被看成是交换价值的放大器。

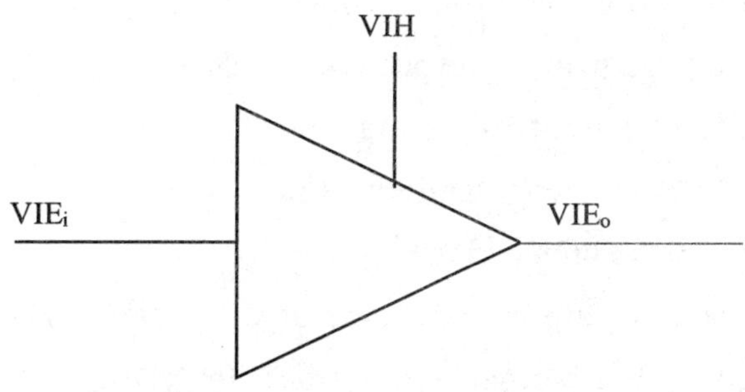

Figure 4. VIE Amplifier 图 4. 交换价值放大器

The input of VIE of the engine is the VIE_i of the fuel, the output in VIE_o is equal to the VIH of the fuel. In an economic situation, the VIH of certain amount of fuel is greater than its VIE. Therefore, the amplification factor (k) of the VIE amplifier is greater than 1.

放大器的输入是燃料的 VIE_i，输出 VIE_o 等于燃料的 VIH。在经济状况下，燃料的 VIH 大于其 VIE，因此，交换价值放大器的放大倍数 k 是大于 1 的。

(4) $VIE_o = k \times VIE_i$

(5) $VIE_o = VIH$

(6) $k = VIH / VIE_i$

Human body is just a kind of bio-engine like body of horse in perspective of VIE amplification. Different from mechanical engines, all the bio-engines are always on running once being ignited because the heart of a bio-engine has to keep pumping blood across all over the body to support the brain thinking, the lung breathing, the guts writhing, and the body moving even if they are on rest.

人体和其他诸如马匹等生物引擎一样，也是一种 VIE 放大器。不同于机械引擎，生物引擎一旦被启动就一直在不停地运行直至死亡，因为生物引擎的心脏必须不停地为脑思维、肺呼吸、肠蠕动以及身体活动提供带有能量的血液，不管休息与否。

XIX. Organizations in Economy

XIX. 经济中的组织

Besides the mental organization in human brain, there are three categories of organizations in the physical world playing different roles in the economy, namely, natural organization, artificial organization, and social organization respectively. Organization is a word of neutral. It may be beneficial sometimes in some sense and evil the other time in other sense to the humankind.

除人脑组织之外，有三种组织在经济中起着不同的作用，这三种组织分别是：自然组织、人造组织和社会组织。组织是中性的，它有时是有益的，有时是有害的。

All the natural resources are in some sort of natural organizations, which are organized by the Mother Nature; and man can influence only a little. A rice grain contains the germ, endosperm, and bran, which arc organized by the Mother Nature for its reproduction, meanwhile for energizing human and many other creatures. When seeded in spring and fostered in the summer according to a well-organized scheme of watering, fertilizing, etc. by man; bathing in the plentiful sunshine for certain period of time, a piece of the rice grain may reproduce more than 300 pieces of new grains.

所有的自然资源都是由自然之母组织的，人的影响极小。一粒稻谷由胚芽、胚乳和糠秕构成，这是由自然之母为稻谷的繁殖，同时为人类和其他动物提供能量而组织的。经过春天播种、夏天培植，人们按照程序浇水施肥，在有足够阳光照射足够时间的条件下，一粒种子可以再生出 300 粒新的稻谷。

All tools fall into the category of artificial

所有的工具都属于人造组织。

organization. For pursuing different utilities, man invented different kinds of tools by changing and connecting necessary materials together by means of dissipation of energy, on which we have discussed in last chapters already.

为了达成不同的效用，人类通过消耗能量，通过对必需材料施以改变和连接，从而创造出了形形色色的工具，前面几节已有讨论。

For keeping the family in peace, people need the extra efforts from the member to manage the family affairs and to develop the family ethics for members to follow. For keeping neighborhood in order, people need chief, policemen and laws. People need school to educate their children, hospital to cure the sickness, market to exchange the goods. People need also the military service involved for defending the wealth of the society. People even need guru to tell where to find right place for next hunting or right timing for next seeding. By end of an exhausting hunting, people need amusement for relaxation.

为了家庭的安稳，人们需要成员们额外的努力来管理家庭事务，制定家庭伦理让成员来遵循。为了邻里的秩序，人们需要里长、警察和法律。人们需要学校教育孩子，医院治疗病人；人们还需要军队保护社会财富；人们甚至需要大师指点下一次狩猎或播种。狩猎结束后，人们还需要娱乐来放松心情。

Families, tribes, firms, governments, militaries, banks, schools, hospitals, etc. are all the social organizations, which mainly connect people for specific purposes; we may also call it the utility here. Not only the organizations of matter have their utilities, but also the organizations of human, which we also call tools of society, together with specific tools have their utilities. The army is such an organization formed with soldiers, weapons and disciplines that a military force is available; a factory is such an organization formed with employees, machines, and procedures so that the productivity is available efficiently and constantly. A government is organized for keeping the society in order; a court is organized for maintaining the

家庭、部落、公司、政府、军队、银行、学校、医院等都是社会组织，它们是为达成某个特定目的——也可以称之为效用，将人们联系在一起构成的组织。不仅物质的组织具有效用，人类的组织即社会组织在运用特定工具时也具有效用。军队是由战士、武器和纪律构成的组织，它因而具有了防务能力；工厂是由雇员、机器和流程构成的组织，它因而具备了长期高效生产的能力。政府是为了维护社会稳定而建立的；法院是为了维持社会公正而建立的；家庭是为了人类的繁衍而建立的。

justice of the society; a family is an organization for human propagation.

The main utility of food is to energize the body of human; the living standard is meanwhile expressed by different forms of food. The main utility of dress is to keep the body of human warm; the social status is meanwhile expressed by different material, different design, and/or different patterns of color. The main utility of a plough is to get the land more puffy; the civilization level of the society is meanwhile expressed by the different styles of plough meanwhile.

食物的主要效用是为人体提供能量，而不同的食物形式又反映了生活水平；服饰的主要效用是为人体保暖，而服饰不同的材料、设计和图案又同时显示其社会地位；犁具的主要效用是松土，而犁具的不同构造和方式又反映了其社会文明的水平。

Even the intelligence is the utility of the organization of the neurons in human brain. Through his sensing organs, man records his impressions on particular things and sometimes their relations by organizing the connection of neurons in his brain so that man learns or sometimes believes he had learnt the law of the outside world. With his knowledge, he organizes himself together with his peers with tools available, or tools made per request, to fetch the living necessaries for his family, tribe and society; by following somewhat pre-designed scheme, which defines the responsibility, action sequence, communication method, and even contingency plan.

甚至智慧也是人脑中神经元组织所产生的效用。由感觉器官感知，人将对特定事物的印象甚至它们之间的关系，通过组织神经元间的连接，确立他对外部世界的掌握或自认为已经掌握了外部世界的规律。运用掌握的知识，他将自己、同伴组织起来，制造并使用必要的工具，遵照预先设定的包含责任、流程、沟通乃至应急的程序，获得他们的家庭、部落和社会所需要的生活必需品。

Different from all material product consumptions, knowledge is always refined and enriched during its interaction with the reality. It is an infinite iterative process, through which knowledge is gradually approaching the truth of the universe. That is the reason why the general productivity of the world is getting higher and higher. We may say that by using

与物质产品的消耗不同，知识总是在与现实世界的交互中得到提炼和丰富。这是一个无限的迭代过程，在此过程中，知识逐渐接近宇宙的真理。这也是这个世界的生产力越来越提高的原因。我们说：根据现有的知识使用现有的工具，人

existing tools according to existing knowledge, man creates new tools and updates knowledge. Both tool making and knowledge updating are in constant iterative processes.

创造新工具，更新知识；工具制造和知识更新两者都是始终处于迭代的过程中。

Marx emphasized the function of tool making. Smith appreciated the division of labor. And Marshall spent five chapters to discuss the industrial organizations. Going more deeply in thinking, we will soon realize that all these three cases are indeed of the same fact that they are the realizations in real world of the organization of knowledge in human brain.

马克思强调工具的作用，斯密赞赏劳动的分工，马歇尔用了五个章节来讨论工业组织。细想起来，他们三人都是在肯定人脑中的知识组织在真实世界中的实现的作用。

All of the social organizations like governmental system, military system, banking system, education system, health care system, etc.; are also the realizations in real world of the organization in human brain; with the existence of which, at least some humans believe, the process of the accumulation of wealth can be going on safely, healthily, efficiently, and steadily in human societies. Man always strives for better organizations to assure that the process of the accumulation of wealth, including health of human, can be going on more safely, more healthily, more efficiently, and more steadily for sustainability through learning by practicing. We call it the optimization of organization.

所有的社会组织，如政府体系、军队体系、银行体系、教育体系、卫生体系等，也都是人脑中组织在真实世界中的实现，由于这些体系的存在，至少有部分人相信社会财富的积累会安全、健康、有效、稳固地进行。人类总是在尽一切努力来建立更好的组织，以保证包括人类健康在内的社会财富的积累会更安全、更健康、更有效、更稳固地进行，我们称之为组织的优化。

The word Organization has two different meanings, and sometimes expresses the pure logic relations of its components, and sometimes a set of objects formed per certain logic relations. The one may be called Organization in Mind (OIM); the other Organization in Reality (OIR).

组织这个词，也有两个不同的含义：有时它表示元素间的纯逻辑关系；有时表示一组按一定逻辑关系形成的事物。前者为脑中组织（OIM）；后者为现实组织（OIR）。

Now, we may say that the whole economy is just a huge organization of varieties of sub-organizations, which are formed by even low level organizations, so on and so forth. And the economy itself is just a sub-system of the whole ecosystem, in a broad sense, which is governed by the Mother Nature.

可以说：整个经济就是一个巨大的由各种子组织组成的组织，其子组织又是由其子组织组成的，以此类推；而经济本身也是由自然之母支配的整个生态系统的一个子系统。

ⅩⅩ. Optimization of Organization

ⅩⅩ. 组织优化

At very beginning, there was not any tool available for man to keep the water. He had to go to the river or pond for drinking water if he felt thirsty. He had to go back and forth, say three times a day, between the pond and where he lived/worked. Suppose it took 10 minutes for him to finish a return trip. He then needed 30 minutes per day just for him to drink enough water for his own. After clay vase or bamboo tube was invented, man needed only go back and forth once to meet his daily requirement on water. Wooden bucket of bigger size was invented afterwards, with which man needed go back and forth only once but could cover the daily needs on water for all of the family members. Later on, the wheeled cart is employed. Together with several buckets on it, one man can satisfy the daily water needs of all of a small village by still one return trip. With the pipeline and powered pump available nowadays, we don't need hauler to transport water for us anymore. Nevertheless, the needs on water of all people in a city are well satisfied.

起初，没有任何盛水的工具，如果渴了，人们必须往返奔走在他（她）的处所与河流或水塘之间才能喝到水解渴。如果一天他（她）需要喝三次水，一次往返需要10分钟，则一天就要花费30分钟用来喝水。后来陶罐或者竹筒被发明用来盛水，往返一次就解决了他（她）一天对水的需求。容量更大的木桶被发明后，一次往返可以解决全家人一天对水的需求。再后来，将数只木桶堆放在一辆手推车上，一次往返能解决全村人一天的喝水问题。如今，机动水泵和水管网络的建立，使我们再也不需要挑水工了，而全城的人却随时都能喝到水。

Before market place was fixed by the villagers, man had to ask for anything he longed for from

在集市没被村民确立之前，某人需要挨家挨户询问是否有他需要

one house after another, which surely wasted a lot of time. The market place makes it possible that the sellers can show their goods for exchange in a fixed place and at one commonly recognized time. The buyers, by going through from the beginning to the end, eventually get what they want hopefully. It is getting better in terms of time saving. But yet, it could be improved further. It saves even more time by categorizing the goods according to their functions/utilities. Therefore, the department store becomes one of the commercial patterns. For some of goods with low value, it is still a heavy burden of hiring couple of shop assistances for each department. Supermarket becomes another commercial pattern with even higher general efficiency.

的物品与其交换，这个过程肯定是浪费时间的。集市可以让买者和卖者在一个约定的时间在这个固定的场所交换商品，买者从头到尾看货问价，最终买到他需要的物品，从节约时间的角度看，这种方式更好。但还有更好的节约时间的方式，如果将商品按其属性分类并分区销售，时间就能更进一步地被节约，因此，百货公司这样的商业模式应运而生了。对于一些低价值的商品，一个货区设置数个营业员仍然是个不小的负担，超市这样的商业形态能产生更高的效率。

Mr. Goldratt and Mr. Cox illustrated a very good case study on their famous management novel of *The Goal*. Let me recite it here in a concise way as following. Suppose, there is a team of 5 people, say P1, P2, P3, P4, P5, with different production efficiencies, say R1=100 pieces per hour, R2=200 pieces per hour, R3=300 pieces per hour, R4=400 pieces per hour, R5=500 pieces per hour. Furthermore, we suppose that the work is to install 5 same parts into a work piece. The production efficiency of the whole team differs per the setup of organization of the team. Just taking two extreme cases for analysis, one case is to let every person finish the whole installation by him alone; the other is to let everyone in line finishing just one part installation sequentially. The output of the team in former case is 100+200+300+400+500=1500 pieces

Goldratt和 Cox先生在他们名为《目标》的管理小说中，举了一个很好的例子，让我在这里以一个简化的例子说明。假设有5个人P1，P2，P3，P4，P5，他们的生产效率不同，分别为R1=100件/小时，R2=200件/小时，R3=300件/小时，R4=400件/小时，R5=500件/小时，我们再进一步假设让他们往某工件上装相同的零件。那么，由这5个人组成的小队的生产效率，会因为组织的不同而不同。以两个极端的组合为例，一个是让他们各干各的，另一个是让他们组成一个串联的流水线；前者的生产效率是每小时能生产100+200+300+400+500=1500件，而后者每小时却只能生产

per hour. The output of the same team in latter is 100+100+100+100+100=500 pieces per hour only, since the station of the lowest efficiency in the production line determines the efficiency of the whole line. What an amazing result!

100+100+100+100+100=500件，因为在串联模式下，生产线中效率最低的那个人决定了该线的效率。多么神奇的结果啊！

Smith was fascinated by the division of labor. He wrote, "To take an example, therefore, from a very trifling manufacture; but one in which the division of labour has been very often taken notice of, the trade of the pin-maker; a workman not educated to this business (which the division of labour has rendered a distinct trade), nor acquainted with the use of the machinery employed in it (to the invention of which the same division of labour has probably given occasion), could scarce, perhaps, with his utmost industry, make one pin in a day, and certainly could not make twenty. But in the way in which this business is now carried on, not only the whole work is a peculiar trade, but it is divided into a number of branches, of which the greater part are likewise peculiar trades. One man draws out the wire, another straights it, a third cuts it, a fourth points it, a fifth grinds it at the top for receiving, the head; to make the head requires two or three distinct operations; to put it on is a peculiar business, to whiten the pins is another; it is even a trade by itself to put them into the paper; and the important business of making a pin is, in this manner, divided into about eighteen distinct operations, which, in some manufactories, are all performed by distinct hands, though in others the same man will sometimes perform two or three of them. I have seen a small manufactory

斯密沉醉于劳动分工产生的结果，他写道："因此，用一个微不足道的加工，但其劳动分工经常受到关注的别针行业作为例子，一个没受过行业整体培训，对使用的设备也不了解的工人一天恐怕只能做出一枚别针，但肯定做不出二十枚。但是以这个行业现在运行的模式，这个模式不仅将整个工作作为一种特定的行当，进而将它分割成的大的分段也同样作为特定的行当来对待。一个专门拉丝，另一个负责矫直，第三个负责切割，第四个负责磨尖，第五个负责磨平另一头；制作针托需要二到三种不同的操作；套上针托是一个行当，漂白别针又是另一个；将它们放在一张纸上甚至都是一个行当；在这种模式下，制针行业最重要的行当是将整个过程划分为大约十八道不同的操作，在有些工厂里，每道操作由不同的人来完成，而另一些工厂里，一个人可能有时完成两到三个工序。我曾经参观一个仅有十人的此类小工厂，其中一些人要完成两到三个相连的操作，尽管处于非常惨淡的环境，只有必要的设备，但他们也能在满负荷情况下一天生产十二磅别

of this kind where ten men only were employed, and where some of them consequently performed two or three distinct operations. But though they were very poor, and therefore but indifferently accommodated with the necessary machinery, they could, when they exerted themselves, make among them about twelve pounds of pins in a day. There are in a pound upwards of four thousand pins of a middling size. Those ten persons, therefore, could make among them upwards of forty-eight thousand pins in a day. Each person, therefore, making a tenth part of forty-eight thousand pins, might be considered as making four thousand eight hundred pins in a day. But if they had all wrought separately and independently, and without any of them having been educated to this peculiar business, they certainly could not each of them have made twenty, perhaps not one pin in a day; that is, certainly, not the two hundred and fortieth, perhaps not the four thousand eight hundredth part of what they are at present capable of performing, in consequence of a proper division and combination of their different operations". (Book I, Chapter 1)

针。四千只中等尺寸的别针差不多为一磅。这十个人一天能制造出四万八千枚别针，取十分之一作为一个人的产能，他能一天生产出四千八百枚别针。但如果让他们在没有接受整体行当培训的情况下，一人从头到尾独立完成别针的制作，估计一天也做不了二十枚即原来的二百四十分之一，也许一只即原来由合理地划分和组合操作所形成的产能的四千八百分之一也做不了。”（第一卷第一章）

The case of pin-making cited by Smith is also a good example of optimization. There are hundreds ways to get the pin done, among which there are two extreme scenarios in contrast, one is to let a single person do all the steps, where he has to master all the knowledge of all the processes; the other of which is dividing the whole process into a set of different simple steps in logic, each of which is done by one person, where each

斯密引证的例子也是一个极好的组织优化的例子。在上百种制造别针的组织方法中，取了两种极端的例子作比较，一种是让一个人独立完成所有的制作步骤，在那里一个人需要掌握制造别针的所有知识；另一种是将制作步骤划分成一系列操作简单的分步，每步由一人完成操作，在那里每人只要掌握一

person needs master only a small piece of specific knowledge. People found then the productivity of latter could be hundreds folds of that of the former just because the different organizations. We all know it is impossible for everyone to be Thomas Edison or James Watt who are outstanding figures out of millions of people. We have to optimize the use of common people for mass production in a way of the least thinking and the least mistaking by breaking a complicated whole piece down to many single simple pieces with a fixed logic frame, which in our case is called the optimization of organization through externalization of knowledge. This story tells us that different organization of the production possesses different productivities. The differentiation could be huge, sometimes even flapping between the impossible and the possible in an extreme case.

小部分特定的知识即可。由于不同的生产组织形式，后者的生产效率是前者的百倍以上。大家都知道，不是所有的人都像爱迪生或是瓦特那样是百万里挑一的聪明人，我们不得不将一件复杂的工作分割成单一简单的步骤，为普通工人优化工作，将工作中思考和出错的机会降到最低，通过知识的外延实现组织的优化。这个例子告诉我们，不同形式的组织具有不同的生产效率，而且差异是显著的，有些极端的事例甚至处于可能与不可能之间。

In the case of simple operations like Mr. Goldratt's case, we found that the organization in parallel is optimal; In the case of complicated operation like Smith's case, we found that the organization of divided operations in cascade can be optimal in general.

在像 Goldratt 的例子那样的简单操作中，我们发现并行操作是最优的；而在像斯密那样的复杂操作中，串行分段操作一般能达到最优。

The net energy required to get certain thing done is constant. However, by using fitter scheme or by eliminating redundancy, it is possible to get thing done in shorter time, which means in a higher time efficiency, comparing with other different schemes. The strategies of optimization in the economic world could be categorized as following.

完成一件特定事务所需的净能量是一定的，但较合理的安排能够使得它在较短时间内完成，即意味着比其他安排有较高的时间效率；消除冗余也能产生同样的效果。在经济世界里，优化策略可以列举如下：

1. To make a combined effort, rather than many times of easy-job, on condition that the capacity

1. 在负载能力允许的情况下，将数次的轻松工作合并成一次性工

allows. If one man is able to carry 50 kg of water in 10 km back and forth once in 4 hours, don't let him carry 25 kg of water twice since it will take 8 hours to finish the job.

2. To avoid the logic judgment in operation by using complex tools.

3. To organize a team of people in a way that every member gets his/her capability fully played a role.

4. To break a complicated process as a whole down to sequential simple steps, one or several of which are done by a single common person; through converting a simple organization of a single person operating the whole process of complexity into a complicated organization of a set of persons, each of which operates one or couple of simple processes. All of the procedure is well organized though. If we treat a production organization as a kind of social tool, the one with labor division is just a good case of application of the concept of complex tool on production, the principle of which is the same as Item 2 just mentioned above, using complex tool instead of simple tool if possible.

5. To use external engine other than human body so that the productivity can be multiple to that of the exertion by only human efforts.

6. To eliminate idle time between effective labor.

The type of the organization of social system affects surely the economy development as well. There have been arguments on issues like, Public Ownership vs. Private Ownership, Socialism vs. Capitalism, and Market Regulation vs. Government Regulation in

作。如果一人能够在 4 小时内一次性搬运 50 公斤到 10 千米以外，就别让他花 8 个小时一次只搬运 25 公斤而用两次来完成。

2. 用复杂工具替代操作中的逻辑判断。

3. 让小组中的每一个成员完全发挥其个人能力。

4. 将一人完成整个复杂过程的简单组织转换成有多人完成各自简单操作的复杂组织，将一个完整的复杂过程分解成一系列简单的顺序操作步骤，每人仅完成其中一个或几个步骤，而整个操作步骤又是经过合理组织的。如果将生产组织也看成一种社会工具的话，劳动分工型组织就是在生产活动中运用了复杂工具的成功案例而已，其实质与上述第2条原理是一样的，即如果有可能，用复杂工具替代简单工具。

5. 用其他引擎替代人力以获得比人力高很多倍的生产力。

6. 在有效劳动之间消除空闲时间。

社会组织的形式当然也会影响经济的发展，公有制与私有制，社会主义与资本主义，市场调节与政府调节的争论曾持续了很长时间。

place.

Most of above mentioned strategies have to have specially designed tools/scheme/firm to make them to be realized. Or, in other words, the level of tools determines the level of optimizations.

The history of the economy is the one of the continuous optimization of the organizations on social relationship, on process, on material, and last but absolutely not the least, on the engine; with which the products can be produced and distributed in a higher and higher efficiency to better serve the wants of human being.

上述的优化策略必须要有特别设计的工具 / 规程 / 组织来实现，换句话说，一定水平的工具决定一定的优化水平。

经济发展史就是一部社会关系、生产流程、构成材料，最后是绝对至关重要的驱动引擎等组织的优化史，优化使得产品的生产和分配以越来越高的效率来满足人类的需求。

XXI. Human in the Economic System

XXI. 经济系统中的人

Man is the initiation, dominant, and meanwhile the destination of the economy. Man is, of cause, the initiator of the value aggregating process firstly, by identifying his wants in varieties of tiers around the core of human subsistence; and thereafter, 1) offering his pre-designed plan of getting external substance organized; 2) forming organization of labor by using his physical power, or by means of external power, together with helps of tools he invented; 3) checking, through his sensing, the products against his expectation he designed in step 1); to finally form a product. The expectation is a mental vision in mind of human. The pre-designed plan is also procedure born in mind of human, too. Surely, the physical power is generated by muscles' and bones' movement in a harmony way coordinated by brain. Marx concluded that: "Labour

人既是经济的起点、主导者，也是经济的终点。首先，人是当然的价值聚集过程的发起者，他（她）自己找出以人类生存为核心的各种层次的需求；然后据此，（1）提出预先设计好的组织利用外部资源的方案；（2）利用自己的体力或外部动力，运用其发明的工具，组织劳动；（3）通过感知将劳动结果与第（1）步设计的要求进行比对；最终形成一个产品。对结果的期待，是大脑中的主观愿景；预设计的方案也是大脑中产生的过程；体力是肌肉和骨骼在大脑的协调下的运动。马克思总结说：“首先劳动是人和自然共同参与的过程，人自愿地发起、调整、控制他与自然之间

is, in the first place, a process in which both man and Nature participate, and in which man of his own accord starts, regulates, and controls the material re-actions between himself and Nature. He opposes himself to Nature as one of her own forces, setting in motion arms and legs, head and hands, the natural forces of his body, in order to appropriate Nature's productions in a form adapted to his own wants. By thus acting on the external world and changing it, he at the same time changes his own nature."

的物质反应，设置臂、腿、头、手和身体中的自然力的运动，以作为自然力之一抵抗其他的自然力，从而让自然的生产结果符合他自己的需求。他在对外部世界的行动和改变的同时也改变了他自己的本性。"

The output of an economy is the wealth for mankind to enjoy solely.

而经济的产出是为人类独享的财富。

At the very beginning, man has to do by himself both physically and mentally. With the division of labor, some of people take the physical part mainly and some others take mental part mainly just like the ploughing case mentioned before. Two men in the front pulling the plough through ropes are mainly laboring physically. The one behind the plough is doing controlling, which is mainly mental part of the job; surely he has to use his muscle to align the plough with a little power involved. Once the animal power is employed, man needs only control with his mental labor no direct muscle driving any more. The motor tractor controlling saves much more man's muscle power than ox-plough, since he needs only rotate the steering wheel by sitting in the cab instead of walking after an ox.

起初，人必须同时从事体力和智力劳动，随着劳动的分工，有些人以体力劳动为主，而另一些人以脑力劳动为主。就以前述耕地的例子来说，两位在前拉犁的人是以体力劳动为主；而在后扶犁控制犁地过程的人则是以智力劳动为主，当然他必须用体力矫正犁的走向。一旦使用了畜力，人就只需要利用脑力和体力进行控制而不再需要自己的直接驱动力了。机动拖拉机的控制能节省更多的体力，因为他只需坐在驾驶室里转动方向盘，而不再需要跟在牛后面行走了。

The role of man in the modern economic world is getting more and more towards to the situation that man controls the tools to operate as per the pre-organized scheme by exertion of his mental labor

随着越来越多的助动工具和智能工具的运用，人在现代经济中的角色越来越趋于由人来控制操作工具，需要的是他的脑力劳动多过

rather than his physical labor of his muscle, bone, and ligament; along with more and more powered and intelligent tools are employed. An automatic production line can produce tons of products under only monitoring by few operators who are managers per se, rather than laborers in the classic sense. Even so, the human plays the dominant role still.

他的体力劳动。一条自动生产线在几个人的监控下可以生产成吨的产品，那几位监控的人与其说是劳动者不如说是管理者，然而人仍然起着主导性的作用。

Man is, secondly, also the designer of the Economic System, in which he participates. This situation forms a close loop system in terms of cybernetics. According to the theory of cybernetics, there is only chance for a system to be stable on condition that the negative feedback regulation in the system plays a major role; however, it is not always true that all the systems with negative feedback regulation are stable. In one word, the structure of the organization of the economic system determines its stability. Man himself is the only influencer of the evolution of the economic system.

另外，人也是自己参与其中的经济体系的设计者。从控制论的角度看，这种状况构成了闭环系统，根据控制理论，闭环系统只有在负反馈调节占主导地位的状态下才有可能达到稳定状态。但不是所有的负反馈调节系统都是稳定的。一句话，经济系统的组织结构决定该系统的稳定性。人是经济系统进化过程中唯一的影响因素。

In the primitive age, food was the produce of nature; everybody went out for finding his/her own food every day. They came back to where their mothers situated every evening. With the invention of the basket, people were able to take some labor surplus back home for juniors and/or the disables to use. With the increasing of the capacity of production and the discovery of ways of preserving food, people were able to accumulate a lot of food for even months' needs of a family. However, a guy in neighborhood, driven by his selfishness, often stole the preserved food for his own use instead of collecting food out in the wood by himself. A powerful man was needed for defending the private

在原始社会，食物是自然的产物，每个人天天外出寻找他们自己的食物，每天晚上，他们回到妈妈所在的地方。箩筐的发明，使得人们可能将劳动剩余带回来供小孩和行动不便者食用。随着生产能力的提高与保存食物方法的发明，人们可以储备数月家庭所需的粮食了。可是，某位邻居出于自利的目的，自己不去劳动，而是从他人家中偷窃食物。一位强有力的男人就需要站出来，同样出于自利的目的，保卫他们家的私有财产。人类因此从母系社会转换到父系社会，父亲因

property of the family, which was also driven by the Self-interested. Human transferred therefore from matriarchal society to patriarchal one. The father had to take more responsibility of raising family though. A pride of lions are still living in this way.

此担起了更多的责任。现在的狮群还一直以这种方式生活着。

Along with the growth of the populations of surrounding villages, the food supplied by the wood was not enough for all of the hunters/collectors. Wars between neighbor tribes happened now and then. The victors killed the losers and enslaved their wives and children to produce food for the victors in the occupied territory. To assure the bloody fruits of conquer lasting forever, the victors built up a hierarchy from king to the peasants. The Self-interested of the super power overwhelmed the Self-interested of the weak. The wealth of the society was controlled by the minorities in the top of the hierarchy. Such caste structure is still somewhat accepted in India as the time being, although it has been officially abolished.

周围村庄的人口在增长，树林中能提供的食物已满足不了所有人的需求，相邻部落之间的战争时常不可避免地发生。战胜者杀死失败者，奴役失败者的妻儿为他们在占领区里生产食物。为了长期保证这血腥的胜利成果，战胜者建立了从国王到贱民的社会阶级结构，强权的自利剥夺了弱者的自利，社会的财富从此由处于统治集团高层的少数人所把持。在印度，尽管官方已经宣布取消了种姓制度，但种姓观念到现在仍或多或少地存在。

Hegemonism is replaced by mercantilism nowadays. Instead of aristocrats, the capitalists take the place. The total wealth of the society has been tremendously increasing though. The living standard is well improved therefore.

在资本主义时代，强权主义已被重商主义代替，资本家取代了贵族的位置，社会的总财富得到了无可比拟的增加，人类的生活水平也因此得到了改善。

Man is, after all, an Economic Machine just like other mechanical machines produced by man, but intellectual in addition. Human is produced by human in the biological sense. It takes more or less than 16 years for a newly born baby to become a fully functioning adult in the modern sense. The child foster is just like the machine building, before it's ready for use/function, it needs many different

归根结底，人是一台经济机器，除了有智慧外，就像人自己发明的机械机器一样。从生物学角度看，人生产人。用现代的标准计，需要大约 16 年将一个刚出生的婴儿培养成一个完全的成人。孩子的抚养就像建造一台机器，需要消耗各种家庭的、社会的劳动以充实孩子的

kinds of labors of the family/society to be bestowed into the body and brain of the child; we may also treat it as in the phase of WIP of the cycle of tool. Therefore, human shall be also regarded as one kind of, but a special, asset of the society.

身体和大脑。我们可以将此阶段理解成处于 WIP 周期。因此，人也应该被理解为一种社会的特殊资产。

Now, we may conclude as the following, man is the participant of the economy from the lowest level to the highest. As the laborer, man is a powered tool; as the operator, man is the most complex tool — full intelligent tool; as the designer, man gets all the elements necessary together to make them tool for either living or producing; as the member of the human society, man participates and influences the dynamic of the society.

我们可以得出如下结论：人是从低层到高层经济活动的参与者。作为劳动者，人是一种动力工具；作为操作者，人是一种最复杂的智能工具；作为设计者，人将可用资源组合起来以制造出用于生活和生产的工具；作为社会成员，人参与和影响社会的进程。

PART FIVE: ON MONEY

第五篇 货 币

XXII. Drive of Exchange

Before Christopher Columbus discovered the new Continent, only those original American Indians had the fortune to enjoy the taste of potato, tomato, maize, and even tobacco. Europeans started to transplant these species and afterwards all over the world are there the potato, tomato, maize, and tobacco.

Tea tastes good but the produce of tea in Europe is not as good as in Asia. The only way for European to enjoy tea in good taste is to trade in tea with their products.

Even the people live in the same area need exchange because it make no economic sense and even impossible for one to make all the things valuable needed by himself, which include crop farming, food preparation, housekeeping, child fostering, making of all kind of tools for both living and producing, medical care, family defense, etc. The division of labor makes exchange necessary for people of the society to enjoy all other products, which are not produced by themselves.

It seems that the trading across the regions has been getting more and more extensive, especially after man was convinced by Ricardo with his famous doctrine of the Comparative Advantage.

XXII. 交换的原动力

在哥伦布发现新大陆之前，只有美洲大陆的原住印第安人有幸品尝土豆、番茄、玉米乃至烟草的味道。欧洲先开始移植这些品种，然后，世界各地都有土豆、番茄、玉米乃至烟草了。

茶味道很好，但欧洲产的茶没有亚洲产的好，欧洲人能享受好茶的唯一方法是用他们的产品交换茶。

甚至是住在同一个地方的人之间也需要交易，因为一个人要从事所有他需要的产品的生产是不经济的，有时甚至是不可能的，他不可能一边种地，一边准备食物、打扫房间、养育孩子、制造所有要用的生产和生活的工具，自己看病，还要保卫家园。劳动的分工使得交换成为必然，只有这样，人们才能享用自己不生产的产品。

自从李嘉图提出了著名的比较优势学说后，跨地区的交易变得越来越频繁了。

So, God creates the unevenness but we are working out ways to make it even through exchange hopefully.

因此，上帝创造了不均，而我们在想办法通过交换得到均匀。

ⅩⅩⅢ. Forms of Exchange

ⅩⅩⅢ. 交换形式

A. Share — the Primitive Exchange

A. 共享——最原始的交换

Hundreds thousands years ago, man, woman and their children went out to different places for collecting different produces of nature. In the evening, the man brought back with fish, the woman brought back with radish, and the children brought back with squash. In the family, they share the food by exchanging the harvests of their individual labors. Product sharing may happen in a family, a tribe, and even in a small society.

数十万年前，男人、女人以及他们的孩子去不同的地方收集大自然的果实，晚上回家，男人带回了鱼，女人挖回了萝卜，孩子拿回了瓜，一家人共享他们的劳动成果。产品共享不仅发生在家庭里，也可以发生在部落内，甚至一个社会中。

B. Barter — the Synchronous Trade

B. 以物换物——及时交易

Sometime the family may barter in a bunch of shrimps with their neighbor for fish they caught. Now the fairness becomes an issue. Out of many possible ways, people eventually realized that it is fairly fair if they exchange things based on the efforts they exerted in general; but the qualities of the goods and the preferences of the participants influence the final exchange rate as well. Once the exchange rates are confirmed, they may keep trading in about the same rates unless something significant happens.

有时，某家庭以自家的虾交换邻家的鱼，这时公平的问题就出现了，从很多可能的办法中，人们最终意识到以他们获得物品花费的精力作为交换的依据是相对公平的，但物品的品质和参与者的偏好也会影响最终的交换比例。一旦交换的比例确定了，人们将依照此比例进行交易，除非有重大的影响产生。

Barter is a direct and effective peer to peer trade, which selling and buying are happening simultaneously. No other intervention is needed.

以物换物是“单对单”的直接的交易，购买和销售同时发生，因此不需要任何其他的介入。但是，

However it is not so effective for multiple to multiple trading like, Person A would like trade with his Product A for some of Product B, some of Product C, and some of Product D; and Person B would like trade with his Product B for some of Product A, some of Product C, and some of Product D; Person C would like trade with his Product C for some of Product A, some of Product B, and some of Product D; Person D would like trade with his Product D for some of Product A, some of Product B, and some of Product C.

应对“多对多”交易的状况，它却显得效率低下，如某A需要以其产品A，与某B交换一些产品B，与某C交换一些产品C，与某D交换一些产品D；某B需要以其产品B，与某A交换一些产品A，与某C交换一些产品C，与某D交换一些产品D；某C需要以其产品C，与某A交换一些产品A，与某B交换一些产品B，与某D交换一些产品D；某D需要以其产品D，与某A交换一些产品A，与某B交换一些产品B，与某C交换一些产品C。

With gold, silver or other metals like copper, which should be some how precious that time so that a small piece of such a metal contains a big value, trade is actually one-step-forwarded barter. Instead of exchanging with Product A for B, C, and D respectively, the Person A may trade out his Product A for certain amount of Silver; and with the silver he may trade in Product B, C, and D thereafter. Now the gold, silver, or copper become the standards for trade. Gold coin, silver coin, and Copper coin, which bear their own values, became the intermediate of trade, which is called commodity money in the classic sense, by using which problems in multiple to multiple barters are well settled. Commodity money itself, in forms of gold coin, silver ingot or copper coin; is wealth with significant value, too.

使用金、银、铜等贵金属作为媒介进行交易，实际上是以物换物的进一步发展，因为一小片金属就包含了很大的价值。某甲现在可以用他的产品 A 换回一定数量的银子，然后用银子换回需要的产品 B、产品 C 和产品 D，而不是用产品 A 直接交换产品 B、产品 C 和产品 D。这样金、银或者铜成了交易中的标准，载着自身价值的金币、银币、铜币成了交易中的介质，即为传统意义上的实物货币。使用实物货币，多对多的交易的问题得到了很好的解决。作为实物货币的金币、银币、铜币本身也是带有很大价值的财富。

C. IOU — the Asynchronous Trade

Person lives on lowland, where rice is the only

C. 欠条——异时交易

住在只能在十月才能收获水稻

crop maturing in October, would like to exchange with his rice for wheat, which is produced on the highland and harvested in June. Besides the issue of the fairness of exchange, there is another issue rising up, which is the lag of time. As the person on lowland gets the wheat in June, he has to leave his counterpart a Credit Note declaring something like, I-Owe-You rice of this much with due date by end of the October.

的洼地的人想用他的水稻，与住在六月就能收获小麦的高地的人换些小麦。除了交易的公平性外，又有另一个时间延迟问题出现了。住在洼地的在六月份拿到小麦后，他必须留下一张欠条作为信用凭证，标明：我欠你多少水稻，到十月归还。

In August, the IOU holder would like to get some bricks to build a house. By endorsing on the Credit Note issued by the person on the lowland, he exchanges again with the brick maker. The brick maker may endorse this IOU again for something else or go to the IOU issuer to ask him to fulfill his promise in October by offering rice of the amount stipulated on the credit note. As long as the IOU issuer gets the credit note back on hand, the IOU is not valid any more. Hereto, the Credit Note finishes its circulation cycle from issuing, assignment to fulfillment.

八月，欠条的持有者需要买砖建房。它可以背书转让洼地人签署的欠条给制砖者，换回所需的砖。制砖者可以继续背书用此欠条换回他所需要的物品，或者等到十月，凭此欠条向洼地的农夫索要相应数量的稻谷。当欠条的签发者拿回这张欠条后，此欠条就从此失效了。至此，信用证完成了它从发行、转让到承兑的循环周期。

The credit is a big issue in IOU trading. Every party involved in the trade has to keep their commitments. Even though everyone would like to keep the commitment, it may also cause problem sometimes when a natural or a man-made disaster happening to the original issuer. Third party guarantee may help reducing the risk. The most trustable third party in such cases is of course the central government.

信用在欠账交易中是个大问题，所有参与者都必须兑现承诺。尽管参与者都愿意兑现承诺，但自然和人为的灾难有时会使得签发者无法兑现承诺。第三方担保是一种降低风险的办法，而最可靠的第三方就是中央政府。

XXIV. Essence of Money

A. Modern Money

We may interpret the modern money as the Universal Credit Note issued by the Central Bank. The Central Bank acts as if it is a huge Virtual Depot of the society. It buys goods from the seller and it sells goods to the buyer with the intervention of the fiat money during the course of value generation and value consumption. Unless the Central Bank loses its credit, people wouldn't be bothered of the credit issue on every trade ideally.

Modern money is just a piece of paper with some number printed on. As a printed paper, it contains very low value itself which is ignorable. The real value it represents is the value of the goods stored in the Virtue Depot of the society. That is to say, how much value in total in the Virtual Depot of the society determines how much value of fiat money in total in the circulation of trade.

B. What are in the Virtual Depot of the Society

We all admit that, money is used for asynchronous trade only. Under the circumstance of synchronous trade, money is not necessary. If a man makes some tools for his own use, the values of these tools were created but money is not needed, either.

A man makes 10 knives and sells them to a grocery dealer. He gets 100 dollars (issuing). He gives money to his wife when home (assignment).

XXIV. 货币的实质

A. 现代货币

我们可以认为法定货币/钞票是由中央银行发行的通用信用证。中央银行就像一个社会虚拟中转库，在价值产生和消费的进程中，它运用钞票从销售者那里购买，向购买者出售商品。理想状态下，除非中央银行失去了信用，否则，人们就不需要为每次交易中的信用担心了。

现代货币只是一张印有数字的纸片，其本身的价值可以忽略不计，其所代表的真正的价值，是储存在社会虚拟中转库中的物品的价值。也就是说：社会虚拟中转库中的总价值决定流通中的法定货币的总价值。

B. 哪些是属社会虚拟中转库中的物品

我们承认只有在异时交易中才需要货币，而在及时交易中，货币是不被需要的。如果一个人为自己做了几样工具，尽管价值被创造了，但却也不需要货币的参与。

某人做了 10 把刀卖给了杂货店老板，他得到了 100 块钱（发行），回到家将钱交给了老婆（转让），

His wife buys a pair of shoes with these 100 dollars (fulfillment). On the way home, one of the her friends sees the shoes and would like to buy from her. She agrees and therefore gets the money back. In this case, we treat it only one cycle of circulation no matter how many times this pair of shoes is resold. That is to say, only 100 dollars are needed for the circulation.

他老婆用这100块钱买了一双鞋(承兑)。可在回家的路上，她遇见一位朋友希望从她那儿买走这双鞋，她同意了，因此拿回了钱。在这种情况下，无论被转卖了多少次，我们都认为仅仅发生了一次流通。也就是说，只有100块钱参与了流通。

Money is means of circulation. It concerns only newly created wealth, which are not yet found their destination (see Chapter XXXVII for further discussion). So long as the goods got into phase of consumption (WIC), money is not needed anymore. So, we have to keep in mind that not all the wealth of the society belong to the Virtual Depot of the society, but only those products which have not yet reached the hands of the end users, meaning that they are still in cycle of value adding, that is to say that they are in phases of WIP and WIS.

货币是流通的工具，它只与新创造出来的还未找到其目的地的财富相关联（进一步讨论请参见第三十七章）。一旦货物进入了WIC阶段，货币即不再被需要了。我们必须记住：并不是所有的社会财富都属于社会虚拟中转库，只有那些仍未到达最终用户之手的产品才是，它们仍处在价值增值的过程中，也就是说处于WIP和WIS阶段。

All the used tools for trade don't belong to the Virtual Depot. It is just the transfer of ownership from one to the other just like the wife sells shoes again to her friend as above mention. And neither a stock for exchange does nor a facility for rent (the rental of the facility does though).

所有用于交易的二手工具都不属于虚拟中转库，它只是物主从一人换成另一人而已，就像上述主妇将鞋转售给她的朋友一样。股票或用于出租的设施也不属于（但设施的租金却是）。

A certain amount of food or other final products of a farmer/producer, which are kept for his own use or for direct donation, even though they have their own VIEs, doesn't belong to the Virtual Depot since it is in WIC already but not in the circulation of trade any more. If a family buys 10 kg of grape for make wine in house for the family use only, the 10 kg of grape belongs to the Depot but the wine

家庭或生产者自用或直接捐献的产品也不属于，尽管这些产品有交换价值，因为它们已经未经流通直接进入了WIC阶段。如果某家庭买了10公斤葡萄酿酒自用，那10公斤葡萄属于虚拟中转库而酿成的酒就不属于。如果主妇拿出一半的酒出售，那么一半的酒属于虚拟中

made out of the grape doesn't. If the wife changes her mind and is willing to sell half of the wine to the market, that half now does.

转库。

Of course, all the products for bartering do not belong to the Virtual Depot since no money is needed for trade.

用作以物换物的产品当然也不属于虚拟中转库，因为交易不需要货币参与。

Intangible product in phase of WIP surely belong to the Virtual Depot. We treat the preparation course of a concert/performance is in phase of WIP. When the concert/performance started, the WIC started as well, that is to say that the concert/performance is out of the Virtual Depot and has been consumed. The same concert/performance can be played many times. The additional activities like rehearsal, advertisement, ticket booking belong to the Virtual Depot as well, but not the original concert/performance anymore. The DVD of this concert/performance on the shelf of the book store is the tangible goods in the Virtual Depot.

处于 WIP 的无形产品当然属于虚拟中转库。我们将一场演出的准备阶段看成处在 WIP 阶段，而当演出开始后，WIC 也即开始，也就是说：演出已经从虚拟中转库中售出并被消费掉了。同样的演出可以表演多次，新增的诸如剧本修改、排练、广告、售票等活动属于虚拟中转库，但原来的表演却再也不属于了。书店货架上的 DVD 制品是有形资产当然属于。

PART SIX: ON PRICE

第六篇 价 格

XXV. Price — the Expression of Exchange and Transfer of Value

XXV. 价格 —— 价值交换和转移的表达

A. Price

Price is the external expression of the transfer of value-in-exchange in terms of money. As Adam Smith described in his book, *The Wealth of Nations*, there are Natural Price (NLP) and Market Price (MTP). The words he used, "neither more nor less than what is sufficient to pay the rent of the land, the wages of the labour, and the profits of the stock employed in raising, preparing, and bringing it to market, according to their natural rates" (Chapter VII, Book One), sounded like a tautology without relevant calculation associated.

The fact is, when people exchange goods according to their VIEs solely, in the other words, 1 to 1 on labor-in-Joule spent onto the goods, then we have,

A. 价格

价格是交换价值转移的货币形式的外部表达。如亚当·斯密在他的《国富论》一书的第一卷第七章中所描述，存在有自然价格（NLP）和市场价格（MTP）。但他使用的文字说明“根据他们的自然比率，不多不少正好支付土地的租金，工人的工资，以及将其提起、加工、引入市场的资材的利润”听起来像是个同义反复的“套套逻辑”，而并没有给出相关的计算公式。

事实是，当人们严格依照商品的交换价值，即按投入这些产品中的焦耳数进行 1 比 1 地交换商品时，我们有如下公式：

$$\text{NLP} = \tau \times \text{VIE} \quad (7)$$

Where: NLP represents the natural price of a product, unit of which is the same as unit of money, say dollar or CNY;

VIE represents the value in exchange of the product, unit of which is Joule;

τ is the coefficient of the transformation,

其中：NLP 表示一个商品的自然价格，以货币为单位，如美元、人民币等；

VIE 表示该商品的交换价值，单位为焦耳；

τ 表示转换系数，我们这里可

which we may call Anchor Chain Coefficient (see explanation in Chapter XXXV), the unit of which is something like dollar/Joule or CNY/Joule;

以称其为锚链系数（详见第三十五章解释），单位为货币 / 焦耳。

τ is a constant for all the products/services in certain society in certain period of time.

τ 在一定时间里对社会中所有的服务和产品是一个常数。

In the real world, because of the degrees of the redundancy of consumers' wealth (not really scarcity of supply as stated by classical economic theories) and the intensity of demand at certain point of time, people are willing to pay a product in higher price or to sell a product in lower price than its NLP. That is to say,

在现实世界里，由于一定时期消费者手中财富的冗余度（而不是古典经济理论中所提的供应的稀缺性）和需求的迫切性，他愿意以比自然价格高的价格购买或愿意以比自然价格低的价格出售产品，也就是说：

$$MTP(t) = NLP + \Delta P(t) \quad (8)$$

Where: MTP(t) is the real market price of a product at time t;

其中：MTP(t) 表示时间 t 时的真实的市场价；

ΔP(t) is a price premium on top of the natural price at time t.

Δ P(t) 是在时间 t 的自然价格之上的超额价格。

B. Price Premium — Merely Transferring of the Ownership of Value

B. 超额价格——仅仅是价值所有权的转移

The price premium is just a pure transfer of the VIE ownership of other product(s). It does not mean the value-in-exchange of such goods is enlarged/depressed although the value-in-money of it looks enlarged/depressed comparing with its natural price.

超额价格纯粹只是产品的部分 VIE 的所有权转移的结果，而不是该产品的交换价值的价格被放大了或者缩小了，尽管它的货币价值比自然价格增大了或者减小了。

Let us suppose that a piece of diamond contains VIE of 1,000 MJ; and natural price of this diamond is worth of $1,000. Say, a gentleman buys such a diamond in market price of $10,000 from the seller. In the VIE world, it means that, this gentleman purchased a diamond worthy of 1,000 MJ while he transferred ownership of another product(s) he owned, in the Virtual Depot, worthy of 9,000 MJ in

假设载有 1000 兆焦耳 VIE 的一颗钻石，它的自然价格为 $1000，如果一位先生在市场上以 $10000 的价格从出售者那里购买了这颗钻石，在 VIE 的世界里，这位先生还只是购买了价值为 1000 兆焦耳的钻石，而除此之外，他还将虚拟中转库中本属于他的价值为 9000 兆

addition to the seller simultaneously. That is to say, those product(s) worthy of 9,000 MJ is still in the Virtual Depot of the Society but only their owner was changed, which was the buyer before but is the seller from now on. Vice versa, if a seller sells a product worthy of natural price of $1,000 in the market price of $900, it means the buyer gets the product still worthy of 1,000 MJ in VIE, but the seller transferred partial ownership worthy of 100 MJ to the buyer free of charge.

焦耳的其他产品的所有权同时转移给了出售者。就是说，那 9000 兆焦耳的产品仍然存在于社会虚拟中转库中，而仅仅是它们的所有者从以前的这位购买者换成了今后的那位出售者而已。反过来，如果一位出售者以 $900 的价格出售自然价格为 $1000 的产品，意味着：购买者仍然得到了 1000 兆焦耳的 VIE，只是那位出售者将价值 100 兆焦耳交换价值的所有权免费送给了这位购买者。

C. Wage — the Price of Labor

As discussed already, all the labors, either mental ones or physical ones which could be conducted by human bodies, animal bodies, or even man made machines, have their VIE based on the gross VIH consumed. Basically, compensation has to be paid for the fuel and service necessary for keeping the engine, in either biological form or mechanical form, and other tools, ever running normally. The compensation for human labor is called wage. The wage is divided into two portions, one of which is for compensating the necessary food and service to the human body; the other of which is the incentive for the contribution of his knowledge, which helps to organize a production in a high efficiency mode, in terms of either energy scale or time scale. We may treat the second portion of the wage as the share of surplus-value, or share of the gross profit in terms of money.

It is obvious that no wealth at all will be

C. 工资——劳动的价格

如前所述，所有形式的劳动，不管是智力的还是体力的，无论是由人、牲畜还是人造的机器的劳动，都有其对应于所消耗的 VIH 的交换价值。从根本上说，保证生物的、机械的引擎及其他工具持久正常地运行所需的燃料和维护必须得到补偿。对人类劳动的补偿就是工资，工资分成两大部分，其一用于补偿给人体提供的必要的食物和维护；其二用于对他的知识贡献的奖赏，知识能帮助人们以高时间效率或高能量效率组织生产。我们可以将第二部分作为剩余价值的分享，或者以货币形式表达毛利润的分享。

显而易见，没有人启动和维持

created without the proper organization initiated and sustained by human. Besides eating grass and laying shit, ox may run all day long, all month long, and all year long with producing nothing else as no man organizes it. Wind can blow all day long, all month long, and all year long. Without human's organization, it produces nothing but destroying. Only under the organization conducted by human being with their knowledge accumulated in their brain; an ox may be employed to drive a plough; the wind may be utilized to drive sailing boats.

适当的组织，财富是不可能被制造出来的。牛可以整天、整月、整年地跑，但没有人的组织，牛除了吃草排粪，却不能生产任何价值；风可以整天、整月、整年地吹，但没有人的组织，风除了摧毁，也不能生产任何价值。只有在人类的组织下，运用积累在大脑里的知识，牛才可能用于驱动犁具；风才可能用于驱动帆船。

Different people at different positions in different organizations contribute their knowledge in different degrees of complexity; therefore the compensations to different people are different, which causes the unevenness in terms of the family income.

在不同组织的不同位置的不同的人以不同的复杂程度贡献知识，因此对不同人的知识的补偿也是有所不同的，这就是产生家庭收入不均的原因。

XXVI. Anchor of Currency

XXVI. 货币之锚

Although being treated as the standards of money in the past; gold, silver, and copper are all pseudo anchors for the currency in deed. Otherwise, we would have been using them as the anchor of currency nowadays still. What is the real anchor of currency behind the curtain, then?

尽管金、银、铜以前都被用作过货币本位，但实际上它们都是伪货币之锚。要不然，我们会依然将它们用作货币之锚了，那么到底什么是货币大幕后面的锚呢？

Let us have a look at a perfect commutative society first, meaning that, all the people in which sell all their products to the Virtual Depot and thereafter buy every product needed from the Virtual Depot as well; as a total, in certain period of time, we will have then the following.

让我们首先分析完全交换的社会，在完全交换社会里，人们出售他们所有的产品给虚拟中转库，然后从虚拟中转库购买所有的产品，从整体上来看，在一定的时间段内，如下关系成立：

$$(9) \qquad \sum_{i=1}^{P} \text{NLP}_i == \tau * \sum_{j=1}^{P} \text{VIE}_i == \tau * (\sum_{j=1}^{M} \text{VIH}_j + \sum_{k=1}^{N} \text{VOT}_k)$$

Where, P represents the total number of the different tangible and intangible products, including work-in-process, in the Virtual Depot of the society;

其中：P 表示包括处于在制品在内的有形、无形产品的总数；

M represents the total number of the different energy carriers for making these products.

M 表示生产这些产品所消耗各种能量载体的总数；

N represents the total number of the different tools in use for making these products.

N 表示生产这些产品所使用到的各种工具的总数。

It is quite obvious that the anchor of the currency is the total energy consumed plus total tool value transfer happened for making the products existing in the Virtual Depot of the Society. The value of a tool is the imaginary energy value accumulated during the production of it. We may say in other words, the anchor of currency is the total real energy consumed plus total imaginary energy consumed in making the products existing in the Virtual Depot of the Society.

很显然，货币之锚是生产暂存于社会虚拟中转库内产品所消耗的总能量与生产工具总价值转移之和。工具的价值是生产该工具的假想的能量积累，我们也可以换句话说：货币之锚就是生产暂存在社会虚拟中转库内的产品所需的真实的与虚拟的能量消耗的总和。

It is still true in the real world, where the trading price fluctuates up and down. As explained above, the price surplus or deficit based on natural price cause only the ownership transfer of the remaining goods in the Virtual Depot of the Society but nothing else.

即便在现实世界里，交易价格会上下波动，上述论断却依然成立，因为正如我们刚刚讨论过的，在自然价格基础上价格的增加或减少，只是引起了社会虚拟中转库中的产品的所有权构成发生变化而已，别无其他。

XXVII. Natural Cause of the Money Devaluation

XXVII. 货币贬值的自然原因

A. Higher Speed Dissipates More Heat

A. 速度越快散热越多

Medical research has already shown a fact

医学研究表明，如果一个人的

that the body temperature of a man will increase by about 1 degree when his heartbeat increases by every 10 counts. When running faster, we feel the higher heartbeat and more heat dissipation.

心跳速度每增加 10 跳，他的体温将增加 1 度，我们跑得越快，会感到心跳得越快，身体越容易发热。

It needs about power of 100 Watts for a man to walk in a normal speed but it needs about power of 1000 W for an athlete to run in a fast speed. The best achievement in the marathon race is a little bit more than 2 hours. It needs about 8.4 hours for a regular man to finish the distance of 42 km in a regular speed of 5 km per hour. The marathon athlete is 4.2 times faster than a regular man but the energy dissipation of the marathon athlete is 2.4 [= 2×1000/(8.4×100)] times higher than a regular man.

一个人以平常速度行走消耗大概100W功率，但当运动员快速奔跑时，大概需要消耗1000W的功率。一个好的运动员可以在2小时多一点的时间内跑完马拉松，而一个以5千米/小时速度行走的普通人需要花8.4个小时来走完42千米的路程。运动员的速度比普通人快4.2倍，而能量消耗则比普通人高2.4［= 2 × 1000/(8.4 × 100)］倍。

From the natural science, we all know that the higher speed an engine runs at, the more heat dissipation generated due to the heavier inner vibration. We all noticed that a car burns more fuel per kilometer when it runs at higher speed especially when the speed is over 120 km/hr, since the wind drag is not linear to the speed.

自然科学也证明，引擎以较高的速度运行会由于较高的内部振动产生较高的热量。我们大家都知道一辆汽车速度越快，特别是超过120千米/小时后，每千米油耗量越来越大，因为风阻与速度是非线性关系。

B. Higher Speed needs Stronger and More Sophisticated Structure

B. 速度越高结构强度要求和复杂程度就越高

A man, who weighs 60 kg, carries a bag of food in 20 kg for distance of 10 km. He needs only to move the total weight of 81 kg (Let us suppose the bag weighs 1 kg). It may take 2 hours to fulfill the work.

一个体重60公斤的人，肩扛20公斤的粮食步行10千米，他只需要移动总重81公斤（假设麻袋重1公斤）的负荷。他可能需要2小时完成任务。

By riding a bicycle, this man needs move total weight of 91 kg (Bicycle weighs 10 kg). It may take 0.5 hour to fulfill the work.

如果骑自行车，这个人需要移动总重为91公斤（假设自行车重10公斤）。他可能在0.5小时内能完成任务。

By driving a car, the engine of the car needs move total weight of 1081 kg (car weighs 1000 kg). It could take less than 0.1 hour to fulfill the work.

如果开车，汽车引擎需要移动总重1081公斤（假设汽车自重1000公斤）的负荷。但它可在0.1小时内完成任务。

To withstand the vibration caused by the high speed, the tool has to be built with stronger materials, usually meaning heavier in weight. Because of the extra burden from the tools, it needs more energy to get the same work done since the higher the speed is, the heavier tool is needed in general.

为了承受高速产生的振动，需要工具由高强度的材料制造，这通常意味着高的重量。由于工具的这种超额负担，需要有更多的能量来完成相同的任务，因为一般而言，速度越快，使用的工具越重。

Moreover, the higher the speed is, the more sophisticated structure of the tool is, and the more energy is needed to make it.

此外，速度越高，工具的结构越复杂，而制造此类工具的能量消耗也越大。

C. Time Efficiency Versus Energy Efficiency of Labor

C. 劳动的时间效率和能量效率

We said before that there are three ways for a farmer to plough his land; the first of which is to hire three persons to do the job, the second of which is to hire one ox to drive the plough in the front and one human to control at the back; or the third of which is to hire a person to drive a motor tractor with a plough. And we said that the total net energy dissipations in three different methods are the same since they need get the work done to overcome the friction caused by the earth through the same distance they drive through. Only difference is that, pure human configuration may take tree days; the human plus ox one may take one day; and the tractor plus human one may take only a few hours. Scenario 3 is faster than scenarios 2 and scenario 2 is faster than scenario 1. So, we say that the

前面我们提到，农夫有三种耕地的方法：其一为雇佣三人来做；其二是雇佣一牛拉犁一人扶犁；其三是雇佣一人开一拖拉机来完成。我们说，这三种方法的净做功是相等的，都是克服同样一段路程的土地的摩擦力做功。唯一的区别是：纯人组合需要3天；人牛组合需要1天；人机组合仅需几小时。第三种状况快于第二种状况，而第二种状况快于第一种状况。因此，我们说第三种状况的时间效率好于第二种状况，而第二种状况的时间效率好于第一种状况。

time efficiency of scenario 3 is higher than that of scenarios 2 and the time efficiency of scenario 2 is higher than that of scenario 1.

If we look at the energy dissipated in total, however, the rank is reversed. That is to say, the energy efficiency of scenario 1 is higher than that of scenarios 2; and the energy efficiency of scenario 2 is higher than that of scenario 3. Why? Besides the one who controls the plough, two men weigh about 150 kg; one ox weighs about 500 kg; and a tractor weighs over 1,000 kg. The energy needed to move two men forward in a certain distance is of cause less than the energy needed to move one ox; the energy needed to move one ox forward in the same distance is of cause less than the energy needed to move a tractor. The total amount of energy dissipation in scenario 1 is less than that of scenario 2; the total amount of energy dissipation in scenario 2 is less than that of scenario 3. Therefore, the energy efficiency in scenario 3 is less than that of scenario 2; the energy efficiency in scenario 2 is less than that of scenario 1.

但如果我们观察一下三种状况的能量总消耗，排名却要反过来了，即第一种状况的能量效率好于第二种状况，而第二种状况的能量效率好于第三种状况。为什么？去除三种状况都有的一人，两个人的重量为150公斤；一头牛的重量为500公斤；一台拖拉机的重量超过1000公斤。用于驱动两人移动一段距离所需的能量肯定小于驱动一头牛移动相同距离的所需；用于驱动一头牛移动一段距离所需的能量肯定小于驱动一台拖拉机移动相同距离的所需。第一种状况所需的总能量小于第二种状况；第二种状况所需的总能量小于第三种状况。所以，第三种状况的能量效率低于第二种状况；第二种状况的能量效率低于第一种状况。

Value is measured according to the aggregated (gross) energy dissipated in whole procedure of getting a certain job done, not the net work (energy) done. Let us suppose that the value of money is constant ever since. The cost of buying a kilogram of rice in 1000 years ago, when people ploughed the land with human power only, could be 5 times cheaper than that of present, when people use machines, artificial fertilizers and pesticides to farm. This is to say that we are spending 5 times of energy as in 1000 years ago to produce the same amount of

价值是以在生产过程中总的（毛）能量消耗，而不是净做功（能量）来计量的。让我们假定货币的价值从古到今固定不变，1000 年前购买由纯人组合犁地生产的一公斤大米可能会比现在用人机组合、化肥和农药来生产的大米便宜 5 倍。也就是说，我们现在使用 5 倍的能量消耗来生产相同数量的大米。

rice.

Generally speaking, human realizes a high time efficiency in value creation by sacrificing the energy efficiency in terms of getting the same thing done. As the consequence of it, so called natural devaluation of money occurs.

总的来讲，在创造价值的过程中，人们用牺牲能量效率的办法来提高时间效率。这也引起了所谓货币的自然贬值。

XXVIII. Consumption Behavior of Homo Economicus

XXVIII. 经济人的消费行为

A. Priority of Human Wants

A. 需求优先顺序

Based on the level of subsistence, human wants are prioritized as the following,

(1) Food and Drug

(2) Garment

(3) Shelter

(4) Transportation

(5) Relaxation

(6) Education

(7) Future Securities

Generally, only the prior wants are basically satisfied, may people consider of the inferior want if there is any income surplus available.

基于生存的状况，人类需求可以划分成如下几个层次：

（1）食品和医药

（2）衣服

（3）居住

（4）行走

（5）娱乐

（6）教育

（7）未来保障

一般来说，只有上一层需求被基本满足后，如果收入还有盈余，下一层的需求才会被考虑。

B. Projected Life Time Balance Sheet

B. 预想中的终生收支平衡表

A whole society is constituted by lots of families and firms, who are producers on one hand and consumers on the other hand. As single person is not capable to produce all kinds of the wealth of the society, it is not possible for him to buy all the wealth of the society, or even just all the portions which is wanted by him, in a short period of time.

整个社会是由许多既是生产者又是消费者的家庭和公司所组成的。一个人无法生产社会所有的财富，他也没能力购买社会所有的财富，甚至短时间内不可能购买所有他需要的部分。他必须根据他的收支平衡表来安排他的购买行为。每

He has to plan his purchase based on his balance sheet. Everyone has his own projected balance sheet of his life in his mind like the following,

个消费者都有一张预想中的终生收支平衡表，表述如下：

$$(10)\quad \sum_{i=1}^{M} PU_i + \sum_{j=1}^{N} GA_j = \sum_{k=1}^{P} IC_k + \sum_{l=1}^{Q} GM_l$$

Where,

PU_i represents the price of his ith Purchase in his life;

GA_j represents his jth Give-away Money in his life;

IC_k represents his kth Income in his life;

GM_l represents his lth Gift Money in his life;

M represents total times of purchase in his life;

N represents total times of give-away money in his life;

P represents total times of income in his life;

Q represents total times of gift money in his life;

The projection is being updated iteratively along with the development of one's life.

Actually, the Life Time Balance Sheet implies a truth that, in a perfect economical world, one can only have the right to dispose of the fruits of his own mental and physical labor.

其中：

PU_i代表他人生中的第i 次采购的价格；

GA_j代表他人生中的第 j 次捐出的金额；

IC_k 代表他人生中的第 k 次的收入；

GM_l代表他人生中的第l 次收到的财礼捐赠的金额；

M 代表他人生中的购买总次数;

N 代表他人生中的捐献总次数;

P 代表他人生中的收入总次数;

Q 代表他人生中的财礼总次数;

这个预想中的平衡表会在其一生中不断调整更新。

实际上，终生收支平衡表印证如下事实：在一个纯经济的世界里，一个人只具有对他自己智力和体力劳动成果的支配权。

C. Price Sensitivity

To measure the price sensitivity of a specific consumer at specific time, we have the following formula,

C. 价格敏感度

一个特定消费者在特定时间阶段的价格敏感度可以用以下公式表达：

$$(11)\quad PS_I = PU_I / MA_t$$

Where,

PS_I represents his price sensitivity on Ith

其中：

PS_I代表其一生中的在时间点t

Purchase in ones life at time t;

MA_t represent the projected total money available for purchase since time t in his life;

We suppose that, when we discuss the Ith purchase of someone at time t, it means all the previous purchase from the 1st, 2nd… through (I-1) th has already fulfilled. Therefore,

的第I 次购买;

MA_t代表其一生中的在时间点t后的预想的总可用金额;

我们假设之前的第1、第2……第I–1次购买都已经完成。因此:

$$(12)\quad MA_t = \sum_{l=1}^{Q} GM_l + \sum_{k=1}^{P} IC_k - \sum_{j=1}^{N} GA_j - \sum_{i=1}^{I-1} PU_i$$

We all know that, a rich man is willing to pay foods like steak, say worth of \$100, every day without any hesitation, while a poor family is hesitating in buying candies, worth of \$1, for kids. What is the cause behind for different consumers to make decisions? It may well explain this scenario by comparing the Price Sensitivities between the rich and the poor instead of absolute numbers of prices. The PS of a steak to a billionaire could be one millionth, while a piece of candy may mean one thousandth worth of PS to the poor.

When PS_I is equal to 1, it means that the consumer has to use all the money he owns in whole rest of his life to pay just this purchase. When PS_I is equal to 0.5, it means that the consumer has to use 50% of his rest of life to pay just this purchase. When PS_I is greater than 1, it means that the consumer's inheritor has to pay part of the price. So, the higher the PS is, the more careful the consumer will be during the purchase decision making. In the reality, the family has to take its own Engel's Coefficient into consideration first of all, which is the floor for the other PSs of the family.

我们都知道,一个富人愿意毫不犹豫地每天购买价值\$100的牛排,而一个贫穷家庭会因花\$1给孩子买糖果而犹豫。背后是什么导致不同的消费者会作不同的消费决定?恐怕比较消费者的价格敏感度就会有一个很好的解释,对一个亿万富翁,一块牛排的价格敏感度(PS)可能只有百万分之一;而对一个贫困家庭,一块糖果的PS可能已是千分之一了。

PS_I等于1,意味着该消费者须用其后一生的收入来进行这次购买;PS_I等于0.5,意味着该消费者须用其后半生一半的收入来进行这次购买;PS_I大于1,意味着该消费者的继承者还需要替该消费者支付这次购买的部分费用。因此,价格敏感度越大,消费者就会在购买之前越小心地作决断。在现实中,一个家庭,必须首先将恩格尔系数考虑进来,因为这是家庭其他采购PS的前提。

D. Purchase Aggressiveness

The psychological aggressiveness of a person is his personal nature formed per his gene and his grow-up atmosphere. But even for the same person, with same psychological aggressiveness, will have different purchase aggressiveness under different circumstances. Not only the total income affects the decision making of a consumer, but also the current income lever and change of the income affects the decision making, too. We might use the following PID regulation formula to express the consumption aggressiveness of a consumer.

D. 购买冲动

一个人的心理冲动性是其遗传基因和成长环境影响的结果，但具有同样的心理冲动性的同样一个人，在不同时期因为当时环境条件不同，其购买冲动也会不同，不仅总收入会影响其消费决定，收入的现状及其改变一样也会影响其消费决定。用PID调节公式表示如下：

$$\text{(13)} \qquad PA(t) = (\alpha * IC(t) + \beta * \int_{i=l}^{\infty} IC(t)dt + \gamma * dIC(t)/dt)$$

Where,

PA(t) represents the purchase aggressiveness at time t;

IC(t) represents the income function;

α, β, γ represent the psychological sensitivity coefficients on the current level of income, the future accumulation of income, and the change of income respectively.

When PA(t) approaches to 0, it means that the consumer has no intention to buy anything; The greater the PA(t) is, the higher intention of buying things the consumer has, sometimes even without any money on hand at the moment.

其中：

PA(t) 表示时间t 时的购买冲动;

IC(t) 表示收入函数;

α，β，γ 分别表示针对收入现状、收入积累和收入变化的心理敏感系数。

PA(t)接近零，则说明此时消费者没有购买愿望。PA(t)越大，消费者的购买愿望就越强烈，哪怕当时手中没钱。

E. Portfolio of Demand

The above mentioned four aspects, namely, the priority of human wants, the projected life time balance sheet, price sensitivity, and the purchase aggressiveness, of a consumer forms his behavior as

E. 总需求构成

上述四个方面，需求优先顺序、终生收支平衡表、价格敏感度和购买冲动构成了一个经济人的消费行为。而全社会经济人的消费行

a homo economicus. And the aggregated behaviors of all homo economicus in the whole society constitute the portfolio of demand of the society in a macro level.

为总和就在宏观上构成了社会的总需求。

If the Portfolio of Supply of the society matches its Portfolio of Demand exactly, the economy will be running constantly and smoothly for sure. In the long term, the Portfolio of Supply of the society and the Portfolio of Demand approaches each other via their self-regulations. But in the short term, the Portfolio of Supply of the society and the Portfolio of Demand in the market do not always agree to each other.

如果社会的总供给构成准确地满足其总需求构成，经济将会平稳发展。从长远看，通过自我调节，社会的总供给构成与总需求构成会相互靠近。但从短期看，市场上社会的总供给构成与总需求构成并不总是相一致。

Roughly, we may know the portfolio of the market needs and the trends through market survey. However, it is a static and snapshot of some point of the time. Before setting up new facilities of production, the entrepreneurs have, of course, made some analysis and the projection. However, they are not able to predict the situation change of competition from both similar production organizations and its product substitutes in the future. The dynamic of the demands of the customers also changes sometimes due to some unpredictable natural or artificial cause(s).

通过调查我们可以大概知道市场需求的构成和趋势，可它是静态的某个时间点上的情势。在设厂之前企业家们肯定都做过分析和预测，但他们没法预计来自未来相似产品或替代产品的竞争。消费者的需求也会因为不可预见的自然的或人为的原因而改变。

Not saying that there is no flexibility at all in the production organizations, we recognize that the production organization will yield its products in a rather fixed rate once the setup is finished if an economical running mode is expected. It is costly to change the production configuration though.

并不是说现存的生产组织缺乏灵活性，但每个生产组织都会有一个固定的经济生产模式，改变生产配置是有额外耗费的。

X X IX. Pricing Mechanism in Exchange

A. Gradient of Value-In-Exchange

In Chapter VI, we have already demonstrated, that the VIE of the rice remotely produced is higher than that locally produced just because additional transportation needed for moving the rice from distance to town, assuming all other production conditions are the same. Geographically, it forms a VIE gradient surrounding the market place of the town. Not only the geographical factor creates the gradient of VIE, but many other factors also create gradient of VIE as well, such as:

- quality of natural resources
- producing tools
- producing methods
- producing organization
- cultural mentality
- waste treatment, etc

The richness of different mines are different. People need to spend different VIH to obtain the same amount of pure iron; some manufacturers possess higher energy efficiency than the other because they keep the know-how as secrete or patented; and prolonging work time of human is a simple way of raising energy efficiency in deed. Even the way how to treat the waste may affect the gradient of VIE. Coal ash and slag is waste of a steam station. It causes the gradient of VIE for the power station if people treat it as the material for making cement/brick versus just discard it away.

X X IX 交换中的定价机制

A. 交换价值梯度

在第六章中，我们已经论证了外地来的稻谷的VIE比本地产的要高，因为需要额外的运输将外地稻谷搬到本地（假设其他生产条件外地本地都一样），从地理分布上看，就形成了一个以本地市场为中心的交换价值梯度。当然不仅地理因素会导致VIE梯度的产生，诸如下列其他因素也会导致VIE梯度的产生：

- 自然资源的质量
- 生产工具
- 生产方式
- 生产组织
- 文化传统
- 废料利用等

不同的矿床的贫富程度并不一样，人们得到同样数量的纯铁需要耗费的VIH也就不一样；有些制造商，因为掌握着秘密的方法，能达到比其他制造商更高的能量效率；实际上延长工作时间也会提高能量效率。甚至如何处置废料也会影响VIE梯度，发电厂的炉渣是废料，而利用炉渣生产水泥/砖块与直接抛弃炉渣就会产生交换价值梯度。

B. Pricing Based on the Gradient of Value-In-Exchange

Let us do a case study first. When the food produced in town is not enough for all the population of the town, say because of a flood, people have to transport food from the neighborhood of the town first since the VIE of the food to the town is just a little bit higher than local one. If the supply of food is still not enough, people have to transport food from the place where is just a little bit further more. Say, through 5 tiers of gradient of VIE; let us call it tier 1, tier 2, tier 3, tier 4, and tier 5; the prices from which are 1%, 2%, 3%, 4%, 5% higher than the original local price of the food respectively; the demand and supply in quantity reaches the point of equilibrium.

Will the price of the food in town be based on the weighted average of 100%, 101%, 102%, 103%, 104%, 105% in the market place in town? No ("comparative advantage" effects), the price of the food will be just based on the highest price, which is 105% of the original local price in such case, if the food shortage is foreseeable in advance. And as a consequence of it, the prices of the areas; covering the tier 1, tier 2, tier 3, and tier 4; will be readjusted to 104%, 103%, 102%, and 101% of the original price in the areas in deed; just because of the self-interested of human; only tier 5 and upper tiers keep the prices unchanged. This is a case of undersupply for a region but sufficient for a society.

The above-mentioned situation is based on the shortage of food is predictable and supply tiers are computable. However, the shortage and the supply

B. 基于交换价值梯度的定价

首先看一个例子，假设由于洪灾，镇上的粮食已不够供应，人们必须从外地运进粮食，首先是从临近的地方运，因为那里来的粮食的VIE 比本地的略高一些。如果粮食供应还不够，人们则必须从更远的地方再运来粮食。假设越过 5 个层次的 VIE 梯度，我们称之为第 1 层、第 2 层、第 3 层、第 4 层、第 5 层，而从各层运来的价格则比本地粮食价格分别高 1%、2%、3%、4%、5%。而直到第 5 层，供需达到了均衡。

镇中的粮食市场价格会使来自包括地产的6个梯度层次的价格100%、101%、102%、103%、104%, 105%的加权平均吗？不会（比较优势机制在起作用）。如果粮食缺口是可预见的话，粮食的市场价格会依照最高的那个价格来定，也就是本地价的105%。而且作为连锁反应，第1层、第2层、第3层、第4层地区的价格会因为人类的自利考量而上涨到原价的104%、103%、102%和101%，只有第5层地区的粮食保持不变。这是一个局部供应欠缺而全社会供应充足的例子。

以上的分析是基于粮食缺口是可预见的，因此粮食的供应梯度层次是可计算的。如果缺口数量和供

tiers cannot be accurately projected in the reality. Based on the fear of the uncertainty of the future, the acceptable market price of food in town in such case are usually higher than 105% of the original price temporarily, based on the assumption that the supply tier could be higher than 5.

应层次无法预计，人们基于对未来不确定性的恐慌心理，基于供给梯度可能会大于 5 层的考虑，粮食可接受的市场价格暂时甚至会高于 105%。

Let us suppose a town was destroyed completely by a strong earthquake. The construction material supplier tiers of 101%, 102%, 103%, 104%, 105% of the original local price based on VIE have been supplying products in the prices based on the 105% of original local price. Along with the completion of the house construction, the demand on the construction material is shrinking from now on. The suppliers with the 105% of the original local price will be phased out the first and the prices of the construction materials will be adjusted based on 104% of the original local price meanwhile. So on and so forth until the demand and the supply reach their new equilibrium, say at 102% of the original local price level, supposing the local construction material plants were destroyed totally and no one wanted to rebuild them; and the capacities of tier 1 suppliers are not enough to cover the needs. This case shows the dynamic of the oversupply. Let's call it Pricing Mechanism Class 1.

假设一个集镇由于地震被完全摧毁了，重建的材料都是从价格基于VIE梯度的分别为101%、102%、103%、104%、105%本地价的货源供应的，销售市场价格为原地产价的105%。而随着重建工程的进展，建筑材料的需求在下降，那些105%的供应商首先被淘汰出局，市场价格会变成104%；如此这般，直到供需达到新的平衡，假设因为无人愿意在当地重建建筑材料生产厂而第1层的供应量又不够，原价的102%是新的价格平衡点。这是一个过剩供给的例子。我们称之为第一类定价机制。

Pricing Mechanism Class 1 functions only when the same product demanded is available from somewhere else in the world, what we call homogeneous redundancy.

第一类定价机制只有在其他地方有所需要的相同产品供应的条件下，即同质冗余的情况下才发挥作用。

C. Pricing based on the Gradient of the Price Sensitivity of Consumers

There could happen sometimes though that the products from all the VIE tiers in the society cannot still serve all the total demand of the society, that is to say, it is in shortage of overall supply. What would determine the price of the goods in scarcity then?

Actually, besides pricing based on VIE gradient which affects the pricing from bottom up when supply is sufficient in the society; there is another sort of price gradient from the top down affects the pricing when supply is in scarcity in the society, which is the price gradient based on Price Sensitivity. Different families/firms have their different income levels (caused by different profit rate) and different Price Sensitivities therefore. The highest acceptable prices to them are different. The highest acceptable prices from different kind of buyers form another kind of price gradient. This price gradient based on Price Sensitivity forms thereby in a similar way of one based on VIE. From the top of the highest down, the lowest price possible in the price gradient based on the Price Sensitivity, considering the coverage of the total amount of possible supply, determines the price of the goods in scarcity.

Due to the limited amount of the supply, if the demand from the upper tier getting bigger, the pricing point will shift upper alone the gradient of the price sensitivity and the price will therefore be going higher; if the demand from the upper tier getting less, the pricing point will shift lower alone

C. 基于消费者价格敏感度梯度的定价

还有一种可能的情况：全社会所有 VIE 层次的产品仍然满足不了社会的需求，即出现了供应短缺的情况，那么是什么在决定这稀缺商品的价格呢?

实际上，在全社会供给充足时，基于由 VIE 梯度引起的从低到高的价格梯度决定定价。在全社会供应不足时，则存在另一种由价格敏感度引起的从高到低的价格梯度决定的定价机制。不同的家庭 / 公司处于不同的收入水平（由不同的利润率导致）并因此具有不同的价格敏感度。某物可接受的最高价格对他们是不一样的，这些可接受的最高价就形成了一个梯度。这个基于价格敏感度形成的价格梯度与基于 VIE 梯度形成的梯度相似。考虑到可能供给的覆盖面，从最高价格往下，处于基于价格敏感度形成的价格梯度最可能低的价格决定稀缺商品的价格。

由于供给的数量有限，如果较高层次的需求量增大，则定价点会沿着价格敏感度梯度上移，价格因此会变高；如果较高层次的需求量减少，则定价点会沿着价格敏感度梯度下移，价格因此会变低。

the gradient of the price sensitivity and the price will be of cause going down.

Pricing based on the gradient of the Price Sensitivity is the cause of the premium price therefore the premium profit. Let's call it the Pricing Mechanism Class 2.

基于价格敏感度的定价是产生超额价格亦即超额利润的根源。我们称之为第二类定价机制。

Pricing Mechanism Class 2 functions only when the availability of a specific product is less than the quantity demanded, but some buyers are willing and capable to trade with some other product he/she owns in extra, what we call heterogeneous redundancy.

第二类定价机制仅在所需特定产品的供给小于需求，但部分购买者愿意并能够用其所拥有的额外的其他产品作为交换条件下，即异质冗余的情况下才发挥作用。

D. Pricing Based on the Gradient of Tolerances to Discount Loss of Suppliers

D. 基于供应商折损耐受度梯度的定价

In a close society, as we mentioned before, food supply has to meet the requirement of the population of the society. Otherwise, there must be partial of the population dies eventually due to the starvation, who are the loser in the competition for food. Pricing Mechanism Class 2 explains the price change under the circumstance of food shortage. It also implies that those who possesses less ownership of the value in the Social Virtual Depot will be the losers first most likely, in the battle for survival.

前面我们已经讲过，在一个封闭的社会中，粮食供应必须满足社会人口的需求。如果不能满足，必定有一定比例的人口终将因饥饿而死亡，即他们是粮食需求竞争中的失败者。第二类定价机制，直接表达的是在供应短缺时，价格的变化规律，而间接表达的是：拥有较少社会虚拟中转库中价值所有权的人，将会较先成为需求竞争中的失败者。

Analogous to the Pricing Mechanism Class 2, there must be partial of suppliers bankrupts eventually because no product is sold under the circumstance that supply is greater than demand. For crowding in the supplying array, suppliers low the price one after another. The price could be lower than its natural price, so that the supplier of it

相对于第二类定价机制中的“消费者价格敏感度”，在需求不足而供应过度的情况下，必定会有一定比例的供应商因产品不能出售而最终导致破产。供应商为了能够挤进供应序列，相继以低于产品自然价格的价格进行交易，希望能够

could be survive hopefully. Now, the tolerances to discount loss of suppliers determines the trade price in the market.

The Tolerance to Discount Loss of a supplier can be expressed as the following,

(14) LTp = TNLPp / TA

Where,

LTp reprents the Tolerance to discount loss on product p of the supplier.

TNLPp represents Natural Price in total of product p of the supplier.

TA represents the total assets of the supplier.

Different company has different product spectrum and different total assets, therefore possesses different Tolerance to Discount Loss. The lowest prices tolerable to different suppliers are therefore different as well. A gradient of the tolerance to discount loss is thereafter formed, contrast to the Gradient of the Sensitivity to Price of consumer. Considering possible coverage on demand, the supply quantity accumulating from the lowest price upwards until it reaches the quantity of total demand, where the highest price possible is seen. Such Highest Price Possible in the gradient of tolerance to the discount loss determines the actual market price of the goods which are over-supplied.

Due to the limited quantity of demand, the market price shifts down alone the gradient of tolerance to discount loss if the quantity of supply in lower price increases; the market price shifts up alone the gradient of tolerance to discount loss if the quantity of supply in lower price decreases;

Pricing based on the tolerance to the discount

得以苟延残喘继续生存。此时，供应商的折损耐受度梯度，就成了决定交易价格的决定因素。

供应商折损耐受度可以用以下公式来表述：

(14) LTp = TNLPp / TA

其中：

LTp 代表某供应商针对某一特定产品 p 的折损耐受度；

TNLPp 代表产品 p 的自然价格总额；

TA 代表该供应商的资产总额。

不同的公司有不同的产品谱和总资产，因此具有不同的折损耐受度。针对产品可接受的最低销售价格也是不一样的，这些可接受的最低价就形成了一个梯度。这个基于折损耐受度形成的价格梯度与基于价格敏感度形成的价格梯度相呼应。考虑到需求可能的覆盖面，从最低可接受价格的供应量开始往上累计，直至需求量刚好被覆盖的尽可能高的可接受价格的供应，这个处于基于折损耐受度形成的价格梯度最可能高的价格决定了此超量供应商品的真正的市场价格。

由于需求的数量有限，如果较低价位的供应量增大，则定价点会沿着折损耐受度梯度下移，价格会因此变低；如果较低价位的供应量减少，则定价点会沿着折损耐受度梯度上移，价格会因此变高。

基于折损耐受度梯度的定价是

loss is the cause of the negative premium price i.e. the loss, which is called the Pricing Mechanism Class 3.

产生负超额价格亦即亏损的根源。我们称之为第三类定价机制。

the Pricing Mechanism Class 3 functions only when the supply of certain product is greater than the demand in the market and the suppliers are willing to offer a price lower than the cost through giving up the ownership of the value.

第三类定价机制仅在特定产品的供给大于需求，而部分供应商愿意用本应属于他自己的产品价值作为馈赠的交换条件下才有可能发生。

XXX. Fluctuation of Price

XXX. 价格波动

A. Demand, Price and Supply

A. 需求价格及供给

We were taught that the fluctuation of price is the reflection of the mismatching between the portfolio of supply and the portfolio of demand in the society. Price rises when the demand is greater than the supply; price declines when the demand is less than the supply. We have found a solid explanation as the above mentioned pricing mechanism.

以前的教科书上说：价格波动是社会供给总构成与需求总构成不匹配的反映，供不应求价格上升；供大于求价格下降。上一节，我们论述的定价机制给出了一个合理的解释。

It was also said that supply increases when price rises; supply decreases when the price decline in general. It was found that this is not always true. A term called Elasticity of Supply was created to describe the correlativeness of supply against the price. When the elasticity of supply equals to 0, the supply will not be affected by the price fluctuation. It sounds like a tautology though. What is the real cause behind then?

以前的教科书还说：总体上，价格上升，供给会提高；价格下降，供给会减少。但又发现，此说法又不是总成立，因此一个叫供给弹性的术语被创造出来，用以描述供给与价格之间的相关性。当供给弹性为零时，供给将不受价格变动的影响。可这似乎是一个自圆其说的办法。真正的原因是什么呢?

Let's do a case study onto a closed village in remote mountains first. Their food is supplied by themselves totally since it's impossible to transport food from outside world. We also suppose that

让我们首先分析一个远处深山里的封闭小山村的案例。因为无法从外部获得食物，他们的食物完全是自给自足的。我们假定他们那里

there is no extra food reserve for contingency. For some reason naturally or artificially, food supply goes down to half its usual level. The price of food will surely goes up. The fact is that no matter how high the price goes, the total supply of food stays in the same level since no additional food supplying channel is available. So the Pricing Mechanism Class 2 dominates the market. Half of the population in the village may soon or later die if the food shortage last for a long while.

没有任何应对突发事件的额外的粮食储备。由于自然或人为的原因，食物供给降到了通常的一半，食物价格肯定会上涨。可实际情况是，无论价格如何上涨，食物的供给却依然如故，因为没有任何外部供应渠道可用。因此第二类定价机制主导着市场。如果食物短缺时间足够长，一半的人口迟早会死亡。

Let's change the scenario a little bit by assuming, that this village is not closed but belongs to a closed society. Food can be move freely in and out of the village within the society. There are two possible situations happening when this village is in short of food.

我们将情景修改一下，假设村庄不是封闭的，而是属于一个封闭的社会，食物可以自由地在本社会的范围内流进或流出这个村庄。如果该村发生了食物短缺，有两种可能的情况会发生：

Situation 1: If the food supply and food demand of the whole society was just well balanced statically with no extra food reserve at all, food shortage of one village means food shortage of the whole society. Pricing Mechanism Class 2 still dominates the market.

情况一：全社会的食物供需正好处于静态平衡，没有任何的额外食物储备，一个村庄的食物短缺就意味着整个社会的食物短缺。第二类定价机制支配着市场。

Situation 2: There is sufficient extra food reserve somewhere in the society just in case. If some of the villages in the society are in short of food, reserved food can be transported to the places where food is needed. Pricing Mechanism Class 1 dominates the market on condition that the extra food reserve is sufficient to cover the shortage. Otherwise, Situation 1 happens again when the food reserve is run out.

情况二：全社会在某处存有足够的以防万一的食物储备，如果某些村庄发生食物短缺，储备的食物就可以被运到需要食物的地方。第一类定价机制在有足够的食物储备的条件下主导市场。否则，当食物储备用完后，情况一定会再次发生。

Such situation happens not only in the food supply but also in all other fuel and tool supplies.

这种情况不仅发生在食物供应也发生在所有其他燃料和工具的供

Let's take house building as the example. Supposing the cement supply, steel bar supply, wood supply for house building are well balanced in a closed society, that means all the building material supplies are just enough for maintaining, replacing old houses, and building new houses for naturally increased families. All of a sudden, a strong earthquake totally destroys several villages of the society. Additional demands other than well balanced regular demands on building materials pop up. The prices will go up for sure. However, the total supplies of these materials will stay the same level if there are no extra direct reserves of building material or indirect reserves of capacity of producing these materials available.

应上。以一个封闭社会的建筑业为例，假设建造房屋所需的水泥、钢筋和木料的供应处于平衡状态，即所有建筑材料正好用于老房屋的维修翻新和建造，以满足社会由于人口自然增长对新房的需求。突然强地震发生了，有几个村庄被完全摧毁了。在原来平衡的需求基础上，社会对建筑材料有了新的需求。建材的价格自然会上涨，但如果没有直接的建材储备或间接的建材生产能力的储备，建材的供应量却只会停留在原水平不动。

Generally speaking, the reserve or redundancy of labors, fuels and tools plays key roles in regulating supply against demand. The price fluctuation is just a presentation caused by the mismatch between supply and demand. Reserve can be kept in national level, company level, and/or family level. Man may build more or less reserves of fuels and tools, based on the price level and shelf life of goods, emergency level of demand, income level of cause, and sometimes pure financing reason.

总的来说，劳动力、燃料和工具的储备或者称之为冗余，是调节供求关系的关键，而价格波动只是供需失衡的一个表象。储备可以发生在国家、公司和家庭等层面。人们应根据商品的价格水平和有效期、需求的紧急程度、收入水平或纯财政原因或多或少地储备商品。

B. Price Fluctuation vs. Money Supply

Let's suppose that all of the products in the Virtual Depot of the society were priced on basis of Anchor Chain Coefficient of 1.5×10-6 Dollar per Joule initially. The total money supply to the market is therefore regulated based on such rate accordingly. Let's say Product A is in shortage in

B. 价格波动与货币供应

假定，最初社会虚拟中转库里的所有产品是按照（1.5 × 10−6）美元/焦耳的锚链系数定价的，而市场上流通的货币总量也是照此响应调节好的。由于某个自然或人为的原因，产品A出现了短缺，其价

the market for some natural or artificial reason. The price of Product A increased by 50% averagely so that the marginal price gradient is reached therefore. Say, the total VIE of Product A in the Virtual Depot took 10% of the aggregate VIEs of the products in the Depot originally. It causes money shortage for the Products other than Product A by 5% (=10%×50%) in average in the same pace of time. That is to say, there will be some of the products detained in the Virtual Depot waiting for being purchased in the next pace or the next nth pace of time hopefully, due to the shortage of the money supply in current pace of trade. It means potential loss on these detained products in deed, because of the time efficiency is lowered. Averagely speaking, the flow rate of value in the circulation is shrinking. This is so called Deflation.

We analyzed above just on the situation of Product A itself. Correlatively, the demands on the raw materials of the Product A will increase as well; the prices of the raw materials could increase along with their own price gradients for their suppliers to share the profit premium with the producers of Product A, which will cause the profit decrease of other producers who produce the products other than Product A but share the materials of Product A partially. So on and so forth goes all the supply chain. The employees of the producers of Product A expect wage increase, too. The money shortage for those, whose product is not Product A, might be even far bigger than 5%. It just like ink penetration in a wet cloth, so long as the intensiveness is strong enough, the color of the ink will spread all over this

格平均上涨了50%后，达到了边界价格梯度。假设：开始时，产品A的总VIE占整个社会虚拟中转库的10%。那么产品A的价格上涨会导致其他非A产品在同一时间节拍中的购买资金不足，平均缺口平均为5% (=10% × 50%)。也就是说，由于在相同交易时间节拍中的资金缺口，有些产品将不得不被滞留在虚拟中转库中，并只能等待下一个或者是下n个时间节拍后有幸被购买。鉴于时间效率因此降低，对被滞留的产品来说，也是一种损失。平均来讲，流通中的价值流量萎缩了，这就是所谓的通货紧缩。

上面只是分析了产品 A 本身。与产品 A 的增加相对应，产品 A 的原材料的需求也必定增加，原材料的价格也就可能会沿着它们各自的价格梯度上涨，原材料的供应商分享到了产品 A 导致的超额利润。而原材料的涨价却会导致其他非 A 产品，但与产品 A 共用一部分原材料的产品的利润下降。这个过程将会沿着供应链一节一节以同样的方式进行。雇员们也会因此要求增加工资。非 A 产品的货币短缺可能远远不止 5%。整个过程就像一块湿抹布上滴入几滴墨水，只要墨水强度足够，则整个抹布上最终会按照一定梯度散布了墨色。

piece of cloth in a certain gradient eventually.

Surely the example above is exaggerated for understanding impressively. Due to the huge amount of value in the Virtual Depot of the society, it usually makes little impact onto rest of the products when some of the products are in shortage and causing the price increase. The Invisible Hand may regulate it quite effectively. Per Murphy's Law, economic crisis happens sometimes though.

当然，为了使读者在理解上印象深刻，上述的例子是被夸大了的。由于社会虚拟中转库体量巨大，由某些产品的短缺而导致的价格上涨对其他非相关产品的影响一般并不太大。看不见的手基本上可以有效地进行调节。但墨菲定律告诉我们：小概率的经济危机有时也是可能发生的。

C. One of the Causes of Economic Recession

C. 经济衰退原因之一

The price premium phenomenon will be gone in certain transient period of time after the flood or earthquake is gone. The prices will be back to where they were, or will reach a new equilibrium close to the original one. Everything is back to normal. There are, however, some kind of price premium due to the VIE gradient may lead to an extreme economic phenomenon, which is economic recession.

一定的过渡时间后，超额价格现象会随着大水或地震的消失而消失，价格会回到它们原来的水平或者达到一个接近原价格的新的平衡点，一切又回到正常。但某些基于交换价值的价格梯度可能会导致一种极端的经济现象，即经济衰退。

The price premium phenomenon is universal. It is actually the drive for technology innovation. Let us conceive a scenario that; the VIE of producing Product A was 10 trillion Joules in the past; due to an innovative invention, the VIE of the replacement of Product A is 1 TJ now. A VIE gradient with the drop of 90% is therefore created. For maximizing his interest, the manufacturer sells his product in the same price level as before. A 90% of price premium will be maintained if the market demand is not saturated. The manufacturer will surely invest

超额价格现象是一种普遍现象，它事实上是技术革新的源动力。来看一个例子，原来产品A的VIE是100亿焦耳，由于技术改良，现在产品A替代品的VIE只有10亿焦耳，一个90亿焦耳的VIE梯度由此而产生了。为了利益最大化，生产商仍然按原价出售他的产品，如果市场的需求没有饱和，90%的超额价格就会得到维持。生产商肯定会将大部分赚回来的超额价格投资到

the most of the price premium owned, back to the same business expecting more price premium. Many manufacturers in other industries might shift their interests to this industry because of high price premium, too. So on and so forth, it will eventually form a local circulation with higher turnover, by sucking up most of the money from the general circulation of the society, which was allocated quite evenly for all the products previously. The redundancy of production capacity reaches eventually unreasonable height. It will cause cash flow slow-down/broken for other productions first and thereafter no money for supporting the premium price of Product A and no money for buying Product A. eventually. A recession could thereby happen.

同样的产业中以期获取更多的超额价格。而在其他行业的制造商也会因为超额价格的诱惑转而进入这个行业的制造，如此这般，依靠吸取社会大流通中早先被均匀分配的资金，一个高回报率的产业投资的局部流转就此形成。生产能力的冗余度最后达到了一个不合理的水平。最终，其他产品生产的现金流会减缓甚至断裂，从而又导致消费者无钱支持产品A的超额价格，甚至无钱购买产品A，一场经济衰退可能就此发生了。

Let’s have a look at the water flow in a river as a reference. When the flow speed is low, we see only laminar flow; when speed of the flow increases over a threshold, small whirlpools are seen here and there; when the speed goes upper and upper, small whirlpools may combine together and generate a maelstrom. Small recession in the economy likes small whirlpool in the river. Overall economic recession in a state likes a maelstrom in a speedy water flow.

让我们以河中的水流作为对比：当水流速度低时，我们仅观察到层流；当流速超过一定的阈值时，可以在这里或那里看到漩涡发生；如果流速再高，则小漩涡会汇集成一个大漩涡。经济中的小衰退就像是河流中的小漩涡，全国范围的经济衰退则是水流中的大漩涡。

Price premium generates the force of acceleration, the higher the price premium is, the higher amount of money will be sucked in and the higher speed the cash flow is.

超额价格是产生加速力的源泉，超额价格越高，吸入的金钱越多，因此现金流的速度越快。

We may say that, high enough price premiums in a large enough scale for a long enough period of time might cause the outbreak of an economic recession.

可以说：足够高的产品超额价格，在足够的规模下，持续足够的时间，可能引发经济衰退。

PART SEVEN: ON CIRCULATION

第七篇 流 通

XXXI. Process of Value Adding

XXXI. 价值增值过程

Even though almost all of the lands and partial of the oceans are already claimed as sovereignties by different nations and further by many private or collective owners, all the substances in natural form on the earth are free for human in deed. Through the organizations by human, these meaningless substances, in so called quasi-chaotic form, become more and more valuable to human along with the exertion of the more and more efforts by human.

尽管几乎所有的陆地和部分的海洋已经被各国瓜分，但所有地球上的自然形态的物质对人类而言其实都是免费的。在人类的组织下，这些毫无意义的、处于准混沌状态的物质，随着越来越多人类精力的投入变得越来越有价值。

Whole value adding happens in phase of WIP and WIS (although not significantly). Starting from collecting natural resources, the process of value adding is a step-by-step or bit-by-bit process of reorganization of the natural resources, along with the material flow, until a meaningful tool/fuel finally formed. Every step of or every bit of change requires proper tools in proper organized sequences and driven by either biological or mechanical engine, both of which need a certain amount of energy as the power source. So, the conversion from VIH to VIE is a gradual process.

整个价值增值过程都发生在WIP和（增量较小的）WIS阶段。从采集自然资源开始，到一个有意义的燃料或工具的形成，价值增值过程就是一个顺着物流方向一步一步、一丝一丝对自然资源进行再组织的过程。每一步每一丝的改变都需要有恰当的工具，在有序的组织下，在生物或机械引擎的驱动下进行，而两种引擎都需要一定的能量作为动力源，因而，VIH向VIE的转换是一个渐进的过程。

It is natural for a man to accept that the more effort man bestows onto a product, the more valuable man treats it. Man tends to neglect the

人很自然会接受这样一种观念，他投入产品的精力越多，他就会觉得该产品越有价值。人倾向于

effort by others. Jumping out of the loop of the self-focus, we may immediately realize that, under human being's proper organizations and with proper tools, the efforts no matter bestowed by biological engines; including man himself, horse, and ox, etc., or by mechanical engines "create" values.

忽略其他方面的努力，如果我们跳出自我关注的怪圈，我们很快就能意识到，在人的恰当的组织下利用合适的工具，不管是包括人、牛、马等在内的生物引擎，还是机械引擎都在“创造”价值。

There are three types of energy available on the earth, namely, the solar energy, the geothermal energy, and the nuclear energy. We are going to focus on solar energy since it is much more widely used than the other two in the world nowadays. The sunshine is the primary form of solar energy. Via atmosphere converter, some secondary form of solar energy, such as wind and stream, are there available; via the biological converter, many other different secondary form of solar energy, such as plants and algae, are there available; via organic converter, the tertiary form of solar energy, such as animals, fishes, and birds, are there available; coal, natural gas, and crude oil are deposited secondary or tertiary form of solar energy. Electricity is a terminal form of energy, which can be available by converting geothermal heat, radioactive energy, or all forms of solar energy.

地球上一共有三种能量形式，太阳能、地热能和核能，我们将专注于太阳能，因为其他两种能量的利用所占比例微乎其微。阳光是太阳能的原始形态；通过大气层的转换有了太阳能的第二形态，如风、水流等；经由生物转换器，又有了第二形态的其他表现，如植物和藻类等；经由有机转换器，有了第三种形态，如动物、鱼类、鸟类等；原煤、天然气、原油等都是储存的第二形态的和第三形态的太阳能。电力是利用包括地热、核能在内的任何形态的能源转变成的一种终端能量形式。

In the nature, the energy carriers have their objective value which we now call it Value-In-Heat (VIH). Along with every step of or every bit of change in the material flow above mentioned, the VIHs of the energy carriers are then transformed into VIEs as so called, which is subjective value, by either the organic engines or mechanical engines and bestowed bit-by-bit onto the subjects of labor, which are fuels or tools eventually.

在自然界，能量载体具有它自己的客观价值，我们称之为热量价值 VIH，通过每一步或每一丝的沿着物流方向的改变，能量载体的 VIH 经由有机或机械引擎转换成称之为交换价值 VIE 的主观价值，并一点一点地注入最终成为燃料或工具的劳动对象中。

Energy flow doesn't form a close loop circulation, which is a one-way trip. Energy may be converted, saved, transferred, but eventually it is gone in forms of heat dissipated back into the space. As we discussed in the previous Chapter, the VIH is the real value of energy, which is measurable, and the VIE is the imaginary value of energy dissipated in gross, which can only be calculated.

能量流并不是一个封闭形式的流通，它是一种单向旅程，能量可以被转换、储存、转移，但最终以热量耗散的形式消失在太空之中。如我们以前所述，VIH 是可以被测量的真实的价值；而 VIE 是想象中的只可以被计算的价值。

Value, as an imaginary measure of the degree of organization, cannot flow by itself alone. It seems to be embedded into some sort of organization of other substances through the process of reorganization. A course of the value flow is actually a chain of value adding, along with the material flow starting from farming/hunting/mining, through varieties of processing in fuel or tool productions, and finally reaching the hands of consumers. All the organizations of substances carry both heat if any (real part) and value (imaginary part) as we pointed out in the previous Chapters.

价值，作为一种组织程度的虚构计量，自己并不会流动，通过对其他物质进行再组织，它似乎是被注入被再组织后的组织中了。一个价值流实际上是一系列沿着物流，从耕种 / 狩猎 / 开采开始，经过各种生产过程而后成为燃料或工具，最终到达消费者手中的价值增加过程。正如我们在以前的章节中所指出的，所有的物质组织都携带着热量（实部）和价值（虚部）。

XXXII. Consumption of Wealth

XXXII. 财富的消费

There are two categories of material wealth in the society, namely, Energy Carrier and Utility Carrier. Basically, besides creating new energy carrier itself, we burn out the energy carriers for creating utility carriers, which are either tools or materials on their ways to be the tools in the end. The essence of the consumption of a tool is that the value of the tool to be evenly transferred to the subjects (WIP) it applies on, which is on the way to be a new utility carrier or new energy carrier, from

社会物质财富分两类，分别为能量载体和效用载体。撇开能量载体自身的再生产不说，我们用燃烧能量载体来创造效用载体，它们不是工具就是最终成为工具的材料。工具消费的实质就是，直至损坏不能再用，工具在使用中将其携带的价值平分转移给其施加的劳动对象，无论是最终成为新的能量载体还是新的效用载体中。工具的价值

the moment of its being made till the moment it is not available any more. The value transferring of a tool could be fulfilled at one time, at many times, or lasting for quite long time.

The consumption of wealth could be happening either inside the Virtual Depot of the society like in a factory, in a shop, in a firm, etc., which we usually call value-adding in other words; or outside the Virtual Depot of the society, like in a family, in a church, or in an army. We call the consumption happening inside the Virtual Depot of the society the Samsaraous Consumption of Wealth, which consumes wealth for creating other form(s) of wealth. And we call the consumption happening outside the Virtual Depot of the society the Terminal Consumption of Wealth, which consumes wealth out eventually for human's being. The consumptions by governments and families are generally the terminal consumptions.

All the social organizations of human, which include families, governments, and varieties of firms including manufactures and trades, hospitals, law firms, media, education and training centers, are both value producers and consumers the same time, each of which produces one or two specific products for the society and meanwhile needs a collection of products from the society for sustaining themselves.

All of the goods in the Virtual Depot of the society are for consumption with only two options, in either samsaraous or terminal manner, no matter part of which goes to governments as the taxations, to banks as the interests, to the owners as the profit, or to the employees as the wages respectively.

转移可以是一次完成，也可以是多次完成，甚至可以持续一个相当长的时间才完成。

财富的消费可以在诸如工厂、商店、公司等属于社会虚拟中转库的内部发生，我们也称之为增值；也可以在诸如家庭、教堂、军队等属于社会虚拟中转库之外的组织内发生。发生在社会虚拟中转库内部的，用以创造另一种形态财富的对财富的消费叫财富的轮回消费；发生在社会虚拟中转库之外的，用以人类存在的财富消费叫财富的终极消费。家庭消费和政府消费通常是终极消费。

所有的人类社会组织，家庭、政府以及各种各样的公司包括工厂、商号、医院、律师行、媒体、教育培训机构既是生产者又是消费者。它们生产一两种特定的产品同时需要从社会上获得一大堆其他产品以维持自己的存在。

社会虚拟中转库中的所有商品仅供两种形式的消费，不是轮回消费就是终极消费，无论其形式是政府的税收、银行的利息、业主的利润还是雇员的工资。

Except the wages to its employees/officials, all of rest of the tax income of the government is purely for samsaraous consumption;

Except the wage to its employees, all of rest of the interest income of a bank is for samsaraous consumption;

The profit income to the owner is usually for investment, which means samsaraous consumption;

The wages to the families could be used for either terminal consumption or investment meaning samsaraous consumption.

除了发给雇员 / 官员的工资，剩余的政府税收基本会被用于轮回消费。

除了发给雇员的工资，剩余的银行利息均会纯粹用于轮回消费。

业主的利息通常会被用于轮回消费。

家庭的工资可以被用于投资，即轮回消费，或终极消费。

XXXⅢ. Economic Circulation

A. Cash Flow

In Robinson Crusoe's island, there is no need of using money since he makes all fuels and tools solely for himself. All the labor value he exerted, are transferred and saved immediately as his own property. Even though there is value flow associated with Robinson's labor, there is no cash flow, and therefore there is no economic circulation at all. The trading of labor value through goods exchange is the cause of the economic circulation. A laborer spends his labor for making something for somebody else meanwhile he needs some other things made by other laborers. So, as the owner of his own labor, he has to have some sort of proof issued against the value flow, saying that he has spent labor worth of some amount of energy so that he can hopefully get something from others worth of the same amount of energy eventually, to keep the labor supply in a

XXXⅢ. 经济流通

A. 现金流

在鲁滨孙的孤岛上，不需要货币，因为他只为他自己生产所有的燃料和工具，所有他投入的劳动价值被转变成他自己的财产得以保存。尽管因鲁滨孙的劳动会有价值流存在，但却没有现金流的存在，因此经济流通也就无从谈起。通过商品交换来实现劳动价值的交易是经济流通的原因。劳动者投入他自己的劳动为其他人制造产品，同时需要从别的劳动者那里获得自己需要的产品。作为自己劳动的所有者，他必须有一个针对价值转移的凭证标明他已投入了一定数额的能量的劳动，借此希望最终能从他人那里获得价值等额能量的其他产品，以保证劳动力供应处于可持续的状

sustainable manner.

态。

Not only the owners of the human labor, who are the laborers themselves, need get compensated for sustainability, but also the owners of other biological engines, mechanical engines, and all other producing tools need get compensated for sustainability of the production systems along with the bit-by-bit value transferring process.

不仅参与劳动的人类所有者，即他自己，需要为可持续得到补偿；而且参与劳动无论是生物引擎还是机械引擎的所有者，还有其他生产工具的所有者都需要随着一点一点的价值转移，为可持续而得到补偿。

What it really means, when a worker gets a monthly wage of $1000 is, in God we trust, that the worker has a portion of wealth worth of $1000 deposited already in the Virtual Depot of the society, which was done by his employer on his behalf, because he has contributed the labor of a certain amount of value-in-exchange, which people believe that deserves a payback worth of $1000, through his labor exerted into the products in the warehouse of his employer or maybe even in their customer's warehouse already in the month. By using the credit note issued by the central bank, he may declare any equivalent goods or combination of goods which worth of $1000 anywhere anytime in the society without any additional conditions attached from the Virtual Depot of the society.

一个工人得到 $1000 报酬的真正含义是，我们相信，在社会虚拟中转库里有一部分价值 $1000 的财富属于这个工人。这部分财富是他的老板，以他的名义，当月存在其老板的甚至是他们客户的仓库里了，因为他已投入了，人们认为值得得到 $1000 报酬的交换价值的劳动到产品中。凭这些由中央银行发行的钞票，他可以在任何时候，任何地点无条件地从社会虚拟中转库换回价值 $1000 的商品或商品组合。

The same principle applies to the interest for the bank, taxation to the government, and the profit to the owner of a firm. Say, the bank gets $10,000 of interest; government gets $20,000 of tax; and the owner gets $30,000 of profit; that means in the Virtual Depot of the society are there portions of wealth of $10,000 at the bank's disposition; of $20,000 at the government's disposition; and of $30,000 at the owner's disposition since through

同样的原理也适用于银行的利息、政府的税收和业主的利润。假设银行得到 $10000 的利息收入，政府得到 $20000 税收，业主得到 $30000 的利润；只是说明在社会虚拟中转库中有价值 $10000 的财富属于银行，有价值 $20000 的财富属于政府和有价值 $30000 的财富属于此业主；因为通过服务，他们

their services to the wealth production, they contributed values to the Virtual Depot worth of $10,000, $20,000, $30,000 respectively.

The costs of materials, which are embedded into the goods, are eventually resolved as the wages to the laborer, interest to banks, taxation to the government, profit to the investor, and the depreciation compensation of tools to the owners, along with the supply chain to the very beginning retrospectively.

已经向社会虚拟中转库分别贡献了数量为 $10000、$20000、$30000 的价值。

装配进商品的原材料的成本，最终被分解成劳动者的工资、银行的利息、政府的税收、投资者的利润以及所有者的折旧补偿，顺着供应链反向追溯到最开始。

B. Circulation in the Real World

The economic circulation is formed with value flow, on basis of natural resources free of charge, and cash flow together. The following diagram illustrates the circulation in whole.

B. 真实世界里的流通

经济流通是由基于免费自然资源的价值流和现金流构成，如下图所示：

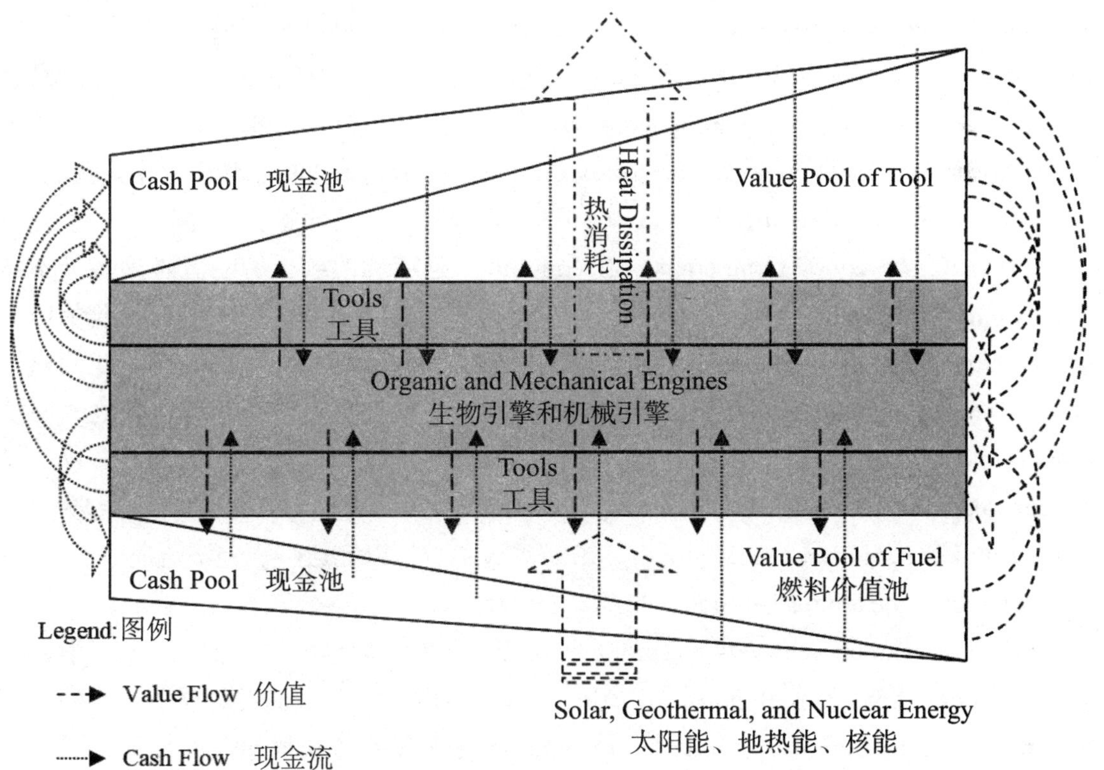

Figure 5. Economic Circulation 图 5. 经济流通

We have already spent a lot of pages to discuss the value and its transferring path. Now, we need to have a further look at the money circulation and therefore the economic circulation as a whole.

前面已经花了很多章节讨论了价值以及它的转移，现在来进一步分析现金流通以及经济流通。

When a laborer gets wage issued by his employer who is the buying representative of the Virtual Depot, by end of the month, it is to say that he has trade out his one month of labor for getting certain amount of money, meaning that there are certain portions of products in the Virtual Depot belonging to him. By paying the money, he got from the employer, to the shops, which are the selling representatives of the Virtual Depot; he can have certain amounts of different living materials being taken home. At this point, it seems to his wife, who never goes out of the house, like that he makes all those living materials himself, just like what Robinson Crusoe does in his island. Now we may say: the course of the trade is completed. As soon as the course of the trade completed, the corresponding money issued by the Virtual Depot goes back to the Virtual Depot. We say that one course of economic circulation is fulfilled. For subsistence and better-off, the laborer has to trade his labor for money and money for living goods again and again so that the economic circulations lasts forever. In a word, the Virtual Depot buys labor results from one by issuing money and sells labor results to the others by collecting the same amount of money back again.

当一个劳动者，月底从作为社会虚拟中转库购买代表的雇主那里拿到工资，表示他已付出一个月的劳动，并据其取得一定数量的货币，用来说明在虚拟中转库里有相应部分的产品是属于他的。通过向作为社会虚拟中转库销售代表的商店，支付从雇主那里得来的货币，取得他所需要的各种生活用品，并拿回家。这时，对于他那位从不出家门的妻子来说，那些生活用品好像与鲁滨孙·克鲁索在他的荒岛上一样，就是他自己生产的。至此我们可以说，一个交易完成了。一旦交易完成，由社会虚拟中转库发出的货币又回到了虚拟中转库手中。我们说，一个经济流通完成了。为了生存的延续和改善，劳动者必须每天不断地以劳动换货币，然后以此货币换取生活用品，经济流通因此而永不停息地进行着。一言以蔽之，虚拟中转库用钱从某人处购买劳动，又向另一些人出售劳动成果收回货币，以完成一次经济流通。

When an entrepreneur gets the profit from the Virtual Depot through realization of sales of his products, certain amount of money corresponding to the profit is issued by the buying representatives

一个企业家通过向虚拟中转库出售产品，而从虚拟中转库的购买代表那里获得相应的货币形式的利润，当他用这笔钱添置了一堆新工

of the Virtual Depot. When this gentleman buys a bunch of new tools with the money he got, the money goes back to the Virtual Depot again in his case. We may also say that one course of economic circulation is fulfilled.

具，这笔钱又回到了虚拟中转库中。这也是一个经济流通的完成。

A laborer or an entrepreneur may treat his money in many ways such as, paying the prices of his own purchase; lending to others through buying bonds, saving in bank. But after all, all the money issued by the Virtual Depot will go either terminal consumption by paying living tools and fuels, or the samsaraous consumption by investing producing tools and fuels.

当然，一个劳动者或者企业家可以多种方式来处置他赚取的钱，可以支付自己的购买活动，可以购买证券将钱借给别人，可以存入银行。但所有发行的货币最终不是被用于购买生活用的工具和燃料的终极消费，就是被用于购买生产用的工具和燃料的轮回消费。

In the reality, there is always a time delay, longer or sooner, between getting money from the Virtual Depot and paying the money back to the Virtual Depot. That is to say that the frequency of the circulation on different goods is different to one the other, just because of the nature of the goods and the preference of the consumers, which makes the economic circulation more or less like a running river, in which there are riptide and slow flow running simultaneously.

现实中，在从虚拟中转库处得到货币到向虚拟中转库支付货币，总是会有或长或短的时间延时，也就是说，不同物品的循环频度，会因为物品的本质和消费者喜好的不同而相互不同，这使得经济流通多多少少像一条奔腾的河流，有激流也有缓流同时流过。

XXXIV. Total Money Demand in Circulation

XXXIV. 流通中的货币总需求

Money is needed only for trade in the economic sense. When trade ends, money is not needed at all. We said in previous Chapter that "the Central Bank acts as a huge Virtual Depot of the society. It buys goods from the seller and it sells goods to the buyer with the intervention of money". The Central

从经济学意义上讲，仅在交易时需要货币，当交易完成了，货币就没用了。前面章节曾说："中央银行就如同一个巨大的社会虚拟中转库，在货币的介入下，它从卖者处购买物品并向买者出售物品。"

Bank doesn't have any depot physically. All of the warehouses and workshops of all the vendors in the society make up the Virtual Depot collectively. When the Central Bank buys goods in, it releases the money out; and when it sells goods out, it calls money back in. If it sells out all the goods in the Virtual Depot, there shall be no money at all in circulation. So, the total amount of the prices of the total inventory of the goods in the Virtual Depot, in both tangible and intangible forms, at any point of time, determines the total money in circulation at that point of time.

而中央银行却不存在实体仓储，所有供应商的仓库和车间在一起构成了一个社会虚拟中转库。当中央银行购买物品时，它付出货币；当中央银行出售物品时，它回收货币。如果虚拟中转库中的所有物品被销售空了，就应该没有货币在流通了。因此，在任何时间点上，虚拟中转库中所有无形和有形物品的总库存数量决定了这个时间点的总货币流通量。

For a society, we have the following equation as,

对一个社会而言，有如下等式：

$$\text{(15)} \qquad TMD(t) = \sum_{i=1}^{N} \left(\sum_i NLP_{rm}(t) + \sum_i NLP_{wip}(t) + \sum_i NLP_{fg}(t) \right)$$

Where: TMD (t) is the total money demanded in circulation at time of t;

N is the total number of the vendors (including farmers, miners, manufactures, traders, and private and public services, etc.) in the society at time of t;

NLP_{rm} (t) is the total natural price of raw materials (including fuel) at time of t;

NLP_{wip} (t) is the total realized natural price of Work-In-Process, consisting of the paid price of its raw materials, paid wage, paid tax and depreciation, etc., if any, at time of t;

NLP_{fg} (t) is the total natural price of finished goods.

其中：TMD (t) 是在时间点 t 所需的货币流通总量；

N 是在时间点 t 社会的供货商（包括农民、采矿者、加工业者、贸易者、私人和公共服务者等在内）的总数；

NLP_{rm} (t) 是时间点 t 的原材料（包括燃料）自然价格总和；

NLP_{wip} (t) 是时间点 t 已实现了的在制品的自然价格，意指其已支付的原材料价格、已支付的工资、已支付的税金及折旧等的总和；

NLP_{fg} (t) 是时间点 t 制成品的自然价格总和。

The equation above is actually a formularized expression that, by paying total amount of money of TMD (t), the Virtual Depot of the Society holds equivalent goods not yet sold at time of t. Or, in

以上公式实际上就是公式化了的以下表述：通过支付总量为TMD (t)的货币，虚拟中转库在时间点t保有总量与之响应的物品仍未售

the other words, there is money of TMD (t) in consumers' hands which are to be used for buying those equivalent goods in the Virtual Depot of the Society sooner or later.

出。或者换句话说，在消费者手中共有数量为TMD (t)的货币，它们早晚会被用于从社会虚拟中转库购买相应的物品。

XXXV. Fiat Money in the Circulation

XXXV. 流通中的法定货币

A. Purpose of the Fiat Money

People gave up the commodity money and had been using fiat money instead just for making the trade more efficiently in time and more sufficiently in scope. According to Mr. Fisher's equation, MV = PT, even one dollar could keep the circulation running theoretically. The only consequence is though that the circulation would be slowed down in an unacceptable creeping speed.

The commodity money was invented thousands years ago. It is usually precious metal with high value in a small volume like gold and silver. After the Industrial Revolution, people gradually realized that, due to the limited supply in total, the commodity monetary system reached its bottleneck since it cannot help making the trade efficiently meanwhile sufficiently any more. The fiat money comes onto the stage.

Ideally, we expect that all the products newly produced can reach the hands of consumers as soon as possible. The word ALL here means the sufficiency and the phrase AS SOON AS POSSIBLE here means the efficiency. Any goods detained in the warehouse are the sacrifice of

A. 法定货币的目的

人们摒弃实物货币而改用法定货币的目的就是使交易在时间上更高效同时在规模上更充分。根据费雪的等式 MV = PT，理论上利用一元钱也能保持循环流转。只不过其结果是：经济流通将以慢到不可思议的蠕动速度进行。

实物货币几千年前就被发明了，它通常是贵金属，即一小片金或银就携带了很高的价值。工业革命以后，人们逐渐意识到，由于可用总量的限制，实物货币体系碰到了自身的“瓶颈”，它无法保证交易高效又充分地进行，法定货币因此走上了舞台。

理想情况下，我们希望所有新生产出来的产品尽可能快地到达消费者之手。这里的“所有”表述是充分性；“尽可能快”表述的是高效率。尽管商品的适量储备以提高经济系统应对意外发生是必须的，

the efficiency and the sufficiency of economic circulation, even though moderate goods reserve is necessary for robustness of the economic system just in case some contingency happens. The longer the goods detained, the worse the efficiency and sufficiency are.

但任何被耽搁在仓库里的商品都是效率和充分性的牺牲，被耽搁的时间越长，效率和充分性就越差。

B. Essential Difference Between the Commodity Money and the Fiat Money

B. 实物货币与法定货币差异的实质

When implementing Gold/Silver Standard System, we are using commodity money, which means the partial (minus the wallet money such as gold jewelry) or total stock of the gold/silver in the society is used to represent the total value flow of the society. The incremental rate of gold/silver supply is limited due to the productivity of the gold/silver production. The society will be in shortage of money supply if the wealth increment is larger than the increment of gold/silver supply, if we keep the value of gold/silver to stay the same. The economic circulation will be therefore slowed down.

在金本位 / 银本位的体系里，我们使用实物货币，这意味着用全社会的金 / 银的部分（减去诸如首饰之类的压箱钱）或全部存量代表全社会的价值流量。金银供应的增速因金银的生产力约束是有限的，如果社会财富的增加速度大于金银供应的增加速度，而如果我们又想保持金银的价值不变，那么社会就可能出现货币短缺的现象，经济流通的速度就要因此下降。

By employing Fiat Money System, the Central Government is able to pour as much money as it likes into the economy. There is no limitation at all in terms of money supply since the fiat money is just printed paper, the productivity of making which is almost unlimited. When fiat money is over issued however, another new phenomenon, which is currency inflation, occurs.

利用法定货币，中央银行可以向经济体里注入任意多的货币，法定货币只是一种印刷品，印制货币的生产力几乎是无限的，因而货币的供应能力也是无限的。当法定货币发行过量时，另一种新现象，即通货膨胀就会发生。

C. How the Fiat Money Regulates the Efficiency and Sufficiency

C. 法定货币如何调节效率和充分性

We described in Chapter XXX that, some

在第三十章中提到，当某些商

goods will be detained in the Virtual Depot when the prices of some other goods increase. That is to say, the speeds of circulations of those detained goods are slowed down. For keeping the efficiency and the sufficiency of the circulations constantly, the central government may increase the money supply to help easing up the situation by following the equation (15).

品价格上涨时，就会有一些商品因此被搁置在虚拟中转库中，也就是说，这些搁置在虚拟中转库中的商品流通速度降低了。为保持流通的效率和充分性不变，中央政府可能会依照公式（15）用增加货币供应的方式来缓和局面。

The total amount of money needed in a society is dynamic; it is a function of time. It is not a practical way for the Central Bank to regulate the scale of currency in real time tough, since the total money in circulation cannot be monitored second by second to trace up the dynamic of the total price in the Virtual Depot of the society. The Central Bank might take the average over month, season, half year, or one year or two as the span of regulation if the economy structure is not changed significantly in such period. Then the averaged total money in circulation ~~MIC~~(T_{I+1}) can be expressed as the following,

社会的货币总需求是动态的，是一个时间的函数。中央银行用实时跟踪的方式来调节货币规模却是不现实的，因为现实中不太可能对社会虚拟中转库中价格的动态，对货币流通的过程进行分分秒秒的跟踪。如果在一段时间内变化不大的前提下，中央银行也许可以根据情况，以一月、一季、半年、一年乃至两年跨度的平均数进行调节。平均货币流通总需求 MIC(T_{I+1}) 可以由下列公式计算：

(16) ~~MIC~~ $(T_{I+1})=\int_{TI}^{TI+1}\left(\sum_{i=1}^{N}\left(\sum_i NLP_{rm}(t)+\sum_i NLP_{wip}(t)+\sum_i NLP_{fg}(t)\right)\right)dt\,/\,T$

Where: ~~MIC~~(T_{I+1}) is the average money in total needed for circulation in the next time span of T_{I+1}.

T is the regulating time span.

其中：~~MIC~~(T_{I+1}) 是下一个时间段所需的平均货币总量；

T 是调节时间跨度。

Or, it may be expressed in a discrete form as the following,

或者，也可以用离散方程式表述为：

(17) ~~MIC~~ $(T_{I+1})=\sum_{j=1}^{Q}\left(\sum_{i=1}^{N}\left(\sum_i NLP_{rm}(T_I+j*v)+\sum_i NLP_{wip}(T_I+j*v)+\sum_i NLP_{fg}(T_I+j*v)\right)\right)/Q$

Where: Q is the total number of sampling intervals in the time span of T;

v represents the sampling interval, which is

其中：Q 是在时间跨度 T 中的样本总数；

v 代表采样分度，等于 T/Q。

equal to T/Q .

Or, it may be expressed in even more sophisticated formula per the theory of cybernetics by following the circle of "trends projection — algorithm determination — implementation — verification".

或者，也可以遵循控制理论采用更复杂的公式，根据"趋势预测—算法确定—实施—验证"的步骤来进行调节。

D. Anchor Chain Coefficient of the Currency and Currency Inflation

D. 货币锚链系数和通货膨胀

If the goods in the Virtual Depot of the society is traded per a constant efficiency and sufficiency, the total value-in-joule of the goods in the Virtual Depot is constant as well at every point of time.

如果虚拟中转库中的货物是以一个恒定的效率和充分性进行交易，那么存储在虚拟中转库中商品的焦耳总价值在各个时间点上都是恒定的。

When people trade goods based on their natural price, in other words, on value-in-exchange, we have the following,

当人们按商品的自然价格，也就是交换价值交易时，我们有：

$$(18)\quad \tau_0 = \Sigma_{i=1}^{P} NLP_i \,/\, (\Sigma_{j=1}^{M} VIH_j + \Sigma_{k=1}^{N} VOT_k)$$

We may call the τ_0 the initial Anchor Chain Coefficient of the currency.

我们将 τ_0 称为货币的初始锚链系数。

In the reality, people trade goods according to their market price. If the aggregation of market prices deviates from the aggregation of natural prices, and then we have,

现实中，人们以市场价格进行交易。如果市场价格的总和偏离了自然价格，我们有：

$$(19)\quad \tau_1 = \Sigma_{i=1}^{P} MTP_i \,/\, (\Sigma_{j=1}^{M} VIH_j + \Sigma_{k=1}^{N} VOT_k)$$

$$= \Sigma_{i=1}^{P} (NLP_i + \Delta P_i) \,/\, (\Sigma_{j=1}^{M} VIH_j + \Sigma_{k=1}^{N} VOT_k)$$

$$= (\Sigma_{i=1}^{P} NLP_i + \Sigma_{i=1}^{P} \Delta P_i) \,/\, (\Sigma_{j=1}^{M} VIH_j + \Sigma_{k=1}^{N} VOT_k)$$

$$= \Sigma_{i=1}^{P} NLP_i \,/\, (\Sigma_{j=1}^{M} VIH_j + \Sigma_{k=1}^{N} VOT_k) + \Sigma_{i=1}^{P} \Delta P_i / (\Sigma_{j=1}^{M} VIH_j + \Sigma_{k=1}^{N} VOT_k)$$

Let $\Delta\tau_1 = \sum_{i=1}^{P} \Delta P_i (\sum_{j=1}^{M} VIH_j + \sum_{k=1}^{N} VOT_k)$ then we have,

令 $\Delta\tau_1 = \sum_{i=1}^{P} \Delta P_i (\sum_{j=1}^{M} VIH_j + \sum_{k=1}^{N} VOT_k)$，则：

$$(20)\quad \tau_1 = \tau_0 + \Delta\tau_1$$

When the total market prices change

当市场价格总和从 $\sum_{i=1}^{P} MTP_i$

from $\sum_{i=1}^{P} MTP_i$ to $\sum_{i=1}^{P}(MTP_i + \Delta MTP_i)$, and let $\Delta\tau_2=\sum_{i=1}^{P}\Delta MTP_i/(\sum_{j=1}^{M}VIH_j+\sum_{k=1}^{N}VOT_k)$, then we have,

变成$\sum_{i=1}^{P}(MTP_i + \Delta MTP_i)$，令$\Delta\tau_2=\sum_{i=1}^{P}\Delta MTP_i/(\sum_{j=1}^{M}VIH_j+\sum_{k=1}^{N}VOT_k)$，则，

$$(21) \quad \tau_2 = \tau_0 + \Delta\tau_1 + \Delta\tau_2$$

We may say that the anchor chain coefficient of the currency is prolonged from τ_1 to τ_2 by increment of $\Delta\tau_2$.

我们说：货币锚链系数以$\Delta\tau_2$的增幅从τ_1增加到τ_2。

Now, we can naturally obtain the formula of the rate of inflation (ROI) as the following,

我们可以自然地得出通货膨胀率（ROI）的计算公式如下：

$$(21) \quad ROI = \Delta\tau_2 / (\tau_0 + \Delta\tau_1)$$

We may conclude as following, if we would like to keep the same efficiency and sufficiency of the circulation, the price increase will cause the total money demand increase, and currency inflation occurs therefore; or, if we would like to keep the value of money constant, the price increase will cause the slow-down of the efficiency and sufficiency of circulation; just because the total value in the Virtual Depot is not changed.

我们可以得出如下结论：因为虚拟中转库中的总价值不变，如果我们希望保持流通的效率和充分性不变，价格上涨会导致货币总需求增加，通货膨胀因此发生；或者，我们希望保持货币的价值不变，价格上涨会导致流通的效率和充分性下降。

XXXVI. Fractal Structure in the Economy

XXXVI. 经济中的分型结构

According to the Fractal Theory, when the structure pattern of the partial is analogous to the structure pattern of the whole, we call such structure fractal structure.

根据数学的分型理论，当局部的结构类似于总体的结构时，此结构被称为分型结构。

From the view point of "In Flow and In Stock", the structure of the economy is fractal structure. Economics is a doctrine about wealth. We call the process of wealth creation production, of wealth worn out consumption; we call the status of wealth kept asset. From the value view, production and

从流量存量的观点看，经济的结构是一种分型结构。经济学是关于财富的学说，创造财富的过程叫生产，财富的耗损叫消费；财富处于保持状态称之为资产。从价值观看，生产和消费是流量价值；资产

consumption is value in flow essentially; and asset is value in stock.

Down to the tier of production, value of labor is bit by bit added to the subject of labor. The value of labor is the value in flow; and subject of labor is the value in stock. As to consumption, all of the producing tools and living tools are value in stock; and the utilization of tools is value in flow.

Assets staying on the same owner's hand are the assets in stock; and assets transferring from one owner to another are the assets in flow. Stock market is the place for exchanging the ownership of the equity. The turnover rate of stock exchange cannot be 100% everyday, so the shares in trade are the equity in flow; and the shares are held on the hands of brokers are equity in stock.

To a family, the money incoming and spending are money in flow; and money kept in pocket, saved in bank or invested in the stock market are money in stock.

Interestingly, the whole economic system is the sub system of the ecosystem, and the ecosystem has the similar structure as economic system as well. Sunshine from the sun is the energy in flow; it is absorbed, converted, transferred, and saved in bodies of plants and animals on the earth, and even in the depth of the earth, which are energy in stock; when these energy carriers are on fire or decayed, energy is released out to the space again, which is energy in flow. Going furthermore, the sun and the earth are the big matter/energy in stock.

For understanding, we may use the following diagram to illustrate the fractal structure of inlet–

是存量价值。

下到生产这个层次，劳动的价值是一点一点增加到劳动对象中的，劳动价值是流量价值，劳动对象是存量价值。对消费，所有的生产生活工具是存量价值；工具的使用是流量价值。

资产留在同一位业主手里的是存量资产；资产从一个业主手里转到另一个业主手里的是流量资产。股市是交换股权的地方，股票的换手率不可能是每天100%，因此，交易的股票是流量股权；留在经纪人手中的股票是存量股权。

对一个家庭，货币的收入和支出是流量货币；放在口袋里的，存在银行的或投资股市的货币是存量货币。

有趣的是，整个经济系统是生态系统的一部分，而生态系统也与经济系统一样有着相同的结构。从太阳来的阳光是流量能量；然后它被吸收、转化、转移并储存在地球上的植物和动物的体内。甚至地球的深处，也有存量能量；当这些能量载体被燃烧或者被腐蚀时，能量又被释放到空中，从而变成了流量能量。更进一步说，太阳和地球是大的存量物质 / 能量。

我们可以用下面的一张图来诠释“流入—储存—流出”的分型结构：

reservoir–outlet.

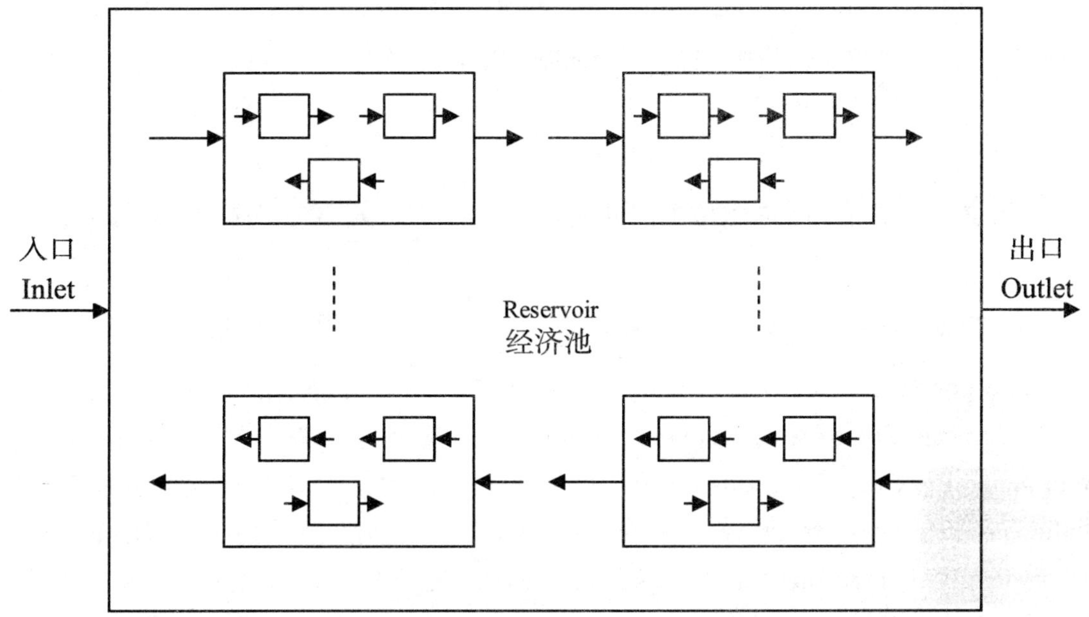

Figure 6. Fractal Structure in the Economy 图 6. 经济分型结构

The fractal structure is a hierarchical structure. We have to realize the fact that there are flows of low layer in stock of higher layer; and there are stocks of low layer in flow of higher layer.

分型结构是有层次的，我们必须认识到以下的事实：上层存量中有低层流量的存在；上层流量中有低层存量的存在。

For example, the money in father's pocket is money in stock; the money transferred from father's pocket to mother's one is money in flow; and money finally in mother's pocket is money in stock again; from the stand point of the family, the money is always in stock though. The wallet given by papa to mama is the money in flow; but the money in wallet is money in stock always from the stand point of view of wallet.

比如，父亲口袋里的钱是钱的存量，钱从父亲口袋转到母亲口袋是钱的流量，落在母亲口袋里的钱又成了钱的存量。可从家庭的角度来看，这笔钱一直是钱的存量而已。爸爸将钱包给妈妈属于钱的流量，但对于钱包来说，里面的钱却一直是钱的存量而已。

For easy understanding, we may just imagine that there is a running river in a high speed. The water flushes down from the high to the low, which is the general trend. But along with the stream,

为理解方便，我们设想有一条高速奔腾的河流，总的运动趋势是水从高处冲向低处。但在水流中存在着许多大漩涡在其中旋转，而在

there are many big whirlpools spinning around. And along with the paths of big spinning whirlpools, there are again many smaller whirlpools spinning around. And so on and so forth.

这些旋转的大漩涡里，又存在着许多旋转的小漩涡，小漩涡里又有更小的漩涡，以此类推。

XXXVII. Exchange in Stock

XXXVII. 存量交换

A. The Cause of Goods in Stock

The goods in stock happen only when the production capacity is greater than the consumption rate generally. Once the goods are finished, their value-in-exchanges are given, and the prices of labors involved in creating such things have already been paid literally. Antiques are extreme examples, the production capacity of which approaches zero (few more antiques may be discovered) and the consumption rate approaches zero as well but the consumption rate is less than the production capacity (otherwise, no antique will be seen in the present); and some of their VIEs were given thousands years ago, and their making laborers died also thousands years ago.

A robust economy needs certain amounts of redundant goods in stock for coping with any contingency. For example, we need keep certain amount of food in stock just in case flood and drought. We need some more dishes in house just in case some of relatives or friends visit the family. A factory needs some products in stock for responding to the fluctuation of the market needs. To a speculator, he keeps goods in stock just for gambling that the price of the goods in future might

A. 货物存量的成因

总的来说，当生产能力大于消费量时，就会产生存量货物。一旦货物完工，它的交换价值就确定了，而且制造这个物品的劳动的价格业已支付。古董是一个极端的例子，古董的出产率几近为零（只有极少数的古董被发掘），而古董的消费速率也几近为零但却小于古董的产出率（否则，当今就没有古董存在了）。一些古董的交换价值在几千年前就确定了，而工匠们的劳动也在千年之前就支付完毕了。

一个健壮的经济需要有一定的货物存量来应对不测的发生。比如，我们需要一定数量的食物存量，以防洪灾和干旱的发生；在家里，我们需要准备更多一些的碗碟用来招待来访的亲戚朋友；一个工厂也需要一定数量的产品存量来应付市场需求的波动。对于一个投机者而言，他保有一部分货物存量是博弈未来的价格会比买入价更高。

go higher than what he bought in.

Generally speaking, the whole wealth of the society is the biggest goods stock of human.

The initial keeper of the goods in stock may not be the final seller of the stock. Through trade, the ownership of the stock is transferred from the one to the other. Besides the possible repacking and transportation, which belong to value-adding, the goods before the stock exchange and goods after are the same goods without any physical change.

总的来说，整个社会的财富就是人类最大的货物存量。

存量货物的最初拥有者，不一定就是最后的出售者，通过交易，存量的物权可以从一人转到另一人手中。除了可能的在包装和搬运属于增值过程外，交易前的货物和交易后的货物的物理属性没有一点被改变。

B. Exchange of Stock

Theoretically, exchange of goods in stock is merely ownership transfer but no value adding from one trade to the next. Security market and futures market are the typical stock exchange market. People don't even need to move whole plant/facility/product actually into the market for exchange; and there are no physical goods seen at all in the futures market when deal is done, although the real subject of trade will be finally transported to the hands of the final users, which falls into the category exchange in flow as the last step of the chain of futures trade.

Now, we know that the goods exchange can be divided into two categories. For distinction, we use term of "Exchange in Flow" to describe the situation that we sale products with certain utility for money and spend the money for buying another products with different utility for further consumption (either samsaraous or terminal), where energy is involved, which is in the "Commodity – Money – Commodity'" (C-M-C') circuit according to Marx's

B. 存量的交换

理论上说，存量货物的交换仅仅是所有权的交换，在两个交易之间却没有价值的增加。证券市场和期货市场是典型的存量交易市场，人们并不需要将整个工厂 / 设施 / 产品搬来现场进行交换，而在期货市场，交易结束后也根本看不见货物，尽管在最后标的物会被运送到最终用户的手中，但那已经是属于期货交易环节的最后一环的流量交换的范畴了。

至此，我们认识到货物交换可以分为两种，为了区分起见，我们用术语“流量交换”来描述如下情景：我们卖掉具备某种效用的产品换回货币，是为了用货币买入其他具有不同效用的产品进行下一步的（轮回或终极）消费，其间有能量的参与，该过程属于马克思交换模型中的“商品—货币—商品”

model; and term of "Exchange in Stock" to describe the situation that we buy goods and sale the same goods in different point of time just for making profit, where no energy is involved literally, which is in the "Money - Commodity - Money" (M-C-M) circuit. Therefore, the exchange in flow is in a process of value adding and stock exchange is just in a process of money appreciation or depreciation but the value of the goods is unchanged.

（C–M–C）循环；用"存量交换"来描述如下情景：我们在不同的时间点买入和卖出同样的物品以谋取利润，其间没有能量的参与，这属于马克思交换模型中的"货币—商品—货币"（M–C–M）循环。因此，流量交换发生在价值增值过程中；而存量交换仅仅是货币自身的增值或贬值过程，而物品的价值并未改变。

In Chapter XXIX, we have discussed the pricing mechanism of exchange in flow. That covers only goods in flow in general though. Once goods put in stock, there will be three different prices associated with them, namely, coming-in price, nominal price and going-out price, even though the value of the goods is not changed at all. The equity stock market is a perfect example for understanding.

在第二十九章中，我们已经讨论了流量交换的定价机制，但它仅仅涵盖了流量货物。一旦货物成了存量，就会有三种价格与之相对应，它们是：进库价格、名义价格和出库价格，尽管该货物的价值一点都没有变化。股票交易市场是一个用于理解的绝好的例子。

When buying in shares, we have to pay certain amount of money for exchange. If shares were purchased in different time and in different unit price, the weighted average unit price of them is therefore their coming-in or cost unit price. The last price in exchange on the market is the reference for upcoming deal, which is the nominal price of all shares on hand. We watch the price on the market and calculation the money value of the share held on our hand. We may sell the shares on hand at some points of time in different prices as we determined. The weighted average unit price we finally got is the going-out price or sales price of the share.

购入股票时，我们支付一定数量的货币作为交换。如果股票分别是在不同时间以不同单价购入的，那么加权平均后单价就是这些股票的入库价或成本价；交易市场上最后一次交易的价格是下一次交易的参考，也就是手中所有股票的名义价格。我们关注着市场的价格并计算手中股票的总货币价值，我们可能会在某些个时间点以不同的我们确定的价格出售股票，加权平均后的单价就是股票的出库价。

Looking at a specific share in whole, there is only a little portion of the whole shares in exchange

再来全面观察一只特定的股票，其实只有占总量的一小部分的

on the market, which are shares in flow. Literally speaking, the last trade of the share determines the nominal price of whole of such a share. People buys share based on the assumption that the price of the share will goes up again; and people sells share based on the assumption that the price of the share will going down further.

股票在市场上流转，我们称之为流量股票，严格说，最后一次的股票交易确定了所有这只股票的名义价格。在股价还会上涨的假设下，人们买入股票；在股价会进一步下跌的假设下，人们抛售股票。

In circumstance that the exchange volume is kept in the same scale, more money is needed, when the price of the share goes up further; less money is needed, when the price of the share goes down further. In other words, the share price goes up when money flows in; goes down when money flows out generally.

在交换的股票总量不变的条件下，如果股票价格进一步上涨，需要更多的货币支持交易；如果股票价格进一步下降，则需要较少的货币支持交易。换句话说，一般情况下，当货币净流入时，股票价格上涨；当货币净流出时，股票价格下跌。

C. Close Market VS Open Market

C. 封闭市场 VS 开放市场

In the reality, there is neither absolute close market (of exchange in stock) nor infinitely open market (of exchange in stock). For easy analysis, we start the analysis with looking at a close market model. Close market means, no quantity change of the subject for exchange and no amount change of money for supporting exchange in the market. We treat the open market with same flow-in and flow-out of either trade subject or money for trade also as the close market.

在现实中不存在绝对的封闭（存量交易）市场也没有无限开放的（存量交易）市场。为了方便分析，我们从一个封闭市场模型开始。封闭市场是指：市场中交易标的的数量不变，用于交易的货币数量不变。我们将交易标的的流入流出量或交易资金的流入流出量相等的开放市场也视同为封闭市场。

Assuming that there are (S) shares in total and ($M) money in total in this specific stock market for exchange. Man might sell his shares at price of $M per share; but only one share can be exchanged since there is only money of $M to support the exchange in the market. Man might sell his shares at price of $M/2 per share; only two shares then can

假设有一只股票共 S 股，共有货币量 M 被用于此股的交易。人们可以将价格定为一股 $M 元，但仅有 1 股可以被交易，因为市场中只有 $M 的货币用于交易。人们也可以一股 $M/2 的价格出售股票，但由于相同的原因，仅有 2 股可以被

be exchanged for the same reason. Or, man might sell his first share at \$M/2; second share at \$M/4; third share at \$M/8; forth share at \$M/16; So on and so forth to exchange all of the shares. However, the no matter how high the nominal price could be, if all of the shares are to be exchanged, the exchange price has to be \$M/S averagely.

交易。或者人们也可以第 1 股 \$M/2 的价格；第 2 股 \$M/4 的价格；第 3 股 \$M/8 的价格；第 4 股 \$M/16 的价格；以此类推来出售所有股票。可是，无论名义价格会有多高，如果我们希望所有的股票得到交换，交易价格平均数必须是 \$M/S。

Situation will be different if more and more money (vice versa) comes from the outside of the market. Suppose there is only one person Mr. A in the market selling his shares of 1,000. Mr. B buys them from Mr. A at price of \$1,000; and Mr. C then buys it from Mr. B at price of \$2,000; and so on and so forth until Mr. E at price of \$8,000. The average price of a share is \$8 instead of \$1 at the beginning, since additional money is poured into the market, which is called open market in this case.

情况将会因为越来越多的货币从外部进入市场而变得不一样（反之亦然）。假定只有A先生出售1000股股票，B先生以\$1000的价格从A先生处购得；而C先生又从B先生处以\$2000购得；如此这般直至E先生以\$8000购得。至此，一股的平均价从开始的1元涨到了8元，这是因为有额外的资金被注入了市场，此时的市场是开放市场。

XXXⅧ. In Stock vs. In Flow

XXXⅧ. 存量与流量

A. The Reserve of goods

Economic circulation is just like a water reservoir system, in which there are three parts, namely, inlet, reservoir and outlet. The reservoir system is utilized for preventing or at least prolonging the happening of the over flower or cutoff of the water supply, caused by the fluctuations of either inlet and/or outlet.

A. 商品储备

经济流通就像水库系统一样，由三个部分组成，分别为：入口、库体和出口。水库系统是用来预防或者至少延缓由入口或出口的流量波动引起的溢流或断流的发生的。

There are all kinds of strategic reserves always available on a national level. There are safety stocks held by all different kinds of vendors here and there in a society just in case. There are more

在国家层面，常年备有各种各样的战略储备。形形色色商品的供应商们也在各处备有安全库存以应对万一。各个家庭也或多或少地备

or less reserves in every family to cope with any contingency.

有储备应对不测。

Normally the flow of outlet has to be the same as the flow of inlet, so the level of reservoir keeps at the same position. When the input from the inlet becomes greater than the output of the outlet, the reservoir takes over the extra portion of the water for keeping the output constant, and the level of the reservoir goes up. In case the upper limit is reached, flood overflow happens. If the input from the inlet becomes less than the output of the outlet, the reservoir will give up some amount of water for keeping the output constant, and the level of the reservoir goes down. In case the bottom of the reservoir is seen, the water supply cutoff happens.

通常，水库的进出流量是相等的，水库的水位能够保持在相同位置。当入口的流量变得大于出口时，水库吸纳多余的流量以保证出口流量的恒定；水库水位上升。如果上限被突破，则会发生洪水溢流。当入口流量小于出口流量，水库释放储存的水以保证出口恒定；水库水位下降。如果水库见底，就会发生断流。

When the output of the outlet becomes less than the input from the inlet, the reservoir takes over the extra portion of the water since the input is constant, and the level of the reservoir goes up. In case the upper limit is reached, flood overflow happens. If the output of the outlet becomes greater than the input from the inlet, the reservoir will give up some amount of water since the input is constant, and the level of the reservoir goes down. In case the bottom of the reservoir is seen, the water supply cutoff happens.

当出口的流量变得小于入口时，水库吸纳多余的流量以应对入口流量的恒定；水库水位上升。如果上限被突破，则会发生洪水溢流。当出口流量大于入口流量，水库释放储存的水以应对入口恒定；水库水位下降。如果水库见底，就会发生断流。

As we call the water in the reservoir the water in stock, and water in the pipelines of inlet and outlet the water in flow; we call the goods in reserve the goods in stock, and goods in trading the goods in flow. The total goods in both stock and flow are goods in circulation.

正如我们称水库中的水为存量水，称入口管道和出口管道里的水为流量水；我们称处于储备状态的商品为存量商品，称交易中的商品为流量商品。存量商品和流量商品之和构成了流通商品。

There is a target level of water set somewhere

根据洪水和干旱的概率和体

around the middle capacity of the reservoir based on the probabilities and the volumes of flood and drought, hoping that the water level fluctuates around this target level. We may call it target of stock. Averagely speaking, the target of stock stays in the reservoir always, which seems not to take part in the water circulation. Similarly, goods in reserve also have their targets of stock, which do not take part in the commercial circulation averagely, although old goods are replaced by new ones just for keeping the goods in reserve always fresh by following first in first out.

量，在库容中间点附近的位置设置有一个目标水位，以期水位在此目标位上下波动。我们称之为目标存量。平均来说，目标存量始终存在于水库中，似乎并不参与流转。同样地，商品储备也有它们的目标存量，似乎也不参与商业流通，尽管为了保鲜，遵循先进先出的原则，老商品一直在被新商品替换。

B. Money in Stock

As we call the water in the reservoir the water in stock, and water in the pipelines of inlet and outlet the water in flow; we can also call the money in reserve the money in stock, and money in trading the money in flow. The total money in both stock and flow are money in circulation.

Assuming that all the money is managed through bank except that individual person and individual firm keep some limited amount of money just for their immediate convenience, which we call wallet money. Everyone has his own bottom line of money as his wallet money. As the wallet money is used out, it will be immediately complemented from the bank account. The wallet money is a kind of money in stock in the economic circulation.

Banks have the obligation to follow the deposit reserve rate defined by the Central Bank, which causes certain amount of money stay in the bank safe untouched; which is also a kind of money in

B. 存量货币

正如我们称水库中的水为存量水，称入口管道和出口管道里的水为流量水；我们称处于储备状态的货币为存量货币，称交易中的货币为流量货币。存量货币和流量货币之和构成了流通货币。

假定所有个人和单位的钱，除了为了方便起见手中保有的有限的钱（我们称之为押包钱）之外，都是由银行来管理的。每个单位每个人都有他们自己的押包钱底线，当押包钱被使用时，不足部分会被立即从其银行账户里取出的钱补上，因此，押包钱是经济流通中的一种存量货币。

银行有义务遵守中央银行的存款准备金的规定，这个规定使得一部分钱会待在银行的金库里不动，这笔钱也是经济流通中的一种存量

stock in the economic circulation.

货币。

Besides the deposit reserve rate, there is another rate called loan-to-deposit ratio determined by bank causing additional money in stock in the economic circulation.

除了存款准备金率外，银行还有一种叫贷存比的规定，从而导致另外一部分钱成为经济流通中的存量货币。

All the wallet money rate, the deposit reserve rate, and the loan-to-deposit ratio are sort of damping coefficients for the economic circulation. The smaller the wallet money rate or the deposit reserve rate is; or the bigger the loan-to-deposit ratio is; the faster the economic circulation moves, since it affects the total effective money in flow in the circulation up and down responding to the decrease or increase of them.

诸如押包钱比率、存款准备金率、贷存比等都是相当于经济流通的阻尼系数。押包钱比率或存款准备金率越小，或者贷存比越大，经济流通就越快，因为它的降低或提高，影响到经济流通中总的有效流量货币的总量的上升和下降。

In other words, there is always some money not really active in economic circulation, which is the money in stock just like goods in stock mentioned above.

换句话说，在经济流通中，总有一部分货币不是真正流动的，就像前面提到的存量货物一样，它们是存量货币。

C. Goods in Circulation VS Money in Circulation

C. 货物流通 VS 货币流通

On the goods side, we have goods in stock (goods in reserve) and goods in flow (goods in trade); on the money side, we have money in stock (money in reserve) and money in flow. Economic circulation now is divided into two sections, one of which is the section of flow and the other is the section of stock. Goods in flow and money in flow form the section of flow in the economic circulation; and goods in stock and money in stock form the section of stock in the economic circulation correspondingly.

在货物一边，我们有存量货物（储备货物）和流量商品（交易货物）；而在货币一边，我们有存量货币（储备货币）和流量货币。经济流通现在被分成了两部分：一部分是流量区，另一部分是存量区。流量货物与流量货币构成经济流通的流量区；存量货物与存量货币相应地构成经济流通的存量区。

Every section has its own anchor chain

每个区都有各自的锚链系数，

coefficient, namely, the anchor chain coefficient of flow τ_f, anchor chain coefficient of stock τ_s. The total money in flow and the total goods in flow determine the anchor chain coefficient of flow τ_f; the total money in stock and the total goods in stock determine the anchor chain coefficient of stock τ_s. Perfectly, the anchor chain coefficient of flow τf and anchor chain coefficient of stock τ_s are all equal to the overall anchor chain coefficient of circulation τ_c. A situation that money in flow matches goods in flow meanwhile money in stock matches goods in stock is reached therefore, which means that the rate of inflation (ROI) in section of flow is the same as the one in the section of stock in the circulation. If more money is transferred from the section of stock to the section of flow, the anchor chain coefficient of flow τf is therefore greater than anchor chain coefficient of stock τ_s. It will cause the average price level of goods in section of flow going up generally. And therefore, the nominal prices of goods in stock go up accordingly. Vice versa.

分别叫：流量锚链系数 τ_f 和存量锚链系数 τ_s。流量货币总量和流量货物总量决定流量锚链系数 τ_f；存量货币总量和存量货物总量决定存量锚链系数 τ_s。理想状态是：流量锚链系数 τ_f 和存量锚链系数 τ_s 都等于整个流通的锚链系数 τ_c。由此形成了一个流量货币匹配于流量货物同时存量货币匹配存量货物的局面，也就是说：流量区的通胀系数(ROI)与存量区的通胀系数相同。如果更多的货币从存量区流入流量区，则流量区的锚链系数 τ_f 就会大于存量区的锚链系数 τ_s，其结果就是流量区的货物的平均价格水平总体上升，因而反过来导致存量物品的名义价格也上升；反之亦然。

This tells us a fact that currency inflation or deflation could happen partially even though the overall anchor chain coefficient of the circulation is kept unchanged, if we didn't keep the money in flow matching the goods in flow.

这告诉我们一个事实：尽管总体经济流通的锚链系数并没有变化，但由于流量货币与流量货物不匹配，局部通胀或者通缩依然可能发生。

When the ratio of total value of goods in stock against total value of goods in circulation equals to the ratio of total money in stock against total money in circulation, we say money in stock matches goods in stock and money in flow matches goods in flow simultaneously. The anchor chain coefficient in flow τ_f and anchor chain coefficient in stock τ_s are

当存量货物总价值在流通货物总价值的占比等于存量货币总额在流通货币总额的占比，我们说：存量货币与存量商品匹配，与此同时，流量货币与流量货物也匹配，此时，流量锚链系数 τ_f 等于存量锚链系数 τ_s 等于总流通锚链系数 τ_c.

all equal to the overall anchor chain coefficient in circulation τ_c.

How could it happen? As we have already known that the labor involved in all goods manufacturing, no matter they are in stock or in flow as the time being, has been paid already upon finish of the production in either cash or credit. The pay-off of labor will be used mostly for purchasing any goods wanted by the laborers/shareholders/governments in the market becoming money in flow.

这怎么可能发生？我们现在已经知道，不管当时是存量商品还是流量商品生产中所用的劳动，在商品完成后都已经按现金或欠账的方式支付完毕。劳动所得的货币大部分会被劳动者/股东/政府在市场上用来购买他们需要的东西而成为流量货币。

If the total goods in stock are still going up, the social labor income increase, and it means that the net money flow is flooding towards the trade in flow; and the prices of the goods in flow increase and therefore the nominal prices of the goods in stock go up surely. Economy looks prosperous during such period of time.

如果存量货物总量一直在增加，社会劳动所得增加，这就意味着有货币净流量涌入流量交易中，流量货物的价格就会因此上涨，而同时存量货物的名义价格也一定是上涨的。在这个时期，经济看上去是繁荣的。

If the total goods in stock are going down for some reason but money in stock unchanged, the social labor income decrease, it means that money in flow decrease, the decrease of the goods in stock may cause the increase of the goods in flow. Less amount of money in flow need to be shared by the part of possible increase of the goods in flow. The prices of the goods in flow in total will go down and therefore the nominal prices of the goods in stock go down for sure. And the economy is depressed during this period of time though.

如果存量货物总量因某种原因而下降，但流量货币不变，社会劳动所得减少，则意味着流量货币减少。存量货物的减少导致流量货物的增加，而较少数额的流量货币还要被可能的流量货物的增量分摊，总的流量货物的价格将会下降，存量货物的名义价格也一定会跟着下降，此时经济进入萧条期。

X X XIX. Economic Cycle

A. Curve of the Aggregated Demand on a Product

To any newly invented product, no matter it is a living tool or a producing tool, the response of the consumers of the market can be illustrated as the following.

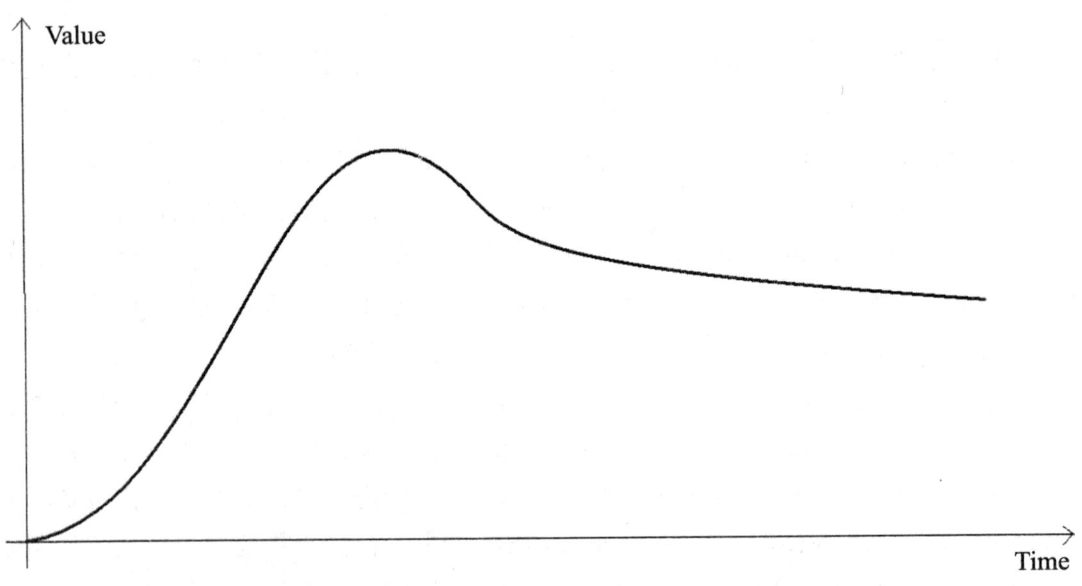

Figure 7. Demand Curve

Most people's feeling that everything seems OK already for life or for production, only a few curious people are interested in using new tool at the very beginning. We call this period of time convincing phase. Realizing the utility of the new product through demonstration, more and more people are interested in and afford to buy it. Gradually, the demand on such a product reaches the peak. We call this period of time uprising phase. Due to the utilization cycle of the product, people

X X XIX. 经济周期

A. 产品的总需求曲线

对一个新发明的产品，无论其是生活工具还是生产工具，市场上消费者的反应可用以下曲线表示：

图 7. 需求曲线

在新工具发明的开始阶段，大多数人以为一切皆足够好了，只有一小部分的人对使用新工具有兴趣，我们称这个阶段为征信期。通过示范，越来越多的人开始对新工具感兴趣也有能力购买它，渐渐地，对这种产品的需求达到了顶峰，我们称此阶段为上升期。由于产品都有一个使用周期，只要手中的工具仍可使用，人们将不会购买新的此

will not buy any more of it when tools on hand are in good condition. The total demand on such product will going down drastically. We call this period of time saturation phase. New families/firms with new needs come up along with the time going on. Plus the replacement requirements from the old users, the demand will be kept in a relative lower level. We call this period time stabilization phase.

工具。市场对此工具的需求显著地下降，我们称此阶段为饱和期。随着时间的推移，出现了新家庭 / 新机构中的新用户，加之一些老用户的替换需求，整个需求会稳定在一个相对较低的水平，我们称此阶段为稳定期。

B. Production Capacity Curve of a Product

B. 产品生产能力曲线

At the very beginning, some smart and brave people build up a few facilities for producing newly invented product just based on such a belief that it is useful to the human being. More and more entrepreneurs invest in building up more and more production capacities to meet the requirement from the market, once market proves that it is true though the uprising of the demand in the market. In the demand uprising phase, there usually is certain period of time when the supply is less than the demand.

最初，基于新发明的产品会对人类有用的信念，某些机敏和勇敢的人开始建立起一些设施用来生产新产品，一旦市场需求在上升期得到证明，越来越多的企业家就会投入资金建造出越来越多的生产能力来满足市场的需求，在需求上升期，通常会有供不应求的情况出现。

Unfortunately, a manufacturing facility setting up is a process with very big inertia in terms of engineering, that is to say, it takes resources and time to build it up; but as long as the production capacity is there, it will be there available for quite a long time, no matter it is utilized or not.

不幸的是，生产实施的建立从工程的角度来看是一个大惯性过程，也就是说：需要资源和时间来建造它，一旦生产能力形成，不管你利用与否，它就会在相当长的一段时间里存在。

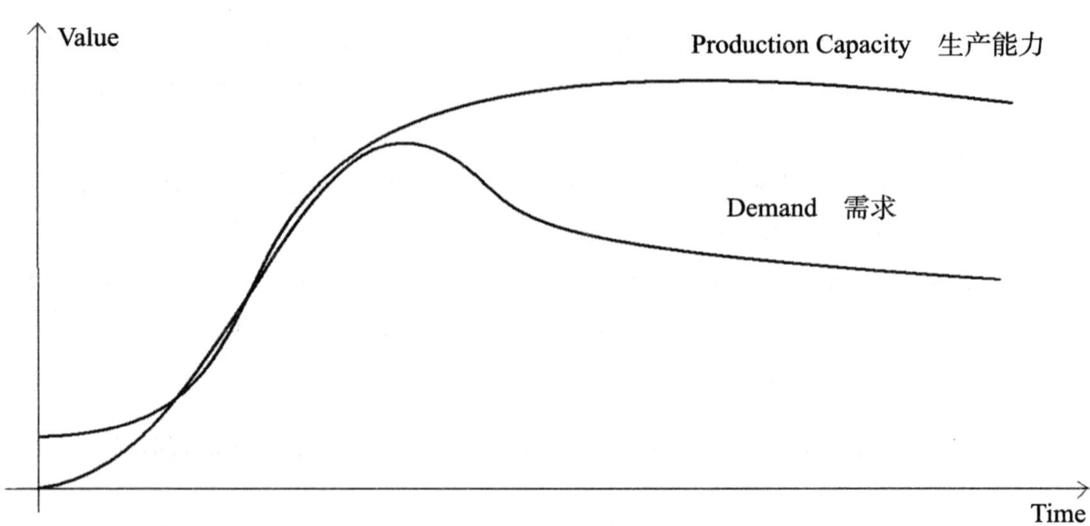

Figure 8. Production Capacity vs. Demand Curve 图 8. 生产能力与需求曲线

C. Economic Cycle

At the very beginning, the profit of making a newly invented product is negative. It turns to positive gradually along with the demand rising up. A new product may generate price premium and therefore profit premium usually in uprising phase; otherwise there is no reason for such a product existing in the market. In return, the profit premium becomes the drive for more investors to pour more money into such industry hoping to share the profit premium with the forerunners. Profit reaches the peak somewhere around the point of the demand peak. Thereafter, profit declines in the saturated phase and stable phase. Because of the inertia, the production capacity could be still increasing for a while until no more money is invested in this industry when investors finally realized that there is no possibility to earn premium profit any more in this industry. However, the existing production capacities will be still utilized as long as the nominal profit is positive even though it is

C. 经济周期

最初，制造新发明的产品的利润是负的，它随着需求的上升逐渐地变成了正数。一个新发明的产品通常会在上升期产生超额价格因而有超额利润，否则为现有市场发明新产品的理由就不成立了。反过来，超额利润促使更多的投资者投入更多的资金进入此产业以期与先行者共享超额利润，利润会在需求顶点附近达到最高峰。此后，利润会在饱和期和稳定期下降。生产能力可能会由于惯性仍然在增长，直到投资者最终意识到不再有可能在此行业赚到超额利润，于是不再投入更多的资金进入此行业。然而，只要名义利润存在并且尽管还在下降，已建立起来的生产能力就会被开动，因为立即停止生产将会给投资者造成更大的损失。而此超额生产的后果却是产品的总存量越来越

going down, since it would cause the investors even bigger loss if stop the production at once. The consequence is however that the overproduction causes surely the total stock of the product going higher and higher until cash flow problem is seen or foreseen someday. Manufacturers have to cut the price down trying to collect necessary money for keeping the factories running. The profit of the product during this period of time could be even negative again shortly. Hopefully, the huge stock could be digested off by the market to a reasonable level. Unfortunately, some of the factories in this period of time had to be shut down or phased out if their cash flows were cut off (we call this period of time stagnancy phase), which forces the production capacity matches the market demand eventually (we call this period of time recovery phase).

高，直到某日现金流问题的发生或发生的迹象显现，制造商不得不降低售价来回收必需的资金以维持工厂的运行。在这个时间段内，利润可能会短暂地再度为负。而大部分产品的存量会被消化掉，存量水平从而降低到一个合理的水平。遗憾的是，在这期间会有一部分工厂因为现金流断流问题被关闭或被淘汰（我们称此阶段为萧条期），这样，生产能力最终被强制地与市场需求匹配（我们称此阶段为平复期）。

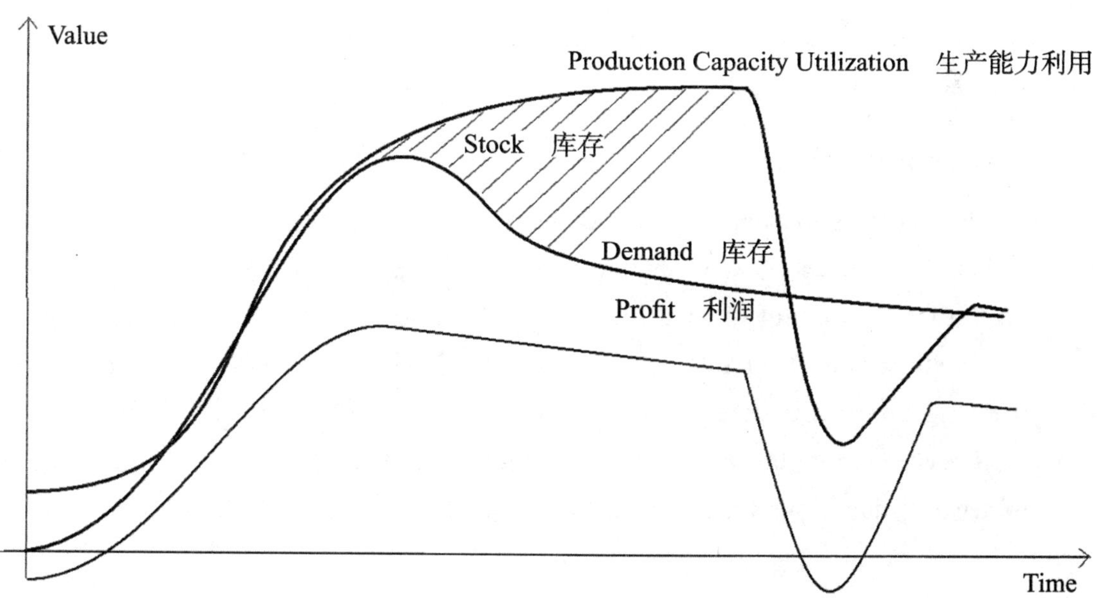

Figure 9. Production Capacity, Demand and Profit Curve 图 9. 生产能力，需求与利润曲线

Now, a product has gone through its whole

至此，一个产品走完了其生命

life cycle, market convincing – market uprising – market saturation – market stabilization – market stagnancy – market recovery. There are a lot of new products emerging up every day here and there in the world. The superposition of the life cycles of all the products forms the overall economic situation of the society.

Generally speaking, it will be averaged off if the new products emerge randomly according to stationary stochastic process ideally. The economic situation is however not a perfect stationary stochastic process in the reality, especially when a revolutionary technology is invented. There will be one leading product and lots of associated product clusters emerging up almost simultaneously upon the invention of such a technology. Together, they form a significant wave of convincing — uprising – saturation – stabilization – stagnancy – recovery superposing on the existing economic situation, which creates an economic cycle.

D. Economic Crisis

Economic crisis is an extreme case of economic cycle. When the product stock accumulation is too fast and too large, it could happen that only the products in stock can cover the market demand for quite long time, which means no production capacity is needed during this period of time. Profit turns to negative due to the fix cost of the existing facility.

的整个周期：市场征信期—市场上升期—市场平稳期—市场萧条期—市场平复期。在这个世界上，每天都有许多新产品在这里或那里出现，也正是这些产品族的生命周期的叠加构成了全社会的经济状况。

总的来说，如果新产品是按照理想的平稳随机过程随机地出现，叠加的结果将是一个被平均的直线。可现实中的经济状况却不是一个完美的平稳随机过程，特别是当一个革命性的技术被发明后，将会有一个主导产品和一系列相关产品族随着此技术的发明，几乎在相同的时间段内出现。它们在一起构成了一个征信—上升—饱和—平稳—萧条—平复的波动叠加到已有的经济状况上，从而形成了一次经济周期现象。

D. 经济危机

经济危机是经济周期的一种极端现象。当产品存量积累得太快太多时，就会发生仅产品存量就能覆盖相当长一段时期的市场需求，这就意味着在这段时间里不需要利用生产能力了，而利润会由于现有设施的固定费用而成为负数。

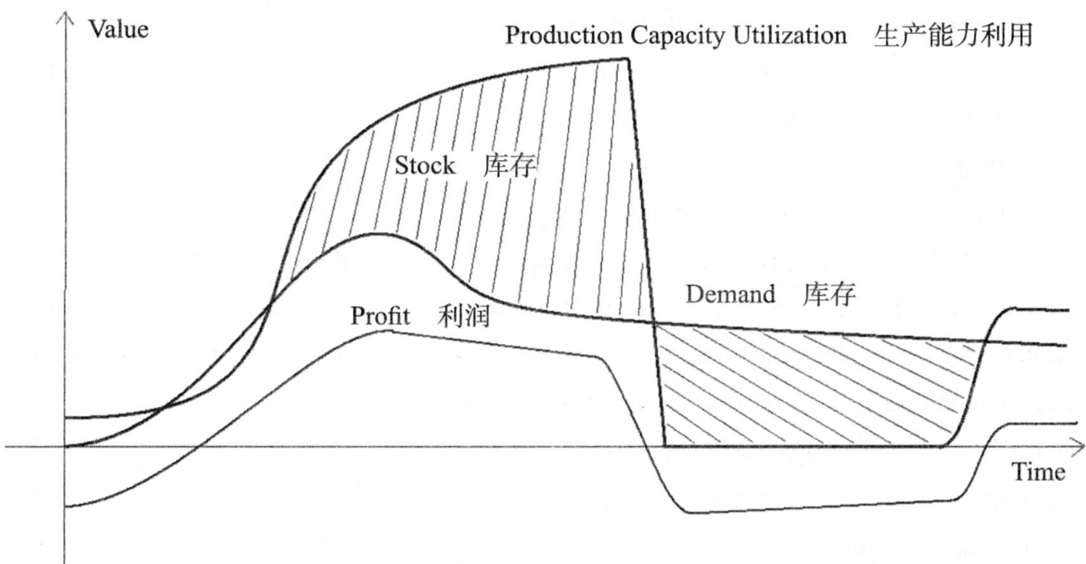

Figure 10. Curve of Economic Crisis 图 10. 经济危机曲线

E.Price Premium and Speculation Accelerate Its Happening

In Chapter XXX, we have discussed that the price premium could lead to an economic recession basically because the price premium may cause an over capacity of production even heavier than common level happening in a relatively short period of time. Once a production facility is set up, it makes economic sense only when it can be run for around 10 years averagely with only limited regular maintenance.

Supply shortage in uprising phase of demand is also a good ground for speculation, if the price premium thereby is attractive enough. Speculator's buying products in lot and keeping them in stock will cause a further shortage in the market; and a price premium with higher price than usual one is therefore forged, and meanwhile, the total stock of the product is much higher than it should be.

E. 超额价格和投机行为是经济危机发生的加速器

在第三十章中，我们已经探讨了超额价格可能会导致一场经济衰退，因为超额价格会在相对较短的时间内就导致超过一般水平的超生产能力的发生。而一旦生产设施建造好，一般需要让它运行差不多 10 年才具有经济意义，其间仅需要有限的日常维护。

在需求上升期的供给短缺也是投机行为的温床，只要超额价格有足够的吸引力。投机者大量购入产品并囤积在库中，从而导致市场短缺的恶化，一个比平常还要高的超额价格被哄抬了出来，而总的产品存量也被推高到不合理的水平。

Usually, the human nature of avoiding risk will prevent people to invest blindly. Unfortunately, another human nature of pursuing interest however will drive people to take the risk if the interest is significant enough. Speculation pumps up the significance although the price premium pumped is an illusion just like a flower in mirror and the moon in water. Once the cash flow is broken one day, an intensive chain reaction occurs fiercely; price drops drastically; and the profit becomes negative.

通常，人类的避险天性会阻止人们的盲目投资，不幸的是，人类另一个逐利的天性会驱使人们去为高额利润而冒险投资，但投机行为却能将超额价格鼓吹到一个如同水中月镜中花的虚幻的境界。一旦某天现金流断裂，一场猛烈的连锁反应就会发生，价格狂跌，利润变负。

We now understand that one of the causes of an economic crisis is the price premium. The higher the rate of price premium is, the higher over-capacity of production could be; the more speculation could happen, too; and the more possible an economic crisis could happen therefore.

现在我们知道，经济危机的原因之一是超额价格，超额价格越高，就越可能导致高的超生产能力；就越可能产生投机行为；就越可能因此导致经济危机的发生。

From the view of cybernetics, a new product invented is a step-function signal excitation to the market; the response of market demand could be roughly described as output of a second order inertia system; and the production capacity build up process is a servo system with an integrator unit (with a none-zero initial state) to follow up the dynamic of the market demand. The rate of the profit premium determines the amplification factor (not constants but variables though), and degree of speculation indicates the degree of the positive feedback of the system.

从控制论的观点看，一个产品的新发明对市场来说就是一个新的激励信号，市场需求的反映可以大概用一个二阶惯性系统的输出来描述，而生产能力的建立过程则是一个带有积分器单元（非零初始状态）的以市场需求为目标的随动系统，超额利润率决定了系统的（非恒定的）放大倍数，而投机程度则反映系统的正反馈的程度。

Basically, this Market Demand & Production Capacity system responding to the invention of a product is an auto-regulating system. When the boundary condition (limitation of the cash flow) is not reached, the fluctuation of the response is

一般讲，市场需求 & 生产能力针对新产品发明的响应系统是自动调节的。当边界条件（现金流的限制）没有触碰到时，系统响应的波动是温和的；如果边界条件不幸被

mild and it causes only economic cycle; when the boundary condition is unfortunately reached, the fluctuation of the response is fierce and it leads to an economic crisis.

打破，系统响应波动将会是剧烈的，它会导致经济危机的发生。

PART EIGHT: EXPLANATIONS, CONCLUSIONS AND INFERENCES

第八篇 解释、结论及推断

XXXX. Retrospection on Value

XXXX. 再论价值

A. Understanding Value

There are many definitions and explanations on Value. My understanding is, Value is the measure of positive contribution to the formation and/or the existence of an organization. As to a natural being, two dimensions, which are of matter and of energy, are needed to express its total value; as to an artificial article, three dimensions which are of knowledge, of matter and of energy, are needed to express its total value. All in all, the value of an object in real world can be described entirely in three aspects, which are knowledge, matter and energy. Nevertheless, knowledge is the process and product of interaction of special matter, which is human brain, and its special activity, which is remembering and thinking.

Actually, there are two perspectives to understand the Value, one of which is to view value from the subject stand point, the other of which is to view its own value from the object stand point.

For instance, rabbit is valuable to tiger; grass is valuable to rabbit.

A. 理解价值

对价值的定义有很多，我的理解是：价值是对某个组织的形成和存在的正面贡献的量度。对于一个自然物的价值，用两个维度，即物质和能量来表述即可；而对人造物则需要用知识、物质和能量三个方面来表述方才全面。总而言之，在现实的世界里，一个事物的价值形成可以从知识、物质和能量三个方面来表述。而知识是特殊物质——人脑的特殊活动——记忆及思考的过程和结果。

其实理解“价值”有两个角度：一是从主体的立场看客体的价值；二是从客体形成的立场来看其自身的价值。

举个例子，对老虎而言，兔子是有价值的；对兔子而言，青草是

From the first perspective, eating a rabbit of 5 kilogram survives a tiger for one day life. A rabbit needs 5 kilograms of grass for survive a day's life. Problem is, is one day life of a tiger equals to one day life of a rabbit?

From the second perspective, a rabbit, weighing 5 kg, needs 5 months to grow. Supposing it eats 5 kg of grass per day averagely, a rabbit of 5 kg is converted from 5×5×30=750 kg of grass. Analogously, a tiger of 5 months old needs to eat out totally 5×30=150 rabbits, which are of 5 months old, and can be converted to grass of 150×750=112500 kg. That is to say, one day life of a tiger is converted from 150 days lives of rabbit. Or, one day life of a tiger is quals to 112500 kg of grass.

It will be clearer to view the value of an object from the stand of its formation. And more understandable and comparable, too.

As to life of a grass, elements like nitrogen, phosphor, kalium, calcium, carbon, hydrogen, oxygen, and energy from soil, water, air and sunlight respectively, are valuable. A piece of seed in soil, bathed in water and warm, starts to burgeon. It strikes root down. And then grow its sprout up and up. Its root develops in soil continuously and absorbs nutritious elements like nitrogen, phosphor, kalium, calcium. By means of energy, they are transported into all parts of the plant,

有价值的。

以第一种立场来看，吃进一只体重 5 公斤的兔子，可以延续老虎一天的生命。而一只兔子一天需要吃 5 公斤青草才能延续一天的生命。问题是，老虎一天的生命等于兔子一天的生命吗？

以第二种立场来看，对一只体重 5 公斤的兔子来说，它需要 5 个月的生长，如果平均一天需要吃 5 公斤青草的话，一只 5 公斤重的兔子是 5 × 5 × 30=750 公斤青草转换来的；依此类推，对一只生长了 5 个月的老虎来说，它需要吃掉总计为 5 × 30=150 只 5 个月大的兔子，也可以折算成 150 × 750=112500 公斤青草。也就是说，老虎一天的生命是用兔子 150 天（5 个月 × 30 天）的生命换来的，或者说是用 112500 公斤青草换来的。

我认为从客体形成的立场来看其自身的价值更加清晰，更加易于理解和比较。

对草而言，土、水、气、光中的氮、磷、钾、钙、碳、氢、氧以及能量，对它的生长是有价值的。一粒种子，落进土里，在水分的浸泡和温度的催动下，开始发芽，首先是往下扎的根，然后是往上长的芽，破土而出。根在土里不断发展，不断汲取氮、磷、钾、钙等元素和水，并借助于能量的作用，将养分送至草的各个部分，空气中的二氧

first of all, stems and leaves, and then flowers and fruits; The carbon dioxide is absorbed by leaves of the plant, through photosynthesis, converted into carbohydrate, which is the supply for the growth of stem and leaf. As to the reproduction of grass, the wind and bee is valuable to help propagating of pollen and seed, which is one of the chain of the circulation of the reproduction of grass. Besides those eaten by animals like goat, rabbit, pig, and cattle, grass itself withers in autumn. By means of germ and enzyme, the yellowed leaves disintegrated into nitrogen, phosphor, kalium, calcium, carbon dioxide, and heat, for recycling.

化碳被叶吸收，经光合作用，转化成碳水化合物，成为其生长的材料。对草的繁衍，风是有价值的，它有助于种子的传播，进入下一个春荣秋枯的循环。除了在生长过程中被羊兔猪牛们吃掉的部分外，草叶也会自行新生老衰，枯黄的叶子会在细菌和酶的作用下，重新分解成氮、磷、钾、钙、二氧化碳和热量，以待再生。

As to animals like goat, rabbit, pig and cattle, grass on land, air and light in sky is valuable to their birth and growth. They eat grass and drink water, and thrive thereby. The goat mothers, rabbit mothers, pig mothers and cattle mothers absorb nitrogen, phosphor, kalium, calcium, carbohydrate and heat from grass to foster their babies for keeping the propagation of the species. Part of the elements absorbed by grasses leave in the bodies of those animals, who eat them partially, and the other part of the elements absorbed are excreted into ground and air through shitting and breathing.

对羊兔猪牛们而言，地上的草和水，空中的气和光，对它们的出生和生长是有价值的。它们吃草喝水，茁壮成长。羊妈妈们、兔妈妈们、猪妈妈们、牛妈妈们，用从草中获取的氮、磷、钾、钙、碳和热量，再孕育下一代，以保证物种得以延续。被草吸收的全部化学元素，一部分留在了羊兔猪牛们的体内，另一部分则经过呼气和排便等被羊兔猪牛们交还给了大地和大气。

As to beasts like wolf, tiger, and leopard, animals like goat, rabbit, pig and cattle are valuable to their birth and growth. They hunt preys and drink water, and thrive thereby. The mother wolves, mother tigers, and mother leopards absorb nitrogen, phosphor, kalium, calcium, and heat from their preys to foster their babies for keeping the propagation of the species. Part of the elements absorbed by preys

对豺狼虎豹们而言，地上的羊兔猪牛，空中的气和光，对它们的出生和生长是有价值的。它们猎杀羊兔猪牛获取食物，茁壮成长。豺妈妈们、狼妈妈们、虎妈妈们、豹妈妈们，用从猎物的身体中获取氮、磷、钾、钙、碳和能量，在肚子里孕育下一代，以保证物种得以

leave in the bodies of those predators partially, who eat them, and the other part of the elements absorbed are excreted into ground and air through shitting and breathing. Old wolves, old tigers, and old leopards die eventually. They turn back the elements contained in their bodies totally into soil and air eventually.

延续。原来留在羊兔猪牛体内的那部分物质则又被豺狼虎豹们吃了，一部分留在了它们的体内，另一部分则经过呼气和排便等被豺狼虎豹们还给了大地和大气；最后，老豺、老狼、老虎、老豹们终将死去，它们把留在了体内那部分化学元素也最终彻彻底底地又交还给了大地和大气。

Only the photo-energy from the sun, in the process of photosynthesis, part of which is dissipated during transportation of nutritious elements from the earth, and other part of which is saved in the body of the grass together with the nutritious elements, so that the grass grows. After eaten by a goat, part of the energy saved in the body of the grass is dissipated during the process of eating, digesting, excreting, and living; the other part of the energy is saved in the body of the goat together with the ingredients of flesh and bone, so that the goat grows. After eaten by a tiger, part of the energy saved in the body of the goat is dissipated during the process of preying, digesting, excreting, and living; the other part of the energy is saved in the body of the tiger together with the ingredients of flesh and bone, so that the tiger grows. After dying, by means of germ and fungus, the body of tiger dissolved. And the energy saved in its body eventually dissipated into the universe.

唯有源于太阳的光能，在光合过程中，部分在传输从土地中汲取的养分的过程中耗散掉了；另一部分则与养分一起储存在草的身上使得草不断地长大。草被羊吃了之后，储存在草中的一部分能量耗散在吃草、消化、排泄以及生存的活动中；另一部分则与构成骨和肉的养分一起储存在羊的身上使得羊不断地长大。羊被虎吃了之后，储存在羊身上的一部分能量耗散在猎杀、消化、排泄以及生存的活动中；另一部分则与构成骨和肉的养分一起储存在虎的身上使得虎不断地长大。虎死后，它的身体在细菌和真菌的作用下分解，所有储存在虎身上的能量最终彻底地耗散在宇宙之中。

The element of iron is distributed over the global. People collect ore rich of iron and transport it to the smeltery with their labor. Under the high temperature by burning coke, iron in high purity is obtained. High temperature is cooled down. Slag

铁元素散布在地球上的各个角落，人们采集富含铁的矿石，花力气将这些铁矿石运到冶炼厂，在燃烧煤焦所产生的高温下，人们提炼出高纯度的铁。高温终究被散尽，

is dumped to the earth (Slag is the waste from smeltery, but not waste at all). Iron can be employed to make a lot of tools. Let's take an iron hammer as an example to survey what is really happening in its life cycle in terms of value. Iron hammer is used to forge a work piece (utility). Its value in broad sense is composed in following three dimension, firstly, all materials forming a hammer which is called value in matter; secondly, all the energy dissipated in forming a hammer from scratch, which is called value in energy; lastly, knowledge of making hammer, which is called value of know-how.

废渣被扔回了地球（其实对炼铁来说的废渣，并非绝对的废），我们可以用铁制造很多工具。这里就以一把铁榔头为例，来细究一下在这把铁榔头的生命周期里，到底发生了什么。铁榔头（效用）是用来捶打锻件的，它的“广义使用价值”应该是组成该榔头的总的“物质价值”加上形成这把榔头的总的“能量价值”和设计制造这把榔头的“知识价值”分摊之总和。

Every strike of forging may cause a little bit iron wearing out of the head of the hammer. Eventually, hammer will be totally scraped due to weight loss. Nevertheless, the total weight of the scraps plus the total worn-out shall be the same as the new hammer is just made up. Even though the value in use, in narrow sense, of a scraped hammer is none, the value in matter of this scraped hammer is always there unchanged, which can be re-collected, re-smelted and re-casted as a new head of a hammer theoretically.

随着锻打的进行，榔头上会有极少量的铁被磨损掉了，落在了地上，直至有一天，该榔头变得太轻而不能再使用了。我们计量一下磨损的铁屑的总量加上被弃用榔头中铁的总量，应该与这把榔头新造出来时铁的总量是相等的。尽管这把榔头的“狭义使用价值”已经消失，但构成这把榔头的“物质价值”仍然存在，它们理论上可以被再收集、再冶炼及再浇注成一把新榔头的头。

The knowledge how to make a hammer doesn't lose at all along with the hammer's utilizing. Oppositely, the know-how of making a hammer could be improved based on the utilization of the hammer in forge through running human's brain (through dissipating heat in brain).

制造榔头的知识不仅没有受到损失，人们开动脑筋（大脑也需要消耗热量），根据榔头在锻打中的使用情况，可能设计出性能更佳的新一代用于锻打的榔头。

So, the only change is the value in energy of that hammer, which is dissipated to none from the maximum as it was just made up.

因此，变化的只是该榔头的“能量价值”，它从形成一把新榔头时的极大，几乎耗散成了“零”。

The total value of all the matters/elements in earth is constant. Through absorbing energy (positive function of energy), matters enter into the state of entropy reduction, where a higher organization is constructed; Through releasing energy (negative function of energy), matters enter into the state of entropy increment, where an organization is deconstructed.

地球上所有物质 / 元素的价值总和是恒定不变的。通过吸收能量（能量的正向作用），物质进入建构组织的熵减状态；或者通过释放能量（能量的反向作用），进入熵增状态。

The energy dissipation is unidirectional, according to the Second Law of Thermo-dynamics. The re-accumulation of the value, which is a process of increasing the degree of order of an organization, needs more energy. During the procedure of accumulation and dissipation of value, values in matter of all the chemical elements are accumulated and distributed in circles. They start from one point of state and end at the same point of state after one circulation. The endless cycles go around and around.

能量的耗散是单向的（热力学第二定律），价值的重新积聚（组织有序度提高），需要有新能量的加入。而所有化学元素的物质价值，在价值的积聚和消耗的过程中从一点开始，跑一圈后，又回到了该点，循环往复，周而复始，永不消失。

When observing the movement of an object standing on the earth, which is spinning in a high speed, we don't take the self-rotation of the earth into consideration. We treat the earth as a relative static reference of the movement (relative speed equals to zero). Analogously, we treat the value in matter of an object as the carrier of value with relatively zero value. We focus only on the value in energy in all the economic activities. We say thereafter, "value is energy" in the study of economics.

当站在快速旋转的地球上观察研究物体的运动规律时，我们并不将地球的自转考虑进来，而只是将地球当作一个相对静止（相对速度为零）的运动载体。同理，在做经济学价值研究时，我们也将物质仅仅看作是“相对价值为零”的价值载体，而只研究能量价值在经济活动中的表现。因此我们说，在经济学范畴里，“价值即能量”。

Therefore, we declare here, there is only one independent variable in economics study besides time, which is energy.

因此我们在这里声明，除时间之外，经济学研究中只有一个自变量，它就是能量。

B.As to Value, Marshall Was Wrong

"But experience has shown that it is not well to use word in the former sense." Marshall commented on Smith's definition of value-in-use and value-in-exchange, "Thus the term value is relative, and expresses the relation between two things at a particular place and time" .

However, through the energy view discussed in this book, we now understand that both value-in-use and value-in-exchange are expressed by the aggregated energy dissipation in the process of the forming of an organization, but with different starting points though. Theoretically speaking, the starting point for measuring value-in-use is the Big Bang of the universe; and the starting point for measuring value-in-exchange is where human's hand touches. Value-in-use covers the whole process of value creation; and Value-in-exchange covers only portion of value creation participated by human.

We can easily measure and/or calculate the total energy dissipation in the process section of a specific organization participated by human, which means that the result of the measurement and calculation are absolute. As to the value-in-use, it is now impossible, or too hard, to measure or calculate the total energy dissipation starting from the Big Bang. We can, I am afraid, only use the virgin status of the earth forming as the quasi starting point instead. The result of measurement and calculation are therefore relative, but it makes sense though.

Unfortunately, however, the notion of "relativeness" of Marshall had laid a keynote for the

B. 就价值论，马歇尔错了

"经验证明，运用前者含义稍欠妥当。"马歇尔对斯密的关于使用价值与交换价值的定义时评论说："因此，价值是相对而言的，它表达在特定时间和地点的两物之间的关系。"

通过本书所论及的能量观，我们现在知道使用价值和交换价值都是以形成某个组织的过程中所耗散的总能量来表述的，只是这个过程的计量起始点的选择不同而已。理论上说，计量使用价值的起始点在宇宙大爆炸；而计量交换价值的起始点则在人手能及的地方。使用价值涵盖了价值形成的全过程；而交换价值只是涵盖了由人参与的那一部分价值的形成过程。

我们可以容易地测量或计算某个组织形成过程中，由人参与的那部分过程的能量总耗散，也就是说，测量和计算的结果是绝对的。至于使用价值，现在人们还不太可能（或者太困难）以宇宙大爆炸作为起点来测量和计算能量的总耗散。我们恐怕仅能以地球形成的初始状态作为准起点来计量，计量的结果因此是相对的。尽管如此，却也不无意义。

可不幸的是，马歇尔的"相对说"却成了此后100年来经济学研

economic research for 100 years thereinafter. People used marginal analysis instead of value calculation; or, ignored theory of value at all.

究的主基调。人们用边际分析替代价值的计算，甚至直接抛弃价值理论。

XXXXI. Theoretical Basis of Economics

XXXXI. 经济学中的理论基础

A. Scientific Principles in Economics

A. 经济学中的科学原理

1. The Law of Conservation of Matter

一、物质守恒定律

Marshall said in his book *Principles of Economics* that "Man cannot create material things. In the mental and moral world indeed he may produce new ideas; but when he is said to produce material things, he really only produces utilities; or in other words, his efforts and sacrifices result in changing the form or arrangement of matter to adapt it better for the satisfaction of wants. All he can do in the physical world is either to readjust matter so as to make it more useful, as when he makes a log of wood into a table; or to put it in the way of being made more useful by nature, as when he puts seed where the forces of nature will make it burst out into life." (Book I, Chapter 3, Sec. 1). Marshall's view is the most explicit interpretation of the Law of Conservation of Matter of natural science in terms of economics.

经济学集大成者马歇尔先生，在他的《经济学原理》的书中说："人是不能创造物质的，他只能在智力层面产生想法。当他说生产物质事物时，实际上是说他在制造效用。或者换句话说：他的努力和牺牲换来了对物质形式的改变或重组以更好地满足人的需求。他所能做的仅仅是在物理世界中，调整物质形态使得它更有用而已，就如他将原木制成了桌子；或者使它在自然的作用下变得更有用，正如他将一粒种子播入土中，自然力会将其催生成一个生命。"（第一册第三章第一节）。马歇尔的论述是经济学理论中对"物质守恒定律"最明晰的表述。

Generally, to an open system, the total amount of matter the system contained, is initial amount of matter it contained plus the difference between the total amount of matter taken in afterwards and the total amount of matter discharged out of the system. So, in scope of the whole economic system,

一般来说，对一个开放系统而言，系统内所含有的物质总量等于该系统初始物质总量加上此后摄入系统物质总量与排出系统物质总量之差。因此，对整个经济系统而言，如下大等式成立：经济系统从自然

the following grand equation is concluded as, the total amount of matter taken in an economical system from the nature equals to the total amount of matter stored in this economical system plus the total amount of matter discharged back to the nature from this economical system.

中摄取的物质总量 = 存储在经济系统中的物质总量 + 经济系统向自然排出的物质总量。

2. The Law of Conservation of Energy

In the above recited discussion by Marshall, there are verbs like, produce, manufacture, effort, sacrifice, change, reorganization, adjust, make, vary, insert, and burst, used to express that economy is the activities by human and even nature in certain frame. As we all know, there must be energy involved when there are activities occurring. The Law of Conservation of Energy, as a universal law, has to be followed. In a similar tone of Marshall, we say, Man cannot create energy. In the mental and moral world indeed, he may produce new ideas. By means of energy externally, he conducts the change of the form or arrangement of matter to adapt it better for the satisfaction of human wants.

Therefore, to an economic system as a whole, we have the following grand equation, the total energy taken into the economic system from the nature equals to the energy saved in the system plus the energy dissipated from the economic system back to the nature.

二、能量守恒定律

在马歇尔的上一段论述中，他提及了“生产”“制造”“努力”“牺牲”“改变”“重组”“调整”“制成”“变得”“播入”以及自然力的“催生”等动词来说明：经济是在某个框架下人类和自然的“活动”。大家都知道，只要有“动”的存在，就必有“能量”的参与，遵循“能量守恒定律”就成了一条铁律。效仿马歇尔的说法，我们可以说：人是不能创造能量的，他只能在智力层面产生想法，借助外来能量，用以完成对物理世界中物质形态的改变和调整使得它对人更有用。

因此，对整个经济系统而言，如下大等式成立：经济系统从自然中摄取的能量总和 = 存储在经济系统中的能量总和 + 经济系统向自然耗散掉的能量总和。

3. The Theory of Dissipative Structure

According to the Second Law of Thermodynamics, under the circumstance of none impact from external environment, all the spontaneous processes are irreversible, which is regard as the

三、耗散结构理论

根据热力学第二定律，宏观体系无外界作用的一切自发过程都具有不可逆性，即所谓的熵增原理（就像石头只能从高处往低处滚一样）。

principle of increase of entropy (it's demonstrated as a rock falling only from the high point to low). However, an entropy decrease can be occurring when an open system takes in matters and energy continuously from the surroundings (just like a pig could be blow up when put on the cusp of wind).

但如果一个开放系统能够不断地从周围环境中汲取并积累能量，那么该系统的有序度就有可能会增高，即产生所谓负熵现象（就好比是风口上的猪，也能被吹抬起来一样）。

In 1969, Mr. Ilya Prigogine published an article with name of "Structure, Dissipation, and Life" in the meeting on *Physical Theory and Biology* 51 years ago. The Theory of Dissipative Structure was formally raised.

伊利亚·普利高津于51年前的1969年，在国际"理论物理与生物学会议"上，发表研究报告《结构、耗散和生命》，正式提出了"耗散结构理论"。

Dissipative Structure is a new concept created by Mr. Prigogine while he was studying the evolution of an ordered system under the umbrella of the Second Law of Thermo-dynamics. Simply speaking, the quantities changes of an open system of multi-components in multi-layers far from the state of equilibrium, triggered by the fluctuation of the surrounding factors over certain threshold, may cause a qualitative change. Through exchanging matters and energy with surroundings, forming a negative entropy flow, an ordered state in time, in space, or in function may be produced from the state of disorder, which is called dissipative structure.

耗散结构是普利高津在研究不违背热力学第二定律的情况下，有序系统自身如何演化时，提出的新概念。简单地说，就是一个远离平衡的包含有多组分多层次的开放系统，在外界条件变化达到一定阈值时，经"涨落"的触发，量变可能引起质变；系统通过不断与外界进行物质和能量交换，在耗散过程中产生负熵流，就可能从原来的无序状态自我转变为一种时间、空间或功能的有序状态。这种非平衡态下自我形成的新的有序结构，就是耗散结构。

From the point view of thermodynamics, dissipative structure suggests that a thermodynamic system of none-equilibrium far from the stable ordered state may transform to an equilibrium state. The theory of dissipative structure is used to study the processes and rules how a system in chaotic state initially developing into a stable ordered structure; moreover, to describe the condition and behavior of

从热力学的观点看，耗散结构是指在远离平衡态的非平衡态下，热力学系统可能出现的一种稳定化的有序结构。耗散结构理论就是研究系统怎样从混沌的初态，向稳定有序的结构组织演化过程和规律，并且力图描述系统在变化临界点附近相变的条件和行为，故也称之为

a system around the critical point of changing. It is also called theory of self-organization of system in none-equilibrium state which is the basis of order.

非平衡系统的自组织理论。非平衡是有序之源。

The Dissipative Structure of Prigogine can be used to understand the evolution of the universe, evolution of species, development of economy and furthermore the human ourselves. Life is in high order. We call a thing towards more order the negative entropy. Otherwise, the positive entropy. It has been discussed that it's possible to obtain a high order partly by sacrificing the order of other part of the whole.

普利高津耗散结构实际可以用来理解宇宙演化、生物演化、经济社会乃至我们人类自身。生命是高度的有序。我们把相对有序的东西称为负熵，反之称为正熵。现代物理学显示，局部的有序是可能的，但必须以其他地方的更大无序为代价。

Human needs a continuous supply of food/energy for survival, which means sacrifice (entropy increase) of a lot of plants and animals. Everything grows on the sun. The order increases of plants and animals the results of the exhaustion (entropy increase) of the sun through nuclear reaction and disordering of other objects.

人生存，就要有食物 / 能量的不断供应，就要以动植物的死亡(熵增)为代价。万物生长靠太阳。动植物的有序又是以太阳核反应的衰竭（熵增）或其他形式的熵增为代价的。

All of the creatures including human and society are open systems far from the equilibrium, which need to exchange matters and energy with the surroundings for maintaining the stability in order.

所有生物包括人类以及社会都是远离平衡态并且与周围环境存在物质和能量交换的开放系统，以维持系统的稳定有序。

As to life, equilibrium means dead. Away from the equilibrium state is the precondition of an ordered life. That is to say, structure in equilibrium is a "dead" structure in order. A dissipative structure is the "alive" structure in order. There is huge difference between the two structures.

对生物体来说，平衡就意味着死亡，只有远离平衡，才能保持有序化的生命。通俗地讲，平衡结构是“死”的有序化结构，而耗散结构却是“活”的有序化结构，两者的有序存在着本质的差别。

There are at least three necessities for a dissipative structure to be formed and maintained, #1, it has to be an open system. A stand alone and close system cannot evolve to a dissipative

一个耗散结构的形成和维持至少需要三个条件：一是系统必须是开放系统，孤立系统和封闭系统都不可能产生耗散结构。二是系统必

structure. #2, the system has to be in a none-linear zone and far from the equilibrium. Experiments and studies have already proved that a mutation from none-ordered state to ordered one is not happening in a system which is in or close to the equilibrium state. Neither a mutation from a low ordered state to a higher state. #3, There must be some none-linear dynamic process, such as, positive feedback mechanism.

须处于远离平衡的非线性区，在平衡态或近平衡态，大量的实验和理论研究都证明其不可能发生质的突变从无序走向有序，也不可能从一种有序走向新的更高级的有序。三是系统中必须有某些非线性动力学过程，如正负反馈机制等。

The economic activities are self-organized by human by means of natural energy from fruits, grains, animals, coal, crude oil, wind, stream, trees, grasses, all in all, energy from the sun; by means of natural substances from nature like water, air, stone, and earth; like trees and grasses; like insects and beast; and all kinds of ores, to change their forms into sheds and houses, bowls and pans, desks and benches, jackets and pants, coaches and boats, swords and guns, spades and shovels, hammers and drills, so on and so forth, so that the performances of which are more convenient for human, who are the son of the nature, to better survive and propagate. Along with the expansion, updating, mutation of the iteration of knowledge, the economic system has been exchanged more and more matters and energy with surroundings continuously. The potentiality of the economic system is therefore getting higher and higher.

人类的经济活动，就是人类“自我组织”起来，借助来自自然的能量（果实、谷物、动物、煤炭、石油、风能、水流、树枝、干草，总而言之，是来自太阳的能量），从自然界获取“自然物”（水气石土、树木花草、飞虫走兽、各种矿藏等），改变它们的形态（成了房舍棚帐、锅碗瓢盆、桌椅床凳、鞋帽衣裤、车骑舰船、刀枪棍棒、锄耙锹勺、锤凿钳钎，等等），以使得它们在某方面的功效更加有利于“人”——这个归根到底也是方便“自然之子”更好地生存和繁衍。随着人类知识迭代的不断扩展、更新、突变，经济系统与外界的物质和能量交换在不断地增大，其本身的有序程度也在不断地提高，经济系统结构的势能也就越涨越高了。

If the process of exchanging matter and energy with surroundings stops, plants and animals die firstly; sheds and houses collapse finally; bowls and pans, spades and shovels, hammers and drills corrupt finally; desks and benches decay; jackets

如果与外界物质和能量交换终止了，首先，植物、动物以及人类将会全部消亡；其次，房舍棚帐最终会坍塌，锅碗瓢盆、锄耙锹勺、锤凿钳钎最终会锈蚀，桌椅床凳最

and pans break; coaches and boats malfunction; swords and guns weather; everything goes to heat-dead eventually.

终会腐朽，鞋帽衣裤最终会崩裂，车骑舰船最终会失灵，刀枪棍棒最终会风化，一切归于“热寂”。

Now we can say, the economic system is a typical dissipative structure at all.

由此可见，经济系统是一个彻头彻尾的，具有“耗散结构”的系统。

B. Engineering Disciplines in Economics

B. 经济学中的工程学基础

1. Energy storage, an ignored critical concept in economics

一、储能，一个在经济学中被忽视的重要概念

When put in fire firstly, a piece of iron absorbs and keeps partial heat of the fire. Put in cold water then, the hot iron releases partial heat into the water and the temperature of the water rises. This is a typical process of energy storagc and release. The iron in this case is an energy storage component in thermodynamic system.

一块铁先被放在火里加热，它吸收并保存一部分热量；然后将烧红的铁放进冷水里，它释放热量，并能将水温提高。这就是一个典型的能量储存和释放的过程，这里的铁块就是一个热力学系统中的储能部件。

In an electrical circuit, batteries, capacitors, inductors are energy storage components, too.

在一个电路里，电池、电容器、电感器也是储能部件。

A reservoir in midway of altitude surely is energy storage component. Water from mountains run down into a reservoir due to the potential energy. Energy is saved in the reservoir, which drives water flushing out through its outlets.

在海拔高度中部的水库肯定是储能部件，由于势能，水从高山上流入水库，能量被储存在水库里，这些能量被用来驱动水从出水口喷涌而出。

A tree is an energy storage component. Energy from the sun is saved in its root, its trunk, its branches, its leaves, and its fruits. The total volume of energy saved in a tree is the function to both the way it grows and the way we treat it.

一棵树也是一个储能部件，来自太阳的能量被储存在它的根、它的干、它的枝、它的叶和它的果中。储存在树中的能量是它如何生长和我们处理它的方式的函数。

All animals and human beings ourselves are energy storage components.

所有的动物包括我们人类在内都是储能部件。

Grains stored in depot certainly are, too.

粮库里的谷物当然也是储能部件。

A sewing needle is another kind of energy storage component, let's call it imaginary energy storage component. Leading the thread, the utility of getting two pieces of clothes together is stored in its tiny body in a special shape. Unless being broken midway, this needle releases the utility, little by little, during the sewing process until it is worn too tiny to be used any more (just like the water level in a reservoir is lower than the bottom level of the outlet gate).

一根缝衣针是另一种类型的储能部件，让我们称它为虚储能部件。穿针引线，将两块布料缝在一起的效用被储存在它小小的有着特别形状的身体中，除非中途被折断，在缝制过程中，这根针一点一点地释放它的效用直到它被磨到细得不能再用了（就像水库里的水面低于了出水闸门的底部）。

We say that, the whole economic system is truly a thermodynamic system, in a broad sense, consist of a variety of energy storage components in different layers.

因此我们可以说，整个经济系统就是一个由各色各样的储能部件组成的有层次的广义热力学系统。

The last but not the least, there are only addition and subtraction in context of energy. Energy storage is a timely procedure. And energy release is a timely procedure, too.

最后，必须强调：在能量的语境里只存在加法和减法。能量的储存是一个随时间逐步积累的过程；能量的释放也是一个随时间逐步耗散的过程。

2. Cybernetics

If you are knowledgeable of system theory and cybernetics, great, it should be easier for you to understand fully and truly this book. If not, fine too, allow me to briefly introduce the cores of both doctrines, which are quite simple though. The core of system theory is based on the second law of thermodynamics, which says, heat transfers automatically only from the object of high temperature to lower one. In other words, if you want to keep a system in a status it was, additional energy is needed more or less. As of the key of understanding cybernetics, it is the energy storage component. Cybernetics deals with the performance

二、控制论

如果您对系统论和控制论方面的知识有所了解，那就太好了，这能帮助您正确地全面地理解本书。如果您没有，也没关系，请允许我简单地给您介绍这两种学说的核心，其实也很简单，系统论的核心就是热力学第二定律，它说：热只会自动地从温度高的物体向温度低的物体转移。换句话说：要维持一个物体的状态不变，或多或少的能量是必须的。至于理解控制论的关键则是储能部件，实际上，控制论研究的是由众多储能部件构成的系

of the system consist of variety of energy storage components in time axis.

统在时间轴上的表现。

The water level of the reservoir, the flow volume of the outlet responds to the way of water coming into the reservoir and the way of man regulating the gates of its outlets. That is the situation where cybernetics functions. And cybernetics works well only when the water level is in between the height of the dam and the bottom of the outlet. It will be out of control when either the water flows over the top of the dam or the water level is lower than the bottom of the gate.

水库的水面高度、出水口的流量，与流入水库的水的动态和人调节水库出水口闸门的动态相关。这就是控制论能发挥作用的场合。而控制论只有当水面介于大坝顶面高度和出水闸门底部高度之间才起作用。如果水从大坝顶面溢出，或者水面高度低于了闸门底部的高度，事态就处于可控状态之外了。

C. Biology in Economics

C. 经济学中的生物学基础

1. Mechanism of Growth

一、成长机制

Dropping into soil, a seed may sprout a radicle first and then a germ, under a suitable circumstance. The germ then grow into stem and leaves. From the stem, branches and more leaves grow up. Upon maturity, flowers and then seeds grow. And seed drops into soil again to start another cycle of multiply.

一粒植物的种子落在土壤里，在合适的条件下，首先长出胚根，然后是胚芽，芽再发育成干和叶，主干又分裂出枝，枝上再长出叶片。成熟后，枝上开花、结籽，种子落地来完成物种的繁衍。

Plant needs be nourished by soil, water, air and sunshine. Plant grows flourishingly, where the soil is fertile. Plant grows fast and strong, where the air goes flowingly. Even in a same tree leaves and branches facing sunshine thrive more than ones are in shadow.

植物需要土地、水、空气和阳光的滋养。哪里土地肥沃，哪里的植物就茂盛；哪边的空气通畅，哪边的植物就茁壮；甚至同一棵树，朝着阳光一面的部分都会比背阳的一面更加枝繁叶茂。

On a higher level, an economy, which consists of lives on earth involving human being, animals, plants, and even viruses and bacteria, is a system fractal analogous to biological world in terms of structure and evolution process.

一个经济体是由地球上的生物（包括人类、动物、植物甚至病毒、细菌）所构成的一个由人类主导的更高层次的与生物有着分形相似的结构和演化过程的系统。

Economic activity starts from the food surplus (the root of the economy). The human ancestors wandered around in the forest for searching food several hundred thousand years ago. If lucky enough, they might harvest more than they immediately needed to fill their stomach. Exchange (the stem of the economy) might happen.

经济活动发端于食物盈余（经济的根），几十万年前，人类的祖先们整天徜徉在茂密的森林里，寻找果腹的食物。幸运的话，他们可能收获比填饱自己肚子需要的食物更多的食物，交换（经济的干）就有可能发生了。

People possess different kinds of food may exchange one another. Person A, possessing peach may exchange with Person B for his pear, with Person C for melon. A stable social surplus makes social labor division possible. Person D exchanges the tools he made (the branches of the economy) with Person E for his rice, with Person F for vegetables, Person G for Clothes, so on and so forth.

拥有不同食物的人们便可以相互进行交换了，某 A 可以用收获到的桃，来换取某 B 的梨，或者某 C 的瓜。稳定的社会总盈余，使得社会分工成了可能，某 D 可以用他专业制造的工具（经济的枝）来换取某 E 的大米、某 F 的蔬菜、某 G 的衣服……

After the industrial revolution, there have been more and more producing tools made, which cause the situation of abundance of living tools and progress (evolution) of producing tools.

工业革命以来，各种生产工具层出不穷，从而导致了生活工具的丰富和生产工具的进步（经济的进化）。

It's only possible for a plant to grow similar roots, similar stem and branches, similar leaves, and similar flowers and seeds. An economy tree, however, can have whole different kind of root (food surplus, firewood surplus, coal surplus, oil surplus, even electricity surplus), grow different types of branches (black smith, machining work, production line, and even robots, so on and so forth).

一棵植物，只能长出相似的根、茎、叶、花及籽，而一棵经济之树在它的演化过程中，却能长出不同种类的根（粮食结余、木柴结余、煤炭结余、燃油结余乃至电力结余），长不同形式的枝，结不同形式的果（榔头、车床、生产线、机器人，等等）。

When broken, a new branch of the plant may grow up around the breaks or root; when drought occurs, the aged leaves and branches will be discarded automatically until only buds are kept. When environment goes even worse, whole part

当植物的枝干被折断后，新的枝干会从断面的周边或者根部生长出来；当遇到干旱时，植物的老枝老叶会首先被遗弃，直至剩下芽胚。在恶劣的环境下，植物的地上部分

above ground of a plant may wither, but from the root, new stem and branches and leaves may grow up next year, in some extreme case, in several years. Flowers and fruit may be expected.

全部枯死，它的根部仍然能够在来年甚至数年之后重新长出枝叶并且开花结果。

Similarly, when economy in depression, the scale of the economy shrinks, many enterprises are closed. Once opportunity comes, there will be a lot of new enterprises pop up and grow vigorously.

同理，当经济萧条时，经济体规模萎缩，企业会关门。可一旦时机来临，经济体又会有许多新的企业会应运而生，蓬勃发展。

2. Gene

二、基因

Generally speaking, Gene is a set of expression with which an organ can duplicate itself partially or wholly by taking matter and energy from surroundings. In this context, all organs carrying gene must be of dissipative structure. A virus multiplies itself according to its own gene by absorbing nutrition and energy of the host cell; A bacterium multiplies itself according to its own gene by absorbing nutrition and energy from surrounding. A tree grows new branches and leaves every year according to its own gene.

广义地讲，基因是某组织携带的在吸收外界物质和能量的条件下能部分或全部复制自身的表述集。由此可见，带有基因的组织一定具有耗散结构。病毒依照它自己的基因，通过汲取宿主细胞的养分和能量，不断地复制自己；细菌可以依照它自己的基因，不断地复制自己；大树依据它自己的基因，每年都会长出一部分新的枝和叶。

An economic organ can reproduce its parts according to the knowledge of human and/or setting of the nature. For instance, when a hammer is broken, another same hammer can be duplicated by human for replacement. If one hammer is not sufficient, many hammers exactly the same can be made for expansion.

一个经济体，同样也会在自己的体内，依照人类的知识以及自然的设定，不断地复制自己构件。如一把榔头用坏了，就会有另一把一模一样的榔头依照图纸被制造出来顶替；如果一把榔头不够用了，另一把一模一样的榔头会被制造出来用于扩产。

The gene of some species may mutate upon external stimulation. The gene of an economic organ can also mutate along with the development of the science and technology. The main drive of a locomotive 100 years ago was steam engine, and

受外部的刺激，自然界的物种有可能发生基因突变。经济体的基因也会随着科学技术的发展而发生突变，100年前火车的主要动力是来自蒸汽机，然后是柴油机，现在

then diesel engine, and now electric motor.

The time span of mutation of the natural species is quite longsome. But the one of economic organ is getting sooner and sooner along with the exponential increase of knowledge of human.

The length of a specific species is fixed. The one of some virus may be only of several thousand bases/base-pairs the shortest, while there are 23 chromosomes with 3 billion DNA base-pairs in human cells. The scale of an economic organ may be thousands of times bigger than one of human, and it expands every day.

是电动机了。

自然界物种的基因突变的频率基本上是很缓慢的，而随着人类知识指数级的增长，经济体的基因突变的频率变得越来越快了。

自然界里的一个特定物种的基因序列是定长的，最短的病毒的基因长度只有几千个碱基/碱基对，而人体细胞的23条染色体DNA总共大约有30亿个碱基对。而一个经济体的基因规模可以是人类基因规模的成千上万倍，而且几乎每天在增长。

D. Sociology in Economics

1. Freedom vs. Constraint

It has been discussed in previous section that no wealth at all will be created without the proper organization initiated and sustained by human. Besides eating grass and laying shit, ox may run all day long, all month long, and all year long freely with producing nothing else, as no man organizes it. Wind can blow all day long, all month long, and all year long freely. Without human's organization, it produces nothing but destroying. Only under the organization conducted by human intelligence with their knowledge accumulated in their brain; an ox may be employed to drive a plough; the wind may be utilized to drive sailing boats; manpower can be organized to produce a variety of products.

One has the freedom of tumbling about on a queen-size bed, but only within the frame of the bed. Supposing there are 10 persons lying on the

D. 经济学中的社会学基础

一、自由与约束

前面已经说过，没有人启动和维持适当的组织，财富是不可能被生产出来的。牛可以整天、整月、整年自由地跑，但没有人的组织，除了吃草排粪，却不能生产任何价值；风可以整天、整月、整年地吹，但没有人的组织，除了摧毁，也不能生产任何价值。只有在人类智慧的组织下，运用积累在大脑里的知识，牛才可能用于驱动犁具；风才可能用于驱动帆船；人力才有可能被组织起来生产出各种各样的产品。

一个人躺在大床上，可以有在床上任意翻滚的自由，但仅限于床边之内。如果在同样一张大床上躺

same bed, The freedom for everyone is reduced down to zero almost. That is to say, Freedom is restrained by the resource available.

着10个人，每个人的自由就会被缩减到近乎没有。也就是说，自由是受资源约束的。

2. Egoism vs. Altruism

二、利己与利他

A man of the extreme egoism will find no wife therefore no children for passing his gene down; One of the extreme altruism couldn't pass his gene down either since he wouldn't survive till the age of marriage. So, we all are the descendants of ones, who are in-between the egoism and altruism, and are therefore more or less in-between the egoism and altruism ourselves with only few exceptions.

一个极端利己的人将会因找不到妻子而没有后代延续他的基因；一个极端利他的人也会因在成年结婚前就已死亡，而基因也无法得到延续。因此，我们都是那些介于利己和利他之间的先人的后代，除极个别例外，我们也是多多少少介于利己和利他之间的人。

Different from robber's using violence, homo economicus uses trade for obtaining stuffs he wants. Therefore, he has to produce something valuable sufficiently for trading with others first of all. Based on self-interested however, he always intents to trade more in with less out.

与强盗使用暴力不同，经济人利用交易来获得所需要的东西，因此，他必须首先生产一些有价值的产品用于交换。出于自利的考虑，他总是倾向于用较少的价值换取别人较多的价值。

3. The Goal of Economy

三、经济的目的

There is no doubt about the ultimate destination of human being, which is the subsistence and propagation of human race, just like the destinations of all other species on the earth, but preferably in a joyful mood in addition meanwhile. Joy is the result of interaction between the receiver and the dispenser. The dispenser could be the other people, the materials, or even pure imagination.

毫无疑问，和其他地球上的所有物种一样，人类的终极目标，是保证人种的生存和繁衍，但最好是在一种愉悦的情景下进行。愉悦是施者与受者交互的结果，施者可以是他人、物甚至纯粹想象。

E. Philosophy in Economics

E. 经济学中的哲学基础

1. Novel Explanation of "Tao gives birth of One, and then One gives birth of Two, Two gives birth of Three, and Three gives birth of

一、"道生一，一生二，二生三，三生万物"新解

everything afterwards"

In the book of *Tao Te Ching* Laozi says, "There was something mixed up, even before the birth of heaven and earth, in loneliness, in silence, standing exclusively and permanently, which is believed as the mother of the universe. I don't know its name. So, I managed to describe it as Tao (the way, roughly in English), and name it Tai (the ether, roughly)." Posteriorly, it came the development of "Tao gives birth of One, and then One gives birth of Two, Two gives birth of Three, and Three gives birth of everything afterwards". For emphasize the unique nature of Tao, Laozi declares at the very beginning of the book that "Tao could be explained, but not in a usual way".

《道德经》说："有物混成，先天地生。寂兮、寥兮，独立不改，周行而不殆，可以为天下母。吾不知其名，字之曰道，强为之名曰大（发音为太）。"在此之后才有了"道生一，一生二，二生三，三生万物"的演变。为了强调"道"的特异性，老子在《道德经》开篇便开宗明义地说："道可道，非常道。"

The Big Bang Model is one which describes the initiation and development of the universe. This model is supported and accepted/proven most widely and precisely in the fields of scientific study and observation. This model suggests that, prior to a limited time scope in past, the universe was created from a initial state at an extremely high temperature, which is called "Odd Point, which may be what Laozi calls Tai". Through continuously expansion, it becomes the world nowadays, which may be what Laozi calls Tao. And I believe that Tao should be a general description of flow and change.

当今的"宇宙大爆炸"模型是描述宇宙诞生初始状态及其后续演化的宇宙学模型，它得到了迄今为止的科学研究和观测最广泛且最精确的支持。该模型认为：宇宙是在过去有限的时间之前，由一个密度极大且温度极高的初始状态（也称作"奇点"，这应该就是老子所谓的"太"吧）演变而来的，并经过不断膨胀发展成今天的样子（这应该就是老子所谓的"道"吧，我总觉得"道"应该是流动和变化的总称）。

According to the Big Bang Theory, one second after the universe was born, the temperature was 10 billion Celsius. In such high temperature, none of matters we know exists; even atoms will be smashed. The universe then can only be a pot

按照"大爆炸理论"，宇宙诞生后约1秒钟各处的温度约为100亿摄氏度。在如此高温下，不仅我们熟悉的物质无法存在，连原子核也会被撕得粉碎。宇宙只能是一锅

of "paste" of elementary particles, which is the ingredients to form protons, neutrons, electrons, etc. afterwards. Such paste called light energy, possessing wave-particle duality, should match what Laozi calls One. Thereafter, this pot, full of paste, is cooling down and down due to expansion. Protons, neutrons, electrons, etc. formed thereafter. And the nuclear reaction happened then. Proton and neutrons combine each other. Helium nucleus is therefore formed with two protons and two neutrons It has been calculated that the total mass of helium takes about one quarters of the total mass of the universe. In the first 3 minutes, the neutrons run out and protons left became nuclei of hydrogen. The total mass of helium and hydrogen takes 99% of the total mass of universe. The rest heavy elements, forming varieties of lives and planets, weighs only less than 1% of the total mass of the universe, most of which are formed inside the stars. Thereafter, there are two types of beings, which are energy and matters. The procedure itself matches what Laozi calls "One gives birth of Two".

由构成质子、中子和电子等的基本粒子形成的“糊”。这种具有波粒二象性的“糊”即光“能量”，这应该就是老子所说的“一”吧。随后这锅糊因膨胀而变冷，质子、中子和电子生成了，随后核反应发生了。中子和质子很容易聚合在一起，产生由两个质子、两个中子组成的氦核。计算表明，氦核形成的过程持续了大约3分钟，形成的氦约占宇宙物质总质量的四分之一。这个过程用完了所有的中子，余下的质子就成了氢原子核。最初3分钟里形成的氢与氦，构成了宇宙中99%以上的物质。而形成行星和生命的丰富多彩的重元素，却只占宇宙总质量的不到1%，它们大部分是在恒星内部形成的。此后的世界，就有了“能量”和“物质”两种形态存在。这个过程正好对应了老子所说的“一生二”。

In a long period of time afterwards, energy drives interactions among matters in the lonely world. And varieties of natural substances in more and more complicated structure were formed, from inorganic to organic; from none-life to life; from germ to mammal; intelligence of high animal is eventually on the stage. Intelligence is what Laozi calls Three. The existence of intelligence causes not only countless artificial objects adding to the categories under name of Two, but also creates a lot of categories under name of Three itself, such

在此后一段漫长的时间里，这个寂寥的世界中，能量促使着物质与物质之间的相互交融，产生出了更多结构越来越复杂的自然物。从无机物到有机物，从无生命物到有生命物逐步演化，最终产生了具有“智慧”的高级动物。“智慧”便是老子所说的“三”，“三”的出现，不仅使得这个世界中属于“二”的名下多出了数不胜数的人造物，而且增添了“三”名下的

as, perception, knowledge, thought, spirit, culture, which are all intangible beings.

"感知"，以及更高层次的"知识""思想""精神"和"文化"等无形的"存在"。

Energy, which may be also named as Mobility, is the measurement of movement of substance. And also the expression of the capability of doing work. All the matters are in continuous movement. Among all characteristics of a substance, mobility is the most essential one, all others are the expression of movement, which may be also named as Presentation. For example, scent is the expression of movement of molecules.

能量（或称"能"）是物质运动的量度，即是表征物理系统做功本领的量度。世界万物是不断运动的，在物质的一切属性中，运动是最基本的属性，其他属性都是运动的具体表现（或称"表"）。例如，气味是分子运动的表现。

The movement of matter is absolute. But we may refer the relative state of unchanged to as Being. An apple tree, growing on the ground, absorbing nutrition and water by root and transporting nutritious juice to its trunk, branches, leaves by means of solar energy; distributing other nutrition produced through photosynthesis in leaves by means of solar energy, too, to its roots, trunk, branches, and fruits. We refer this continuous growing tree to as "being" at some place. An unmatured apple fruit on a tree is referred to as "being" on the tree, even though it is growing day by day towards maturity in certain period of time. We refer a matured apple fruit "being" on the ground when an apple dropped. We refer this dropping process to as "flowing" to the ground. From such a procedure, we realize that there is a change of Mobility. And therefore this apple is "being" on ground unless someone pick it away.

事物的运动是绝对的，我们把事物相对不变的状态称作该事物的"存"。一棵苹果树，长在地上，虽然它天天都在成长（在太阳能的助力下，将树根吸收的含养分的水提升到干、枝、叶；同样是在太阳能的助力下，将树叶光合作用下产生的养分分散到根、干、枝、果中），但在一段时间内，我们认为此树是"存"在于某地的；一枚未成熟的苹果长在树枝上，虽然它日趋成熟，但在一段时间内，我们认为此苹果是"存"在于苹果树上的；果熟蒂落，苹果掉到了地上，我们看到了"苹果""流"动到了地上，在这个"流"的过程中，我们认知到有了"能"的变化；从此之后，该苹果就"存"在于地上，直至有人把它捡走。

To move a trolley of apple from Place A to Place B, energy is needed for the porter to get the

将一小车苹果用人力从A地推往B地，推车人需要消耗能量做

work done. Along with the moving step by step of the porter, the value of the work done by the porter is "flowing" dip by dip to the apples on that trolley.

功。随着推车人一步一步地前移，推车人劳动（做功）的（交换）价值也一点一点地"流"向那一小车的苹果中。

Arriving in Place B, the value in exchange of apples on this trolley at Place A, plus the value "flowed" in during the transportation done by the porter, is now "being" inside the apples of the trolley. However, the value in use "being" with these apples at Place B is the same as one at Place A without change in general(or to be precisely, a little bit "flowing" out if corruption happening).

到达B地后，该车苹果"存"在于原来A地的"交换价值"，加上推车人劳动（做功）的总"交换价值"，就"存"在于B地的这车苹果中了。而"存"于B地的这车苹果中用于"果腹"的"使用价值"，对于人而言，还是与"存"于A地时的这车苹果中的"使用价值"一样，几乎没变（甚至是有些"流"失，如果有腐败的话）。

It is also a process from "flowing" to "being" and then "flowing" again, from sensing to knowledge and then to intelligence by human. The brain of a new baby just born is almost in void with only instinct embedded according to his/her gene. Through intrinsic sensing organs, he smells the flow of sent, hears the flow of sound, touches the flow on skin, sees the flow of light, tastes the flow of flavor to recognize the external world in multi-dimension.

从"认知"到"知识"再到"智慧"也是一个信息"流"到"存"再到"流"的过程。刚刚出生的婴儿，除了由基因组织形成的本能外，大脑几乎都是空白。透过自身的感觉器官，他（她）（透过分子的"流"动）嗅、（透过音"流"）听、（透过压"流"）触然后是（透过光"流"）视、（透过味"流"）尝，来认知外部的世界，即对世界进行多维的观察。

With the capability of his brain, he organizes neurons in his amazing brain to make the outside world "being" reflected and connected. Along with his growth second by second, hour by hour, day by day, and year by year, he surveys through varieties of "flowing", memorizes them "being" in brain, and then compares the images in memory and makes some adjustment and abstraction for his future reference. He does even induction and deduction

借助大脑的能力，将神经元组织起来用以"存"储反映外部世界的映像和关联。随着分分秒秒、日日夜夜、月月年年的生长，他（她）观察（各种"流"）、记忆（"存"）于脑中，然后比较记忆中的映像并做出调整和抽象，以备今后之用。他（她）甚至能够采用演绎和归纳（更高一层次的"流"）的方法来

("flow" in higher level) trying to conclude a reason behind and to predict a tendency ahead of the development of a thing. A logic sequence is therefore organized(flow) and memorized(being) in his mind, and the knowledge is therefore created. The presentation(flow) of the knowledge is intelligence.

琢磨一件事情的前因和后果。一个逻辑顺序因此而形成（“流”）并被记忆（“存”）成为“知识”。而“知识”的对外表述乃是“智慧”。

It is approved in modern medicine that human brain is an organ in high metabolic and high oxygen consumption. In case blood supply stopping, for 30 seconds, fuzzy thinking happens; for 40–50 seconds, consciousness lost; for 2 minutes, brain cells dying; for 4–6 minutes, brain function totally lost and body is dead thereafter due to severe cerebral edema; So, the "being" of consciousness is based on a fresh brain "being" existing and the continuous supply "flow" of blood full of nutritious matters and energy. None of these two facts can be missing.

现代医学已经证明：人脑是个高代谢、高耗氧的器官，一旦切断血液供应，30秒人就开始意识模糊，40–50秒基本就失去意识，2分钟，人脑细胞开始不可逆的大面积死亡，4–6分钟严重脑水肿，导致人脑彻底失去功能，而死亡。因此，“意识”的“存”在是建立在脑组织这样一个鲜活的物质存在和血液中携带的养分和“能量”的持续不断的供给（“流”）的基础上的，两者缺一不可。

Man is such a creature that he possesses not only the capacity of learning the world passively, but also the capacity of designing and producing tools and thereby changing the world by organizing his body with his peers and tools in a high efficiency actively. By means of energy obtained in proper ways, he creates and accumulates more and more varieties of tools with more and more durability. He therefore makes the treasure of human society "being" accumulated gradually.

人是这样一种生物，他（她）不仅具有被动地认知世界的能力，而且具有设计和制造工具，并主动地将他（她）自己和同伴以及工具组织起来，形成高效率的改变世界的能力。借助于对获得能量的恰当利用，创造并积累了越来越多的用于生产和生活的且越来越耐用的工具，导致了人类社会的财富积累（“存”）越滚越大。

Tool itself is "being" of organization in higher level. It is the realization of the "knowledge" and "intelligence" inside human brain. The economic system, a higher system embracing all systems in

工具本身是一种“组织”（“存”的更高阶次的形式），它是人类大脑中的“知识”和“智慧”在现实世界中的实现。因而一个集能量

high level, assembled with energy (flow), natural objects (being), and human intelligence, is therefore "being" there in the world.

It seems now more relevant to describe the forming (flowing) and existing (being) of the whole world, including culture and economy, by modifying the description in *Tao Te Ching* that "Tao gives birth of One, and then One gives birth of Two, Two gives birth of Three, and Three gives birth of everything afterwards." to "Tao gives birth of One; and then One gives birth of Two; Two, together with One, gives birth of Three; and Three, together with One and Two, gives birth of everything afterwards." In such context, the first layer of the world is world of energy; the second one is world of matter; and the third one is world of consciousness. The intercourse of these three layers produces the whole world, of which economic world is just a part.

Reference:

Tao Te Ching by Laozi

The First Three Minutes: A Modern View of The Origin of the Universe by Steven Weinberg

（"流"）、自然物（"存"）、人类及其智慧（"组织"—"存"的更高阶次的形式）于一体的几乎包罗万象的高级系统——经济系统也成了这个世界的一种"存"在。

现在看来，将《道德经》中"道生一，一生二，二生三，三生万物"的说法，改成"道生一，一生二，一二合生三，一二三合生万物"，似乎能更确切地描述这个完整（包括人文和经济的）世界的形成（"流"）与"存"在。在此语境下，第一重的世界属于"能量"世界；第二重的世界属于"物质"世界；第三重的世界属于"意识"世界。这三重世界的"合"便生成了这个我们能认知的完整世界，而经济世界仅仅是其中的一部分。

参考：

《道德经》老子

《宇宙最初三分钟——关于宇宙起源的现代观点》(美)史蒂文·温伯格

2. Potentiality and Releasing in Economy

After its dam is built up, the potentiality of a reservoir system is formed. Through releasing the water on the bottom of the dam, electricity, as a kind of energy, is therefore generated. We may increase the height of the dam to increase the potentiality of the reservoir system, therefore more power can be obtained. Or, we may build a lot of reservoirs here and there, to increase the total potentiality of all

二、经济中的"势"与"释"

大坝建成后，一个水库系统的"势"就形成了，在大坝的底部"释"放存水，就能发电获得能量。我们可以靠增加大坝的高度来提高水库系统的"势"以获得更大的动力；也可以用在各处建造很多的水库来增加水库系统的总"势"值，来得到同样多的动力。

reservoirs, therefore more power can be obtained, too.

There are a lot of potentialities of varieties of subsystems forming the general potentiality of the economic system. High population creates a situation of high manpower; Rich wealth creates a trend of making everything easy; A wealth of knowledge creates strong drive of development. The larger the potentiality is, the more energy is demanded, and the more value is created.

Releasing processes, such as, activities of human, utilization of wealth, application of knowledges, cause again the increase of the potentiality of the economic system.

The Potentiality is the capacity of energy (in both real and imaginary) reserving, in the other words, Potentiality is capability of wealth creation. The Releasing is the process of energy dissipating, in the other words, Releasing is consuming.

3. We Are All the Porters of Nature

Let's guess what the God has been seeing under his feet.

An apple tree grows from a seed. With help of the sunshine, it transports nutrition sucked from its root to all the parts of its body; it distributes hydrocarbon photosynthesized by its leaves, with help of the sunshine again, to all the parts of its body, too. It blooms flowers. It invites bees to transport the pollen around. And then bears fruits. It invites birds to eat the fruits together with its seeds and then to transport the seeds to someplace else and drop them onto the ground for next generation's growth.

在经济系统中，形形色色的子系统的“势”就构成了经济系统的总“势”。人口多能形成人多势众的局面；财富多能形成财大气粗的态势；知识多能形成加速发展的动力。“势”越大，能量的需求就越大，能产生的价值就越大。

人类的活动、财富的利用、知识的运用，这些“释”的过程，又反过来导致经济系统的“势”的增加。

“势”是能量（实部和虚部）存储的总量，换句话说，“势”即创造财富的能力；“释”是能量耗散的过程，换句话说，“释”即消费。

三、我们都是大自然的搬运工

让我们来猜猜上帝看到的发生在他脚下的情景：

一棵苹果树从一粒种子开始生长，在阳光的帮助下，养分由根部吸收并被传送至树身的各部分；也是在阳光的帮助下，将树叶通过光合作用产生的碳水化合物送至全身。它开花，并邀请蜜蜂传播花粉；它结果，并邀请鸟儿将果子连同种子一道吃进肚里，再将种子撒在某个地方，然后长出下一代。

For hatching next generation, parent bird has to build up a nest first. She/he picks branches from tree, stems from grass here and there. And a nest is built thereby.

为了孵出下一代，鸟父母们必须先建巢穴，它们收集树的枝丫，各处草的茎叶，用来建造鸟巢。

For survive and propagation, human being does the same thing. Initially, we collect and store the seeds of wheat, of rice, of maize, etc. as food for survival. We then cultivate wheat, rice, maize, etc. through collecting natural fertilizer here and there for keeping the harvest rich. Nowadays, we make chemical fertilizer and pesticide instead, by using chemical elements available on the earth, to maintain good harvest every year. For making the chemical fertilizer and pesticide available, we have to build chemical reaction facilities by using reactors, pipelines, pumps, motors, etc., etc.; For making reactors, pipelines, pumps, motors, we have to smelt iron and steel, copper, aluminum, etc., etc., by using varieties of ores, burning cokes, so on and so forth. An economy of collecting, transporting, transforming, and storing resources available on the earth is therefore formed.

为了生存和繁衍，人类做的也是相同的事。起初，我们收集储存小麦的种子、水稻的种子、玉米的种子用以养家糊口。而后，我们种植小麦、水稻、玉米，通过收集和施放天然肥料来保证收成。现今，我们利用地球上的化学元素制造化肥和农药来维系每年的好收成。为了制造出化肥和农药，我们必须建设由反应釜、管道、泵、马达等构成的化工设施；为了制造反应釜、管道、泵、马达，我们必须用各类矿石、焦炭等材料冶炼出钢铁、铜材、铝材等。一个集收集、运送、转换和储存地球上可利用的资源的经济体由此而形成了。

On eyes of the God, all his creatures are porters driven by his sunshine directly or indirectly. The value, as so called, is just measure of energy involved in the process of moving in and moving out.

在上帝的眼里，所有他创造的生物都是由他的阳光直接或间接驱动的搬运工。所谓价值，只不过是搬进搬出过程中涉及能量的量度。

Strictly speaking, human beings don't CREATE value from scratch. They just recollect values from the sun through plants which collect energy from the sun via photosynthesis, through animals who transform value collected by plants; in fresh or in fossil; and make them more useful to

严格地讲，人类并不能凭空创造价值。他们只是再次集聚由植物通过光合作用集聚的以及动物通过转换植物价值而聚集的，以新鲜的或者是已成化石形式存在的来自太阳的价值，并使得它们直接或间接

human beings directly and indirectly.

地有利于人类。

F. Measurement in Macroeconomics

F. 宏观经济学中的度量

1. Why Is It Improper Using GDP to Measure the Performance of an Economy?

一、为什么用 GDP 来衡量经济体不靠谱

Let's start with a simplified case study. Suppose there are three producers A, B, C produce products a, b, c respectively. For convenience, we suppose that the gross energy (including real part and imagine part) spent to produce a, b, c, are all the same, say, 1 million Joules. The natural prices of these three are the same as well, say $1 per piece.

从一个简化了的例子开始：假设有三个生产者 A、B、C 分别生产不同的产品 a、b、c，为了方便起见，我们假设生产 a、b、c 三种产品所消耗的总能量（实部与虚部）都相同，都是 1 兆焦耳。因此，它们的自然价格也相同，假定每个产品的自然价格为 $1。

Again, suppose producers A, B, C had produced 1000 pieces each of a, b, c in certain period of time and had put them into the Social Virtual Depot. It means that A, B, C owns value worth of $1000 respectively. The central bank needed to issue loan to its purchasing reps (A, B, C) $3000 in total to reflect the total value of goods in the Depot, which is 3000 MJ.

再假设在某个特定的时段里，A、B、C 各生产 1000 个产品 a、b、c 放在社会虚拟中转库内，A、B、C 分别拥有等值于 $1000 元对应的价值的所有权。中央银行共需发行（贷出）$3000 的法定货币给其采购代理（A、B、C）来与 3000 兆焦耳的库存价值对应。

Say, A needs 100 pieces of b; B needs 100 pieces of c; C needs 100 pieces of a, and A will to sell 100 pieces of a in total price of $100 to C; B will to sell 100 pieces of b in total price of $100 to A; C will to sell 100 pieces of c in total price of $100 to B. That is to say, all the deals are done according to the natural prices and following the principle of exchange at equal (in price). After exchanges are finished, There are 100 pieces of A, 100 B, 100 C entering the phase of consumption. There should be value worth of 2700 MJ still left in the Social Virtual Depot. The central bank has to call back

假设A需要100个b；B需要100个c；C需要100个a，而A愿意以$100的总价，向C出售100个a；B愿意以$100的总价，向A出售100个b；C愿意以$100的总价，向B出售100个c，即交易是遵照自然价格进行的，交易符合古典经济学所谓等价（格）交换的原则。交易结束后，由于社会虚拟中转库里有100个a、100个b、100个c进入了消费过程，此时仍有2700兆焦耳价值的货物在社会虚拟中转库中，中央银行

currency worth of $300 from its sales reps (A, B, C). Upon the fulfillment of the course, counting in currency, the total trade is done in $300 and the total inventory in the Depot is $2700.

必须从其销售代理（A、B、C）处回收$300的货币。一圈下来，以货币计算的总交易量为$300，以货币价格计算的库存量还有$2700。

Now, Mr. A, Mr. B, Mr. C changed their mind. A only will to sell 100 pieces of a in total price of $200 to C and C accepted; B only will to sell 100 pieces of b in total price of $200 to A and A accepted; C only will to sell 100 pieces of c in total price of $200 to B and B accepted. That is to say, all the deals are done according to the market prices and following the principle of exchange at equal (in price). After exchanges are finished, there are 100 pieces of A, 100 B, 100 C entering thc phasc of consumption. There should be value worth of 2700 MJ still left in the Social Virtual Depot. The central bank has to call back currency worth of $300 from its sales reps (A, B, C). Another $300 in total goes back to the hands of A, B, C respectively. Upon the fulfillment of the course, counting in currency, the total trade is done in $600 and the total inventory in the Depot is $5400 in price now.

现在，A先生、B先生、C先生改变了主意。A只愿意以$200的总价，向C出售100个a，C也接受；B只愿意以$200的总价，向A出售100个b，A也接受；C只愿意以$200的总价，向B出售100个c，B也接受，即交易是遵照A、B、C规定的市场价格进行的，交易仍然符合古典经济学所谓等价（格）交换的原则。交易结束后，由于社会虚拟中转库里有100个a、100个b、100个c进入了消费过程，此时仍有2700兆焦耳价值的货物在社会虚拟中转库中，中央银行必须从其销售代理（A、B、C）处回收$300的货币，而参与交易的另外的$300重新分别回到了A、B、C的手中。但一圈下来，以货币计算的总交易量却变成了$600，而以货币价格计算的库存量成了$5400。

Supposing, A only will to sell 100 pieces of a in total price of $400 to C and C accepted; B only will to sell 100 pieces of b in total price of $400 to A and A accepted; C only will to sell 100 pieces of c in total price of $400 to B and B accepted. That is to say, all the deals are done according to another market prices, and following the principle of exchange at equal (in price), too. After exchanges

如果A只愿意以$400的总价，向C出售100个a，C也接受；B只愿意以$400的总价，向A出售100个b，A也接受；C只愿意以$400的总价，向B出售100个c，B也接受，即交易是遵照A、B、C规定的另一种市场价格进行的，交易依然符合古典经济学所谓等价交换的原则。

are finished, there are 100 pieces of A, 100 B, 100 C entering the phase of consumption. There should be value worth of 2700 MJ still left in the Social Virtual Depot. The central bank has to call back currency worth of $300 from its sales reps (A, B, C). Another $900 in total goes back to the hands of A, B, C respectively. Upon the fulfillment of the course, counting in currency, the total trade is done in $1200 and the total inventory in the Depot is $10800 in price now.

交易结束后，由于社会虚拟中转库里有100个a、100个b、100个c进入了消费过程，此时仍有2700兆焦耳价值的货物在社会虚拟中转库中，中央银行必须从其销售代理（A、B、C）处回收$300的货币，而参与交易的另外的$900重新分别回到了A、B、C的手中。但一圈下来，以货币计算的总交易量却变成了$1200，而以货币价格计算的库存量现在却成了$10800。

Is it OK to deal in total price of $50? It follows, of course, the principle of exchange at equal (price) of the classic economics. We will have the same result but the total trade is done only in $150 and the total inventory in the Depot is $1350.

以 $50 的总价来进行交易，行不行呢？当然也符合古典经济学所谓等价交换的原则，其结果还是一样。只是一圈下来，以货币计算的总交易量却变成了 $150，而以货币价格计算的库存量却只有 $1350 了。

General Domestic Production is calculated according to the fixed (market) prices and the market price of current year. Therefore, it is improper to measure the economy by using GDP.

国民生产总值 GDP 计算是按照某年的不变价和当年的市场价来计算的，因此用 GDP 来计量经济总规模是不靠谱的。

It will look more prosperous (bubble) to sell the same goods in $400 than in $100. And it will look more sluggish to sell the same goods in $50 than in $100. We may use the following formula to calculate the bubble rate in certain period of time,

同样的货物，以$400交易显然看上去要比以$100交易繁荣（泡沫）得多；而以$50元交易则显得萧条了。我们可以用以下公式来计算某一时间点的泡沫系数：

$$(23) \quad Rbb(t) = \Sigma MTP(t) / \Sigma NLP$$

Where:

MTP(t) market prices in certain period of time;

NLP is natural price.

其中：

MTP(t) 某时间点的市场价格；

NLP 为自然价格。

2. Macroeconomics Shall Focus on Value (in Joule)

二、宏观经济学应该专注于（以焦耳计的）价值

When you drive a car on highway, it takes 8

当你在高速公路上开车，100

liters of gasoline for running 100 km. It cost you $16 when the unit price of gasoline is $2 per liter, or $32 when the unit price of gasoline is $4 per liter. The cost in energy to run a certain car on certain highway for certain distance are certain. But the cost in money to run a certain car on certain highway for certain distance are variable on the price of gasoline even the volume of consumption is certain.

千米需要烧 8 升汽油。如果汽油的单价是 $2/ 升，则要花费你 $16；如果汽油的单价是 $4/ 升，则要花费你 $32；在某段高速公路上驾驶某车开一段路所花费的能量是确定的；但在某段高速公路上驾驶某车开一段路所花费的货币却是随着汽油单价的变化而变化的，尽管油耗是确定的。

A driver needs certain food, containing certain amount of Calories, per day. It may cost him $5 if he eats only bread and pickle, or over $100 if he eats steak in a Michelin-starred restaurant.

一个司机一天需要摄入一定数量卡路里的食物，如果仅仅吃面包和酸菜，也许只要花费 $5；如果吃米其林星级饭店的牛排恐怕需要超过 $100。

From energy stand point of view, economy is a dynamic entity of constantly iteration of collecting and storing value based on existing potentiality and then distributing, exchanging and consuming value to enter another cycle of maintaining and improving the potentiality of the entity.

从能量的观点来看，经济体就是一个在现有“势”的基础上集聚和储存价值，然后又分配、交换和消费价值以维持和改进该经济体“势”的不断迭代的动态实体。

Macroeconomics should be a theory of studying the general potentiality of an economy as a whole entity. It has to trace the energy flow in the endless iteration from value collection, transportation, transformation, reservation and consumption, instead of focusing on the cash flow same as in microeconomics study.

宏观经济学应该是一门研究经济体“势”的整体表现的理论，它应该以跟踪从能量集聚、传送、转换、储存到消费处在不断迭代中的能量流动，而不是像微观经济学那样跟踪资金的流动。

ⅩⅩⅩⅩⅫ. Equilibriums in the Economy

ⅩⅩⅩⅩⅫ. 经济中的均衡

A. The Equilibrium of Population Against Food Supply

A. 人口与食物供给间的均衡

As Malthus pointed out in Chapter One of his book, *An Essay on the Principle of Population*, the total supply of food determines the scale of human population in a nation; and the total population in a nation determines total food needed. We call it Malthus Equilibrium. It is true in not only the human world but also in all other animated nature.

正如马尔萨斯在他的《人口论》中指出的，一个国家的食物的总供给决定着其人口规模；而一个国家的总人口又决定着其食物需求的总量。我们称之为马尔萨斯均衡，它不但在人类社会中成立，在任何动物世界也成立。

B. The Equilibrium of Potentiality against Releasing

B. “势”与“释”间的均衡

It is obvious that the level of wealth determines the level of consumption. It may be a little bit elusive that the level of consumption also determines the level of wealth needed.

财富的水平决定着消费的水平是很显然的，而消费的水平也决定着所需财富的水平就不那么显而易见了。

A leopard has a limited appetite. When it captures a prey containing energy over its appetite, it will keep its wealth left over on the tree for next time enjoyment and do not prey until its wealth is totally eaten up, since over preying makes no sense.

一只猎豹只有有限的胃口，当它捕获的猎物超过了它的胃口时，它便将它的剩余财富储存在树上，以便下次享用。它没吃完现有的食物之前是不会再去捕猎的，因为那样对它已无意义。

It might make sense for a leopard to save one more prey on the tree just in case food is temporarily in short. But it makes absolutely nonsense for a leopard to hang on the tree with full of dead animals it preyed.

一只猎豹，在树上再存储一只猎物以备不时之需也许有些道理，但在树上挂满它捕来的死动物对它而言，是绝对没有任何意义的。

It is quite complicated for understanding in case of human world since there are varieties of wealth

人类的世界就复杂得多了，因为人类需要创造各色各样的财富来

created by human to serve varieties of demands of human. We have also varieties of producing tools in stock for samsaraous consumption and varieties of living tools in stock for terminal consumption.

Let's take a hammer as an example. To a man, a single hammer can be used for knocking a nail into wood; for cracking a walnut; and also for smashing a stone into powder. Until it is worn out, he basically doesn't need another hammer. He may have a special hammer for knocking nail; another special hammer for cracking walnut; another special hammer for smashing stone, but the life times of these three hammers will be three times longer as the hammer in the first case averagely. During this threefold time, he doesn't need to add any more hammers.

Actually, the Equilibrium of Population against Food-supply is a special case of the Equilibrium of Potentiality against Releasing, if we realize that both deal with the same essential characteristics of a dissipative structure.

满足其各色各样的需求。另外我们还有各色各样的用于轮回消费的生产工具存量和各色各样的用于终极消费的生活工具存量。

让我们来分析一下锤子的例子：对一个人来说，锤子可以用来将钉子敲进木块；敲裂核桃壳；或者将石块敲打成粉末。在锤子被全部磨损掉之前，他是不再需要另一个锤子的。他也可以拥有一个锤子专门用于敲钉；一个锤子专门用于敲核桃；另一个锤子专门用于敲碎石块。尽管如此，平均来说，这三把锤子的总寿命会是一把锤子的 3 倍。而在这 3 倍长的时间里，他不再需要增添任何锤子了。

其实，人口对食物供应的均衡是“势”与“释”的均衡的特例，因为两者都是对耗散结构的同一个基本特性的描述。

C. A Philosophical Pondering on the Necessary Conditions of Economic Crisis

Along with the development of the technology, both the energy efficiency and time efficiency of the Economy are getting higher and higher. Only when the capability of the production of the society is times higher than the capacity of the consumption of the society, and the Society keeps production on going even if the supply is over the demand, an economic crisis will surely happen. Taking still above mentioned hammer as the example, If it takes

C. 对经济危机必要条件的哲学思考

随着技术水平的发展，经济活动中能量效率和时间效率变得越来越高。只有当社会的生产能力数倍于社会的消费能力。在供应大过需求的情况下，如果社会仍然坚持生产，那么经济危机就会发生。依然用上述的锤子做例子，如果制造三把锤子需要一个人花费3周，而用坏所有这三把锤子需要3年。他应

a man three weeks to finish the production of those tree hammers, but it takes three years for the man to use out those three hammers at all. He shouldn't make any more hammer until the time span of three years are about over just like a leopard doesn't prey any more until the food hidden on the tree is eaten out. Otherwise, he will have 51 pieces of hammer in extra on his hand but contributing no utility at all. Or, he doesn't need to make any more hammers in coming 51 years.

该像猎豹不吃完藏在树上的食物就不再捕食那样，在这3年的里不再制造任何锤子。否则，他会有51把多余的锤子在手上发挥不了任何新作用。或者他在今后的51年内都不需要制造锤子了。

The existence of surplus-value makes the accumulation of social wealth possible. The existing utility carriers of the social wealth forms organically a society wise monster, in which all the new products are produced, distributed, and consumed terminally and samsaraously. Nevertheless, the samsaraous portion of the society goes to the body of the monster for its growing. Along with the development of the innovation of technologies, the surplus-value rate is going higher and higher; and more and more social wealth is therefore accumulated correspondingly. When the monster eats too much, its body will be too obese. It has to be on diet and do more exercise for a while just like the way we treat our human bodies.

剩余价值的存在，使得社会财富的积累有了可能。而社会财富中的效用载体有机地构成了一个社会级的大怪物，在这个大怪物里面所有的新产品被生产、分配和以最终的和轮回的方式被消费掉。而被轮回消费掉的社会财富，又进入大怪物的体内促进它自己身体的成长。由于剩余价值率的不断提高，社会财富的积累变得越来越大。如果大怪物吃得太多，它的身体就会过于肥胖，因而需要像我们对待自己的身体一样进行一段时间的节食和多运动。

D. The Effect of the Technology of Organization

D. 组织技术的影响

The Equilibrium of Population against Food-supply (EOPAF) and Equilibrium of Potentiality against Releasing (EOPAR) are all dynamic. They depend solely on the level of technology of organizing of both human society and objective

人口对食物供给的均衡（EOPAF）和“势”对“释”的均衡（EOPAR）都是动态的均衡。他们都仅依赖于组织人类社会和物质世界的技术水平。

world.

It was said that the total population of the world was only about 20,000 in a million years ago; about 7.5 million in 8000 B.C. due to preliminary farming implemented; about 85 million in 4000 BC; and 560 million in 1650 A.C. In 1950 A.C., the population of the world reached 2.52 billion, thanks to the industrial revolution.

据说100万年前的世界总人口只有2万；公元前8000年时只有750万，当时已有初级的农业技术；公元前4000年时只有8500万；在公元1650年约为5.6亿。在工业革命后的1950年，世界人口达到了25.2亿。

There were only two bicycles available as the regular transportation tools in my family 30 years ago. Then, We had motor scooter. Now, We have two motor cars. These happened just because of the reform/improvement of the social organizations and producing organizations, making the Potentiality of the economy entity increase therefore, in China since the Open Policy is implemented.

30年前我家只有2辆自行车作为交通工具；随后我家有了摩托车；现在我家有了2部汽车。这些都是在中国开放政策实施后，改革与改善社会组织和生产组织而导致经济体“势”的增加的结果。

The invention of the internal combustion engine, motor car replaced animal driven cart. Standardization of part and production line makes it possible for a common family to possess cars.

内燃机的发明以及标准化生产线的运用使得普通家庭拥有汽车成为可能。

XXXXⅢ. Wealth Model of Robinson Crusoe

XXXXⅢ. 鲁滨孙的财富模型

Robinson Crusoe is alone on a tropic island. He has to find/produce enough food for himself. So, he has to make tools for hunting fishes first. Say, half day per day for Robinson to find enough food averagely by using his fishing tools. His Duty Factor of Obtaining Energy (DFOE) is 25%. Upon being full, he can do many things for himself afterwards. At very beginning, he has to find a place for sleeping. Ground is not safe enough from the bugs and snakes.

鲁滨孙一个人在一座热带海岛上，他必须为自己找到/生产足够的食物，因此他必须首先制作捕鱼工具，假设鲁滨孙平均需要半个白天时间用捕鱼工具捕捉足够的食物，他的获能占空比是25%。吃饱后，就可以干很多其他事情。最初，他必须寻找一个睡觉的地方，睡地面很容易被虫蛇叮咬，即便在

Even in a cave, he has to make a bed with high legs by cutting some bamboo and ivy. For keeping his knife sharp, he has to find a sharpener for sure. It takes, say10 days for him to build a quite good bed, which can be in use for five years at least, with a little maintenance. It makes no sense at all for Robinson to make another bed in coming five years, since there is only one man on his island. He might spend another 5 days to collect some soft grasses to weave a mattress to keep him comfortable when sleeping. Once the grass mattress is done, it can be used for quite long time, say half year. So, it takes 10 days out of 365 in a year for Robinson to make grass mattress for sleeping. He may make some more mattresses for reserve as long as these mattresses don't decay themselves. But averagely speaking, he needs spend only 10/365 of his life on the island for making enough mattresses for himself. If he makes 10 pieces mattresses once, he doesn't need to make any mattresses in coming 5 years practically, unless Robinson feels it's just fun for making them even it makes no substantial sense to him.

一个山洞里，他也必须用藤和毛竹制作一张高脚床。为了保持砍刀锋利，他肯定又必须找到一个磨刀石。假定他花了 10 天，做好了一张不错的床，在少量适当的维护下，它至少可以用 5 年。对鲁滨孙来说，在未来的 5 年中就没有任何必要再制作另外的床了，因为岛上就他一人。他倒是可以花上另外 5 天去收集一些细软的草，编织一张床垫使自己睡得舒服些。一旦草垫做好了，他就可以用上差不多半年。因此，一年中他要花 10 天去编织草垫用于睡觉。他也可以制造更多的草垫作为储备只要这些垫子不会朽坏。但平均说来，他每年还是只需要花 10/365 在岛上的时间为自己编织足够草垫。如果他一次做成 10 张垫子，那么 5 年之内实际上就不再需要编制草垫了，除非鲁滨孙把编制草垫当作一个乐子而并不在意它实质性的意义。

Generally speaking, it may keep him busy at the very beginning upon his landing on the island. He has to build up a shed, a bed, a grass mattress, a blanket, a table, a stool, and some big and small clay pots for storage of water, food, etc. Because the life cycle of these furniture are more or less longer than the time necessary for making them, once after a while, Robinson will feel more and more relaxed since nothing more is substantially needed. What else he can do? The trail to the peak of cliff is too narrow and rugged as well. Robinson got a plan to blaze a

一般来说，登岛之初他必定很忙，他必须建造棚屋、床、草垫、毯子、桌子、凳子以及一些大大小小的陶罐用以储存水、食物等物品。因为这些家具的使用期限多多少少要比制造它们需要的时间长，鲁滨孙将会越来越感到轻松，因为已没有什么东西是实质性需要的了。那么他还能干些什么呢？通往悬崖顶的小道崎岖狭窄，鲁滨孙打算花两年开辟出一条方便的新小道；他

good trail by spending whole rest of 2 years; He may spend some months to level a square in the front of his shed; He may also build some bird nests near his shed and feed birds with some worms and bugs just for fun. He may, of course, sit on the top of the cliff to lookout the possible bypassing boat; meanwhile he can enjoy the sunrise and sunset, listen to the wind blowing over the surface of the sea as well.

也可以花几个月将棚屋前的场地整平；他更可以仅仅是为了好玩，在棚屋附近建几个鸟巢，并捉些虫子来喂小鸟；他当然也可以坐在悬崖顶上往外瞭望，寻找可能路过的船只，同时，可以欣赏日出日落的美景，聆听风掠过海面的声音。

Making a flute and playing it is a good way for entertaining himself; or, weaving tons of mattresses for nothing but fun or just for killing time; or simply lying down on his bed for extra rest on top of essential rest, as the essential rest is of cause a must of life. We may call it enriched life, but it is still the life.

自制一管笛子来自娱自乐也不失为一个好办法；或者，编制一大堆用不着的草垫，用来打发时间；或者就躺在他的床上做基本休息之外的额外的休息（基本休息当然是生命的必须）。我们可以称之为生活中的富余生活。

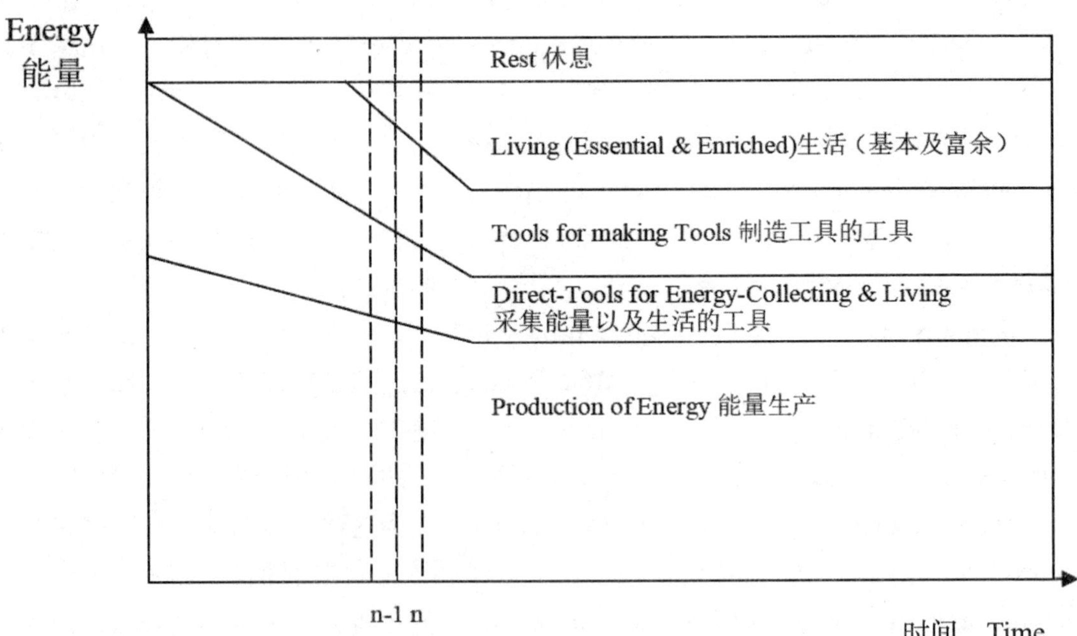

Figure 11. Wealth Model of Robinson Crusoe 图11. 鲁滨逊的财富曲线

At the very beginning, upon enough food is found, Robinson has to spend all his energy

最初，在找到足够的食物后，鲁滨孙不得不用他除休息之外的所

possible to make necessary living tools besides rest. The producing tools are only made on condition that they are helping the efficiency of the production of food or living tools.

有精力来制作必需的生活用品。生产工具仅会根据能否帮助提高食物生产或生活工具的生产效率来确定制作与否。

At anytime, the following equation is always true in a closed society, no matter which is formed by only one man or many as,

在一个由一人或多人构成的封闭社会中，以下的等式在任何情况下都成立：

$$(24) \quad E(n\text{-}1) = C_p(n) + C_d(n) + C_t(n) + C_l(n) + C_r$$

Where, E(n−1) represents the total energy created in time slot (n−1) and for consumption in time slot (n);

其中：E(n−1) 代表时段 (n−1) 创造出的总能量并用以在时段 (n) 消费掉；

$C_p(n)$ represents the portion of energy consumption for creating energy in time slot (n) and for consumption in time slot (n+1);

$C_p(n)$ 代表时段 (n) 内生产用以在时段 (n+1) 内消费掉的总能量所消耗的能量；

$C_d(n)$ represents the portion of energy consumption for creating and maintaining farming and living tools in time slot (n);

$C_d(n)$ 代表时段 (n) 内用以制造和维护农业和生活工具所消耗的能量；

$C_t(n)$ represents the portion of energy consumption for creating and maintaining producing tools for tools in time slot (n);

$C_t(n)$ 代表时段 (n) 内用以制造和维护生产工具的工具所消耗的能量；

$C_l(n)$ represents the portion of energy consumption for essential and enriched living in time slot (n);

$C_l(n)$ 代表时段 (n) 内用以基本和富余生活所消耗的能量；

C_r represents the portion of energy consumption for necessary rest in every time slot, which is a constant to a man. (We include extra rest into the enriched living);

C_r 代表每个时段内用以必要休息所消耗的能量，它基本为常量（我们将额外的休息纳入富余生活中）；

If the Rate of Surplus-value is Rsv, then, we have,

如果剩余价值率为 Rsv，则我们有：

$$(25) \quad E(n\text{-}1) = (R_{sv} + 1) \times C_p(n\text{-}1)$$

$$(26) \quad (R_{sv} + 1) \times C_p(n\text{-}1) = C_p(n) + C_d(n) + C_t(n) + C_l(n) + C_r$$

When Robinson Crusoe is rescued out of that island back to his home town, he has to leave almost all of his property on the island and to begin his life again in the society. To that island, Robinson Crusoe is just like being dead. His legacy on the island hopefully can be inherited by next unfortunate drifter.

Actually, every one in the world has the same wealth pattern as Robinson Crusoe has. It seems like that we can simply come up with a pattern of a whole society by adding up everybody's pattern alone the time axle considering the fact that people is propagated generation by generation through day by day and year by year.

当鲁滨孙获救离开那个海岛回到他的故乡时，他几乎带不走多少东西，他只能在他的家乡又重新开始。对于那座海岛，鲁滨孙就等于是死了，他在岛上留下的“遗产”只能由下一个不幸的漂流者来继承了。

现实中，世上的每一个人都有一个与鲁滨孙差不多的财富模型。我们应该可以将所有人的财富模型按照一代一代的人口繁衍在时间轴上进行叠加，即可得到整个社会的财富模型。

XXXXIV. Wealth Model of a Society

XXXXIV. 社会的财富模型

A. The Static Wealth Model of a Society

In the real world, every normal person has almost the same capability of production and has almost the same structure of consumption. If we freeze-frame the progress of technology, which means we consider the technology is kept un-upgraded in a certain long period of time, the Static Wealth Model of a society can be derived by superposing all the individual models together alone the time axle. Supposing the supersedure of the generation is even, in a perfect world, we will have the following diagram.

A. 社会财富的静态模型

在现实世界里，每个普通人具有几乎相同的生产能力和几乎相同的消费结构。如果我们冻结技术进步，也就是说在一定时间段里技术没有一点进步，那么，一个社会的财富的静态模型可以将个体的模型按时间轴叠加便可获得。假定在一个完美社会中，其人口更替是均匀的，我们便可以得到如下图形。

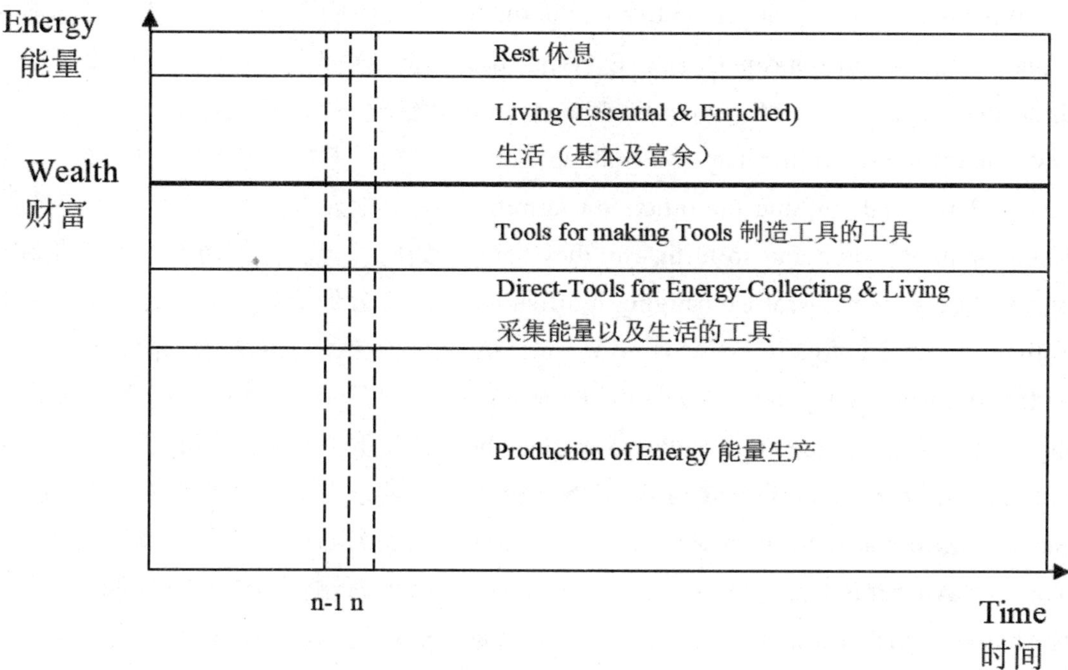

Figure 12. The static Wealth Model of a Society　图12. 静态社会财富模型

Under the circumstance of a society with fixed technologies, all the parameters in stable state are constants, so we have the following equation as,

在固定的技术情况下，所有的参数在静态下都是常数，因此我们有如下等式：

$$(27) \qquad (R_{sv}+1) \times C_p = C_p + C_d + C_t + C_l + C_r$$

$$(28) \qquad R_{sv} \times C_p = C_d + C_t + C_l + C_r$$

B. The Dynamic Model of Tool Making

B. 工具制造的动态模型

On the isolated island, Robinson Crusoe makes food, producing tools, furniture, and entertaining tools for himself. He consumes himself produced food, producing tools, furniture, and entertaining tools. and he even cures his sickness himself. He knows what he wants and what the priority is, since he has only limited capability of production. Literally speaking, he doesn't over produce anything he doesn't use.

在与世隔绝的海岛上，鲁滨孙为自己找食物，制作生产工具、家具、娱乐工具；他消费这些食物、生产工具、家具和娱乐工具。他甚至为自己治病。他知道自己的需求以及优先顺序，因为他只有有限的生产能力。严格来说，他不会生产他不需要的任何东西。

We suppose a group of people live on the small island together with Robinson Crusoe. Everyone has his special responsibility of making livelihood. One may concentrate on knife sharpener making; some ones on knife making; and the others on farming, fishing, hunting, so on and so forth. But they come together every evening for exchanging information sufficiently, that is to say, there is no extra man-made information delay at all. When the knife goes blunt, the hunter asks the knife maker to sharpen the knife again; or if the knife was broken, the hunter asks the knife maker to make a new one for him. When a sharpener is worn out, the knife maker asks the sharpener maker to make a new one for him as well. We see a natural lag always existing between the supply and the demand.

我们设想有一群人与鲁滨孙一起住在那个海岛上，每人各负其责维持生计。某人可能专注于制作磨刀石；某些人专注于刀具制作；还有其他人专注于农耕、捕鱼、狩猎，如此等等。他们每天晚上聚集在一起充分地交换信息，也就是说：信息传递不存在人为的附加延迟。如果刀具钝了，猎人就会要求制刀者帮忙磨刀；如果刀具损坏了，则可以要求制刀者重新制作一柄新刀。当磨刀石磨损完了，制刀者则要求磨刀石制作者为其重新制作一块新的磨刀石。我们能看出供给和需求之间存在着一种天然的迟滞。

We categorize the lag between the demands and supplies of direct-tools the first order lag according to the cybernetic theory. The Transfer Function of the supply of direct-tools against the energy demand of the society, which is the independent variable, is described in Laplace Transform as following,

根据控制论，我们将直接工具的供需之间的迟滞确定为一阶迟滞。以社会能量需求为自变量的直接工具供给的传递函数可以下列拉普拉斯变换形式表达：

$$(29) \qquad T_d(S) = k_d / (S+p_d)$$

Comparing with the direct-tool, the supply of “tools for making tools” is in the second order of lag if we treat the energy demand of the society as the independent variable. We then have the following Transfer Function of the supply of the “Tools of making tools” against the energy demand of the society as,

与直接工具相比，制造工具之工具供给相对于社会能量需求这个自变量来说就是二阶迟滞。我们然后可以有如下形式的传递函数来描述制造工具的工具与社会能量需求的关系：

$$(30) \qquad T_t(S) = k_d * k_t / (S+p_d)(S+p_t)$$

Now, we can naturally come up with the

至此，我们可以自然而然地得

Transfer Function in Laplace Transform of Dynamic Wealth (in Joule) Model of the human society, with perfect information communication and ignoring any pre-action of human per his prediction, as the following described,

出，在完全信息交流并忽略人类根据其预见能力而采取的预先措施的情况下，以焦耳为单位的人类社会的动态财富模型的拉普拉斯传递函数形式如下：

$$(31) \qquad T_w(S) = k_p + k_d / (S+p_d) + k_d \times k_t / (S+p_d)(S+p_t)$$

And the characteristic polynomial of the transfer function in Laplace Transform is a second order polynomial as,

传递函数的拉普拉斯特征多项式有如下形式：

$$(32) \qquad C(S) = S^2 + (p_d + p_t)S + p_d p_t$$

(Note: It is necessary to have some basic knowledge of cybernetic theory to understand this chapter.)

（注：理解本章内容需要有基本的控制论知识。）

In our modern society of labor division however, everybody concentrates on only one or two kinds of production in certain period of time. A group of people keep producing one product all days long, all months long, or even all years long almost indomitably only according to their experiences on, their understandings of, and the demand information from the market. In the reality, there is always a pure time delay of the demand information transferring in the market, which affects the dynamic performance of the wealth system drastically. Plus the intelligent regulation by human, the real dynamic model of tool making could be described as the following,

然而，在我们这个劳动分工协作的现代社会里，一段时间内，每个人只专注于某一两种事物的生产。一群人在一起，仅仅凭借他们对市场的经验和理解以及市场的需求信息，整日整月整年地，始终不屈不挠地生产一种产品。现实中，市场需求信息的传递总是存在纯延时，而纯延时会极大地影响财富系统的表现。加之人类智能的调节，真正的工具制造的动态模型应该如下图所示：

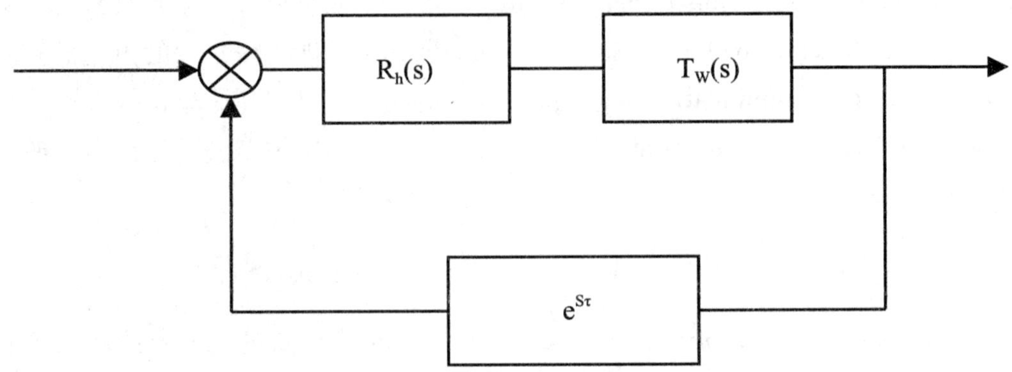

Figure 13. Block Diagram of Tool Production

图13. 工具生产框图

Where, $R_h(S)$ represents the transfer function of human intelligent regulation.

$e^{S\tau}$ represents the transfer function of pure time delay of market information feedback.

Under the circumstance of the Malthus Equilibrium, we know how much food/energy is needed for sure, giving the known population in the society. Supposing the rate of surplus-value is constant in certain period of time, we can easily come up with the maximal surplus-value available for tool making and entertaining. This forms the boundary condition for the dynamic system of the wealth of human society.

Let's suppose that there is a virginal land, like the new world found in 520 years ago, is just found for whatever reason. It needs people to migrate to the new land and to cultivate. Farming tools, such as, spade, shovel, plough, basket, etc., and living tools, such as, house, bed, stool, blanket, cloth, shoes, stove, pan, bow, spoon, vase, knife, etc. are therefore needed. Then, all different plants and works are needed to make these farming or living

其中：$R_h(S)$ 代表人类智能调节的传递函数。

$e^{S\tau}$ 代表市场信息反馈中的纯延时的传递函数；

在马尔萨斯均衡下，在给定的社会人口数量的情况下，我们明确地知道需要多少食物 / 能量。假定剩余价值率在一定时期内不变，我们可以很容易地计算出用于制造工具和娱乐的最大剩余价值。这构成了人类社会财富动态系统的边界条件。

假设由于某种原因，有一片新的土地被发现（就如 520 年前发现的新世界），它需要新移民来开垦。人们对诸如锹、锨、犁、箩等农具，诸如房、床、凳、被、衣、鞋、炉子及锅、碗、瓢、盆、刀等生活用具有了新的需求。而这些农作和生活工具需要由不同的工厂和作坊来制作，为了制作这些工具，又需要

tools, for making which whole bunch of other tools, such as, smelting furnace, hammer, grinder, spindle, loom, scissor, needle, etc. are needed, too.

另一些诸如熔炉、锤子、磨刀石、纺锤、织布机、剪刀、缝衣针等工具。

From the value/energy stand point of view, we need energy directly to plough, to seed, to weed, to harvest; we need tools like plough, basket, spade, sickle, which are literally value transferred and saved from labor directly and manufacturing tools indirectly, which are again energy transferred and saved from labor directly and other manufacturing tools indirectly.

从价值/能量的观点来看，我们需要直接的能量来耕地、播种、除草和收获；我们需要像犁、箩、铲、镰等工具，这些是工人的直接劳动和生产工具间接转移的价值的载体，而生产工具又是其他直接劳动和生产工具间接转移的价值的载体。

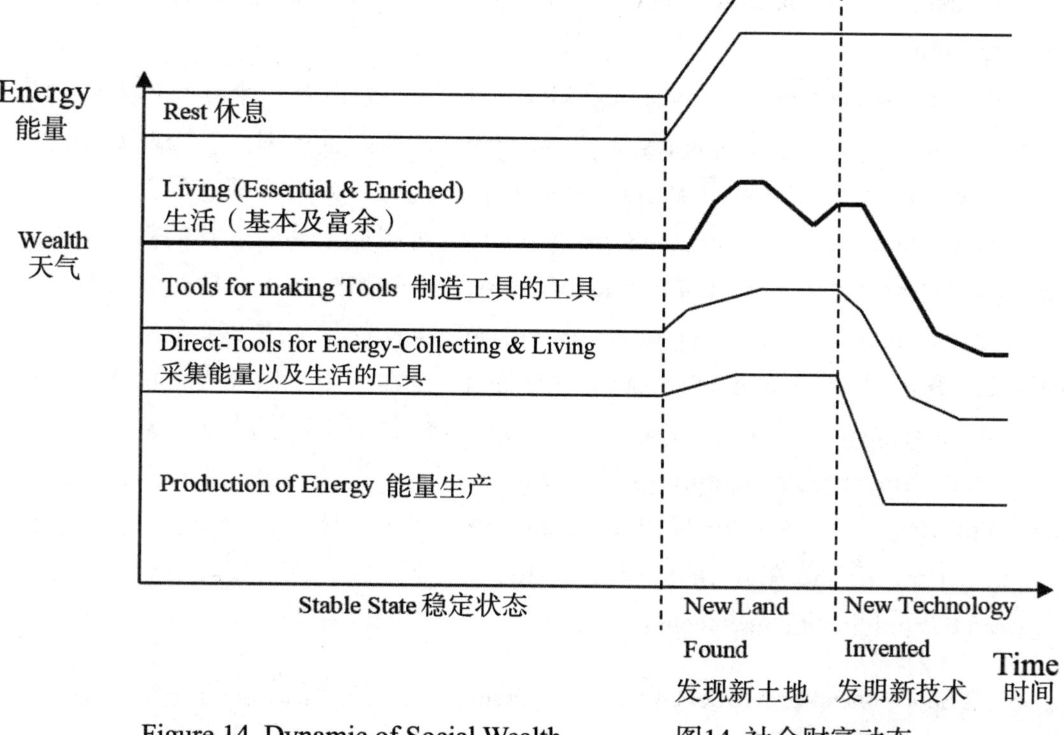

Figure 14. Dynamic of Social Wealth

图14. 社会财富动态

C. The Effect of Technology Innovation

Producing tools are invented for improving either the energy-efficiency, which means improvement of the Rate of Surplus-Value eventually, or time-efficiency, which means that the

C. 技术进步的影响

生产工具的发明，不是为了提高能量效率，即最终提高剩余价值率；就是为了提高时间效率，即相同的能量可以在比以前更短的时间

same amount of energy can be produced in shorter time than before so that man can have more time for enjoying life; otherwise it makes no sense for human to use a new producing tool. Living tools are invented for improving the convenience, comfort, and joy of human life; and there is nothing to do with the efficiency of production though since it consumes value/energy anyway. In the real world, there are many tools serve as producing tools but improve the convenience, comfort, and joy meanwhile.

内被生产出来，也就是人们可以有更多的时间来享受生活；否则，人们就没有必要使用新的生产工具。生活工具的发明是为了改善人类生活的便利性、舒适性和愉悦性，这里却没有对生产效率的任何考量，因为它是用来将价值/能量消费掉。现实中，许多生产工具也可以同时兼顾改善便利性、舒适性和愉悦性。

New tools are associated with new technologies of organization.

新工具总是和新的组织技术相关。

Supposing a new technology is just invented for improving the energy efficiency, a set of new tools are needed for realizing it at very beginning. New needs upon tools for making tools are therefore increased. After a certain period of transient process, the energy required for energy reproduction will be stable on a lower level than in the past for sure; and the total energy required for energy reproduction, production of direct-tools, and production of tools-for-tool-making will be on a lower level than ever for sure. It means the Rate of Surplus-Value is increased by applying the new technology.

假设有一个新技术发明是为了提高能量效率的，因此开始时，需要有一套为实现它的新工具，因而对制造工具的工具的需求也有了一个新增长。在一段过渡过程后，再生产能量所需的能量需求肯定会稳定在一个比以前更低的水平；因而能量再生产、直接工具的生产加制造工具的工具的生产所需的总能量肯定会稳定在一个比以前更低的水平。新技术的运用导致了剩余价值率的提升。

D. The Cybernetic Model of the Economic System

D. 经济系统的控制学模型

The whole existing producing system can be treated as a cascade of three first order inertial sections, the first of which is the production section of the energy carrier, the second is production section of tool for tool, the third is production

整个现行的社会生产系统从控制论的角度来看，可以被粗略地看作由三个一阶惯性系统的串联而成的：第二个是一阶能量载体的生产环节；第二个是一阶生产工具的工

section of tool for terminal consumption, in terms of cybernetics. The whole economic system of a society can be roughly treated as a third order inertial system.

具的环节；最后一个是一阶用于终端消费的工具的生产环节。整个社会的经济系统应该可以用一个三阶惯性系统的模型来予以粗略描述。

XXXXV. Salute to the Upcoming Neo Era of Energy

XXXXV. 向正在来临的能源新纪元致敬

A. The Era of Photosynthesis

Hundreds of thousands of years ago, living only in warm place, naked men, women and even their children hunted for fruits on trees, fish in water, and animal on ground all day long. The result of all day's labor could support only the propagation of the family. The rate of surplus-value was just a little bit great than 0. We may call this period of time the Hunting Age.

Thousands years of years ago, wearing clothes made of animal skin and plant fabric, people farmed crops and domestic animals all day long. The result of twelve hour's labor could support not only the family but also the society. The rate of surplus-value was somewhere around 5. We may call this period of time the Farming Age.

Hundreds years ago, employing the idled out of farming, people started mass production of varieties of tools. The result of eight hour's labor caused a tremendous wealth accumulation of the society. The rate of surplus-value is somewhere around 50. We may call this period of time the Manufacturing Age.

In the Hunting Age, people utilized the result

A. 光合纪元

数十万年前，赤裸的男人、女人和他们的孩子们，生活在温暖的地区，整天在树上寻找果实、水中寻找鱼虾、地上猎取动物。而整天劳动的成果也只能维持家族的繁衍。此时的剩余价值率只是少许比 0 大点，我们称这个时期为狩猎时代。

数千年前，人们身穿由动物皮革和植物纤维制成的衣服，整天种植农作物，豢养家畜家禽，整天 12 小时的劳作的结果不仅能够供应家庭而且能够供应社会。剩余价值率在 5 左右，我们称这个时期为农耕时代。

数百年前，通过雇用农业闲置人员，人们开始了各种各样工具批量的生产，而 8 小时的劳动成果使得社会财富的积累获得了巨大飞跃。此时的剩余价值率达到 50 倍左右，我们称此时期为制造时代。

在狩猎时代，人们仅仅利用光合作用的成果如果实、谷物和肉类

of photosynthesis, which are mainly fruit, grain, and meat, only as food; in the Farming Age, people utilized the results of photosynthesis, which are mainly fruit, grain, meat, as well as fabric and trunk of plant, skin and fur of animal, not only as food but also as means of warm keeping; in the Manufacturing Age, people utilized the result of photosynthesis with fossil fuel in addition as the power source for manufacturing. We may call all the ages of hunting, farming, and manufacturing together the Era of Photosynthesis, since the energy is mostly sourced from photosynthesis with only few exceptions.

作为食物；在农耕时代，人们利用光合作用的成果如果实、谷物和肉类，以及动物的皮毛、植物的纤维和枝干不仅作为食物也作为保暖的工具；在制造时代，利用包括化石燃料在内的光合作用的成果作为制造的动力，我们将狩猎时代、农耕时代、制造时代一起统称为光合纪元，因为除了极少的例外情况，能量大部分来自光合作用。

B. The Era of Photovoltage

Photosynthesis is a slow biological process. It takes at least several months to aggregate the energy from the Sun available for human being's utilization. And the conversion efficiency is quite low.

The invention of the technology of photo-voltage conversion let us see the Neo Era of energy coming, which we may call the Era of Photovoltage. In this Neo Era, the sunshine today can be converted to electrical power for today. The conversion efficiency is improved tremendously. The rate of surplus-value is therefore increased sharply. And therefore, the accumulation velocity of social wealth can be increased sharply for sure. We are stepping into a new age, which we may call the Semi-liberating Age of the Era of Photovoltage, when people are liberated from mining fossil fuel and farming biological fuel; but still have to farm

B. 光伏纪元

光合作用是一个缓慢的生物过程，它至少需要数月来聚集来自太阳的能量以提供人类使用，转换效率相当的低。

光电转换技术的发明，让我们看见了一个能源新纪元的到来，我们可称之为光伏纪元。在这个纪元里，今天的阳光被转换成今天的电力，转换效率被大幅地提升，剩余价值率也因此得到了急剧的增加，社会财富积累速度也一定会因此得到可观的提高。我们正跨入一个新的我们可称之为光伏纪元的半解放时代，在这个时代里，人们不再为获得机械能而从事开采或耕作，但粮食的耕作还是需要的。

foods.

C. Adam Chen's Conjecture

There is no way so far for human to manufacture their food through compounding hydrocarbon, carbohydrate, protein, and other necessary nutrition directly from natural resources by skipping the photosynthesis process. I, Adam Chen, would bet here that it would become true someday in the future. Then, the rate of surplus-value will be increased tremendously once again. And therefore, the accumulation velocity of social wealth is increased once more. People will be totally liberated from energy mining and farming; and will have a lot of leisure time in addition for enjoying their lives, for example, gardening instead of farming, rock-climbing instead of coal mining. We may therefore call it the Utmost-liberating Age of the Era of Photovoltage.

C. 陈亚君猜想

到目前为止还没有直接利用自然资源来合成碳氢化合物、碳水化合物、蛋白质以及其他人类必需营养的可以跳过光合过程的生产方法。我陈亞君斗胆在这里推测，它必将会在未来成为现实。到那时，剩余价值率会再一次被大幅度提升，而社会财富积累的速度也会因此再一次提高。人们就会彻底从能源的开采和耕作中解放出来，并因此而拥有很多的空余时间来享受他们的生活，比如从事园艺而不是农耕；攀岩而不是采煤。我们称这个时期为光伏纪元里的终极解脱时代。

D. Ratiopia

The measure of the Rate of Surplus-value (ROSV) and the measure of the Duty Factor of Obtaining Energy (DFOE) indicate the same phenomenon but in different terms. ROSV is calculated in value and DFOE is calculated in time. Generally speaking, the higher the rate of surplus-value is, the lower the duty factor of obtaining energy is. They are both the key indicators of the social situation.

When the ROSV is close to 0, people consume all of what they got and there is not much properties leftover to worry about. People form family for

D. 理性国

剩余价值率和获能占空比是以不同量纲测量同一现象的两种指标，剩余价值率（ROSV）以价值计算，而获能占空比是以时间计算的。一般来说，剩余价值率越高，获能占空比就越低。它们都是反映社会水平的关键指标。

当 ROSV 接近零，人们将消费掉几乎所有他们摄取的，因此也就没有什么资产剩余来操心了。人们

propagation and tribe for hunting. Everybody is the laborer. It was a primitive society of human.

When the ROSV is close to 1, only half of the time of a man is needed for food production averagely, or in other words, only half of the population has to work for food. There will some properties accumulated if more than half of the total population works. The need to manage and to protect the property of the family/tribe/society rises up. Gradually, people had social hierarchy based on the possession of the wealth.

If the ROSV reaches 999, what will happen? For sure, only one thousandth of the time of a man is needed for food production averagely, or in other words, only one thousandth of the population has to work for survival of the whole society; or the social property would be increased 1000 times as all of the people worked in full time. Base on the constraints of the previously mentioned equilibriums; the higher the ROSV is, the shorter the transit process of economic cycle (uprising phase) will be, the sooner the new equilibrium can be reached, the more leisure time people then will have. In one word, people will be liberated from both poverties of substance and time.

Is it what Saint Confucius called World Commonwealth; or, what Sir Thomas More called Utopia; or, what Dr. Karl Marx called Communism? I would like call it the Ratiopia (meaning Rational State) instead, when, due to the numerous rate of surplus-value already available, people eventually realized that, following a general plan, there should be plans for individual persons, for individual

为繁衍组成家庭，为狩猎组成族群，这就是人类的原始社会。

当ROSV接近1时，一个人只需要花一半时间从事食物生产，或者换句话说，只有一半的人口必须为食物去工作。如果大于半数人口都在工作，那么就会有财产的积累产生，管理和保护这些属于家族的/族群的/社会的财产的需求就会产生，根据财产的多少，社会被分化成了很多阶层。

如果 ROSV 达到 999，会发生什么呢？当然，一个人只需要花其千分之一的时间从事食物生产，或者换句话说，只有千分之一的人口必须去为整个社会的生存而劳动；或者如果所有人都去劳动，社会财富积累的速度将会提高 1000 倍。根据以前所述的各种均衡描述，ROSV 越高经济周期中的过渡过程（上升期）就越短，新的均衡点就越快，人们从而就会拥有越多的空闲时间。一句话，人们将从物质匮乏和时间匮乏的状态中解放出来。

这就是孔圣人所说的“天下大同”吗？抑或是托马斯·摩尔爵士所说的“乌托邦”？还是卡尔·马克思博士所说的“共产主义”？我想将它称作“理性国”，到那时，基于极高的剩余价值率已成现实，人们终于意识到有必要在一个总规划的框架下，每个人、每个家庭、每个单位、每个社团乃至整个世界

families, for individual firms, for individual communities, and even for whole world to be developed, implemented, and adjusted to regulate their lives of the wealth accumulation, wealth consumption, and leisured live rationally.

需要有一个各自生命中的理性的"积累财富、消费财富以及休闲生活"的规划，并加以执行及完善。

AFTERWORD
How I realize "Value is Energy"

后　记
我是怎样意识到"价值即能量"的

Starting in October, 2013, I had a period of time unemployed. For killing time, I resumed reading on *Economics in 300 Years* written by Mr. He Zhengbin. My previous mindset full of product design and business management was replaced by economic concepts like value, price, money, market, regulation and hands tangible and intangible gradually. Soon after, I found blogs of Mr. Steven N.S. Cheung in www.sina.com by accident. I then read them through from the beginning to the end. The book *The Explanations on economics* published afterwards is basically assembly of his blogs. Mr. Cheung's view was pretty new to me and helped expanding my understanding of economics.

2013年10月，我开始了一段在家赋闲的日子。为消磨时光，便将以前利用零散时间读过的何正斌先生所著的《经济学三百年》重新找出来再阅读。以前装满脑子的产品设计、经营管理，渐渐地被"价值""价格""货币""市场""调节""有形无形的手"等经济学概念挤出了脑瓜。稍后，在网上偶尔发现张五常先生在新浪网上的博客，便又从头到尾通读了一遍（张老先生后来的《经济学解释》其实就是以这些博文为基础编辑而成的），感觉有些观点还颇有新意，也扩大了我对经济学的理解。

One day in that winter, I was lying on a cane armchair on the balcony, bathing in sunshine, meditating in silence. Three scenarios of ploughing land by peasant coming into my mind gradually.

就在这年冬日的一个正午，我躺坐在阳台的藤椅里，沐浴着冬日温暖的阳光，闭目静思。渐渐地，有三种农民耕地的场景进入了我的脑海。

Scenario 1, two peasants drawing the plough ahead and one peasant controlling it behind;

场景一：两个农民在前拉犁，一个农民在后扶犁；

Scenario 2, one ox drawing the plough ahead and one peasant controlling it behind;

场景二：一头牛在前拉犁，一个农民在后扶犁；

Scenario 3, one peasant driving a tractor

场景三：一个农民坐在拖拉机

equipped with plough.

Based on the knowledge learned from physics, I knew, the works done in these three scenarios should be the same since they are all doing the same job of overcoming the same resistance of the earth in the same distance. The value contributions to the final harvests on this very land in three scenarios shall be about the same (reason for not being exactly the same has been discussed in this book). In English, WORK and LABOR are synonyms. Let's continue the case study as following,

Scenario 1: There are three peasants doing work, while they are laboring;

Scenario 2: There are one ox and one peasant doing work, while the only one peasant is laboring;

Scenario 3: There is one tractor doing work, while one peasant is laboring but the work his doing is ignorable almost;

If we take only the labor implemented by human into account, the values of labor in three scenarios couldn't be the same. I was therefore convinced that, in economic activities, not only the labor by human, but also labors by animal like cattle, by machine like tractor, even by the nature, such as windmill shall take into account to calculate the value, which brings us to the theory of labor value in a broad sense. It should be more scientific, precise and proper to measure value by using WORK(energy dissipated) done in course of labor instead of consumption of time in average social homogeneous labor suggested by Karl Marx (even though these two calculations are essentially the

上操纵机器耕地。

学过物理的我意识到，这三种场景下，耕完一块地，所做的功应该是相同的，都是在相同的路程中，克服相同的泥土阻力，因而做了相同的功，而这三种场景，对最终从这块土地获得收成所贡献的劳动价值应该是相近的（为什么不是相等？书中已有解释）。在英文中，做功为WORK，而WORK与LABOR（劳动）是同义词。继续分析一下这三个场景：

场景一：有三个农民在做功，即有三个农民在劳动；

场景二：有一头牛和一个农民在做功，但只有一个农民在劳动；

场景三：拖拉机在做功，而有一位坐在拖拉机上的农民在劳动，但他所做的功几乎可以被忽略。

如果只将人类的劳动计入价值，以上三种场景的劳动价值是不可能相同的。因而我认定：在经济活动中，不光是人的劳动应该被纳入价值计算，生物（比如牛）的、机械（拖拉机）的甚至是自然的劳动（比如风车）也应该被纳入价值计算（这是广义的劳动价值论）。用计量劳动活动中所做的功，即消耗的能量来替代马克思建议的用社会无差别化的平均劳动时间来计量劳动价值的方法，应该更科学、更准确、更适用（虽然两个方法的理论基础是相同的）。

same).

Doing work dissipates energy. It is easy and concise to measure the energy dissipation in course of certain economic activity.

Finally, I realized that "VALUE IS ENERGY". The unit of measure on value shall be the same as one on energy, which is Joule. And, as the carrier of labor value, the value of product shall also be measured in Joule of cause.

The word ENERGY was introduced by Thomas Young in 1807 when he gave lecture at King's College London. Only after the Law of Conservation of Energy was widely recognized around 1850, people realized then the importance and the use of the concept of "ENERGY". Although the work done by labor can be calculated by multiplying the average social homogeneous labor (power) with labor time, it is too early for Marx, who started writing the book of *Das Kapital* in 1843, and economists prior to him to associate labor value with energy, when the concept of energy were not widely accepted in the science field.

做功需要消耗能量，而计量在某个经济活动中所消耗的总能量则更为方便和简捷。

因而我意识到，“价值即能量”，价值的计量单位应该与能量的计量单位相同，即焦耳。而作为劳动价值载体的产品价值的计量单位自然也应该是焦耳。

能量这个词是托马斯·杨于1807年在伦敦国王学院讲自然哲学时引入的。直到能量守恒定律在1850年左右被普遍确认后，人们才认识到能量概念的重要意义和实用价值。虽然社会无差别化的平均劳动（劳动的强度即功率）乘以劳动时间即可得出劳动做的功，但马克思于1843年开始《资本论》的创作时，能量的概念在科学界还未被全面接受，因而是不可能将价值与做功和能量关联起来的。

REFERENCES 参考书目

[1] He, Zhengbin. Economics 300 Years 3rd ed. Changsha: Hunan Sci-tech Press.2009.

[2] Marshall, Alfred. Principles of Economics. 1890. http://ishare.iask.sina.com.cn/f/5858980.html?from=dl.

[3] Goudsbiom, Johan. Fire and Civilization. Guangzhou: Huacheng Publishing Co., Ltd.2006.

[4] Smith, Adam. An Inquiry into the Nature and Causes of the Wealth of Nations. 1776. http://ishare.iask.sina.com.cn/f/11819081.html.

[5] Marx, Karl. Das Kapital. Moscow: Progress Publishers,1867. http://ishare.iask.sina.com.cn/f/4505153.html.

[6] Cheung, Steven N.S. Blogs of Steven N.S. Cheung. http://blog.sina.com.cn/zhangwuchang.

[7] Goldratt, Eliyahu and Cox, Jeff. "The Goal". Great Barrington: North River Press, 2004.

[8] Malthus, Thomas Robert. "An Essay on the Principle of Population" 6th ed, 1826. http://ishare.iask.sina.com.cn/download/explain.php?fileid=6456704.

[9] Keynes, John Maynard. The General Theory of Employment, Interest, and Money. 1935, http://etext.library.adelaide.edu.au/k/k44g/k44g.html.

[10] Ricardo, David. 1817 On the Principles of Political Economy and Taxation" 3re ed. Batoche Books, Kitchener, Ontario, Canada.